M12/7   In Print @ £40   £15

THE MORNING CHRONICLE
SURVEY OF LABOUR AND THE POOR:
THE METROPOLITAN DISTRICTS

VOLUME 5

THE MORNING CHRONICLE
SURVEY OF LABOUR AND THE POOR:
THE METROPOLITAN DISTRICTS

Volume 5

HENRY MAYHEW

CALIBAN BOOKS

This edition first published 1982
by Caliban Books
c/o Biblios Ltd., Glenside Industrial Estate,
Star Road, Partridge Green, Horsham, Sussex

ISBN 0 904573 24 9

Typesetting by
Planet Press Ltd., 50 Providence Place, Brighton, Sussex

Printed and bound in Great Britain by
REDWOOD BURN LIMITED
Trowbridge, Wiltshire

CONTENTS

LETTER LV
Thursday, June 6, 1850

I now come to the Street Musicians and Street Vocalists of London. These are a more numerous class than any other of the street performers that I have yet dealt with. The Musicians are estimated at 1,000, and the Ballad Singers at 250.

The Street Musicians are of two kinds – the skilful and the blind. The former obtain their money by the agreeableness of their performance, and the latter in pity for their application rather than of their harmony. The blind Street Musicians, it must be confessed, belong generally to the rudest class of performers. Music is not used by them as a means of pleasing, but rather as a mode of soliciting attention. Such individuals are known in the "profession" by the name of "pensioners;" they have their regular rounds to make, and particular houses at which to call on certain days of the week, and from which they generally obtain a "small trifle." They form, however, a most peculiar class of individuals. They are mostly well-known characters, and many of them have been performing in the streets of London for many years. They are also remarkable for the religious cast of their thoughts, and the comparative refinement of their tastes and feelings.

I shall begin with the more skilful class of Street Musicians. Among these are the London Street Bands, English and German – the Highland Performers on the Bagpipes, and a few others. First of the English Street Bands:

Concerning these, a respectable man gave me the following details:

"I was brought up to the musical 'profession,' and have been a street performer twenty-two years, tho' I'm now only twenty-six. I sang and played the guitar in the streets with my mother when I was only four years old. We were greatly patronized by the nobility at that time. It was a good business when I was a child. A younger brother and I would go out into the streets for a few hours of an evening from five to eight, and make 7s. or 8s. for the two of us. Ours was and is the highest class of street music. For the last ten years I have been a member of a street band. Our band is now four in number. I have been in bands of eight, and in some composed of as many as twenty-five; but a small band answers best for regularity. With eight in the band it's not easy to get 3s. a piece on a fine day, and play all day too. I consider that there are 1,000 musicians now performing in the streets of London; and as very few play singly, 1,000 performers, not reckoning persons who play with niggers or such like, will give not quite 250 street bands. Four in number is a fair average for a street band; but I think the greater number of bands have more than four in them. All the better sort of these bands play at concerts, balls, parties, processions, and water excursions, as well as in the streets. The class of men in the street bands is, very generally, those who can't read music, but play by the ear; and their being unable to read music prevents their obtaining employment in theatres or places where a musical education is necessary; and yet numbers of street musicians (playing by the ear) are better instrumentalists than many educated musicians in the theatres. I only know a few who have left other businesses to become musicians. The great majority — nineteen-twentieths of us — I should say, have been brought regularly up to be street performers. Children now are taught very early, and seldom leave the profession for any other business. Every year the street musicians increase. The better sort are, I think, prudent men, and struggle hard for a decent living. All the street performers of wind instruments are short-lived. Wind performers drink more, too, than the others. They must have their mouths wet, and they need some stimulant or restorative after blowing an hour in the streets. There are now twice as many wind as stringed instruments played in the streets; 15 or 16 years ago there used to be more stringed instruments. Within that time new wind instruments have been used in the streets. Cornopeans, or cornet-à-pistons, came into vogue about fourteeen years ago; ophicleides about ten years ago (I'm speaking of the streets); and saxhorns about two years since. The cornopean has now quite superseded the bugle. The worst part of the street-performers, in point of character, are those who play before or in public-houses. They drink a great deal, but I never heard of them being charged with dishonesty. In fact, I believe that there's no honester set of men breathing than street musicians. The better class of musicians are nearly all married men, and they generally dislike to teach their wives music; indeed, in my band, and in similar bands, we wouldn't employ a man who was teaching his wife music, that she might play in the streets, and so be exposed to every insult and every temptation, if she's young and pretty. Many of the musicians wives have to work very hard with their needles for the slop-shops, and earn very little in such employ; 3s. a week is reckoned good earnings, but it all helps. The German bands injure our trade much. They'll play for half what we ask. They are very mean, feed dirtily, and the best band of them, whom I met at Dover, I know slept three in a bed in a common lodging-house, one of the lowest. They now block us out of all the country places to which we used to go in the summer. The German bands have now possession of the whole coast of Kent and Sussex, and wherever there are watering places. I don't know anything about their morals excepting that they don't drink. An English street performer in a good and respectable band will now average 25s. a week the year through. Fifteen years ago he could have had made £3 a week. Inferior performers make from 12s. to 15s. a week. I consider Regent-street and such places our best pitches. Our principal patrons in the parties line are tradesmen and professional men, such as attorneys. 10s. a night is our regular charge."

Next come the German Bands. I had the following statement concerning these from a young flaxen-haired and fresh coloured German, who spoke English very fairly:

"I am German, and have been six year in zis country. I was nearly fourteen when I come. I come from Oberfeld, eighteen miles from Hanover. I come because I would like to see how it was here. I heard zat London was a goot place for foreign music. London is as goot a place as I expect to find him. There was other six come over with me, boys and men. We come to Hull and play in ze country about half a year; we do middling, and zen we come to London. I didn't make money at first when I come; I had much to learn, but ze band, oh! it did well, We was seven. I play ze clarionet, and so did two others; two play French horns, one ze trombone, and one ze saxhorn. Sometime we make 7s. or 8s. a piece in a day now, but the business is not so goot. I reckon 6s. a day is goot now. We never play at fairs, not for caravans. We play at private parties or public ball-rooms, and are paid so much a dance – sixpence a dance for ze seven of us. If zare is many dances it is goot; if not it is bad. We play sheaper zan ze English, and we don't spend so much. Ze English players insult us, but we don't care about that. Zey abuse us for playing sheap. I don't know what zeir terms for dances are. I have saved money in zis country, but very little of it. I want to save enough to take me back to Hanover. We all live togezer, ze seven of us. We have three rooms to sleep in, and one to eat in. We are all single men but one; and his wife, a German woman, lives wis us, and cooks for us. She and her husband have a bedroom to zemselves. Anysing does for us to eat. We all join in housekeeping and lodging and pay alike. Our lodging costs 2s. a week each; our board costs us about 15s. a week each; sometime rather less. But zat includes beer, and ze London beer is very goot, and sometime we drink a goot deal of it. We drink very little gin, but we live very well, and have goot meals every day. We play in ze streets, and I sink most places are alike to us. Ladies and gentlemen are our best frients; ze working people give us very little. We play opera tunes chiefly. We don't don't associate with any Englishmen. Zare are three public-houses kept by Germans, where we Germans meet. Sugar bakers and other trades are of ze number. There are now five German brass-bands, with thirty-seven performers in zem, reckoning our own, in London. Our band lives near Whitechapel. I sink zare is one or two more German bands in the country. I sink my countrymen, some of them, save money; but I have not saved much yet."

The Highlanders, with their bagpipes, are next in order. A well-looking young man, dressed in full Highland costume, with modest manners, and of slow speech, as if translating his words from the Gaelic before he uttered them, gave me these details:

"I am a native of Inverness, and a Grant. My father was a soldier and a piper in the 42d. In my youth I was shepherd in the hills until my father was unable to support me any longer. He had 9d. a day pension for 17 years' service, and had been thrice wounded. He taught me and my brither the pipes; he was too poor to have us taught any trade, so we started on our own accounts. We travelled up to London, having only our pipes to depend upon. We came in full Highland dress. The tartan is cheap there, and we mak it up oursels. My dress as I sit here, without my pipes, would cost about £4 in London. Our mithers spin the tartan in Inverness-shire, and the dress comes to may-be 30s., and is better than the London. My pipes cost me 3 guineas new. It is between five and six years since I first come to London and I was twenty-four last November. When I started I thought of making a fortune in London, there was such great talk of it in Inverness-shire, as a fine place with plenty of money; but when I came I found the difference. I was rather a novelty at first, and did pretty well. I could make £1 a week then; but now I can't make 2s. a day, not even in summer. There are so many Irishmen going about London and dressed as Scotch Highlanders, that I really think I could do better as a piper even in Scotland. A Scotch family will sometimes give me a shilling or two when they find out I am a Scotchman. Chelsea is my best place, where there are many Scotchmen. There are now only five real Scotch Highlanders playing the bagpipes in the streets of London, and seven or eight Irishmen that I know of. The Irishmen do better than I do because they have more face. We have our own rooms. I pay 4s. a week for an empty room, and have my ain furniture. We are all married men, and have no connection with any other street musicians. 'Tullochgorum,' are among the performances best liked in London. I'm very seldom insulted in the streets; and then mostly by being called an Irishman, which I don't like; but I pass it off just as weel as I can."

Of the Irish Pipes, a well-dressed, middle-aged man, of good appearance, wearing large green spectacles, led by a young girl, his daughter, gave me the following account:

"I was eleven years old when I lost my sight from cold, and I was brought up to the musical profession, and practised it several years in Ireland, of which country I am a native. I was a man of private property – small property – and only played occasionally at the gentle-people's places; and then more as a guest – yes, more indeed than professionally. In 1838 I married, and began to give concerts regularly; I was the performer, and played only on the Union pipes at my concerts. I'm acknowledged to be the best performer in the world, even by my own craft – excuse what seems self-praise. The union pipes are the old Irish pipes improved. In former times there was no chromatic scale; now we have eight keys to the chanter, which produce the chromatic scale as on the flute, and so the pipes are improved in the melody, and more particularly in the harmony. We have had fine performers of old. I may mention Caroll O'Daly, who flourished in the fifteenth century, and was the composer of the air that the Scotch want to steal from us – Robin Adair, which is 'Aileen ma ruen,' or 'Ellen my dear.' My concerts in Ireland answered very well indeed, but the famine reduced me so much that I was fain to get to England with my family, wife and four children – and in this visit I have been disappointed, completely so. Now I'm reduced to play in the streets, and make very little by it. I may average 15s. in the week in summer, and not half that in winter. There are many of my countrymen now in England playing the pipes, but I don't know one respectable enough to associate with, so I keep to myself; and so I cannot tell how many there are.''

A very handsome man, swarthy even for a native of Bengal, with his black glossy hair most picturesquely disposed, alike in his head and in his whiskers and moustache, gave me, after an oriental salute, the following statement. His teeth were exquisitely white, and his laugh or smile lighted up his countenance to an expression of great intelligence. His dress was a garb of dark brown cloth, fitting close to his body and extending to his knee. His trowsers were of the same coloured cloth, and he wore a girdle of black and white cotton round his waist. He was accompanied by his son (whom he sometimes addressed in Hindostanee), a round-faced boy, with large bright black eyes and rosy cheeks. The father said –

''I was born in Calcutta, and was Mussulman – my parents was Mussulman – but I Christian now. I have been in dis contree ten year. I come first as servant to military officer, an Englishman. I live wit him in Scotland six seven mont. He left Scotland, saying he come back, but he not, and in a mont I hear he dead, and den I come London. London is very great place, and Indian city little if you look upon London. I use tink it plenty pleasure look upon London, as de great Government place, but now I look upon London and it is plenty bad pleasure. I wish very often return to my own contree, where every ting sheap, living sheap, rice sheap. I suffer from climate in dis contree. I suffer dis winter more dan ever I did. I have no flannels, no drawers, no waistcoat, and have cold upon my chest. It is now near five year I come London. I try get service, but no get service. I have character, but not from my last master. He could not give me; he dead ven I want it. I put up many insult in dis contree. I struck sometime in street. Magistrate punish man gave me blow dat left mark on my chin here. Gentlemen sometime save me from harm, sometime not. De boys call me black dis or de oder. Wen I get no service I not live, and I not beg in street, so I buy tom-tom for 10s. De man want 30s. De 10s. my last money left, and I start to play in streets for daily bread. I beat tom-tom and sing song about greatness of God, in my own language. I had den wife, Engliswoman, and dis little boy. I done pretty well first wid tom-tom, but it is very bad to do it now. When I began first I make 3s., 4s., 5s., or 6s. a day. It was someting new den, but nine or ten monts it was something old, and I took less and less, until now I hardly get piece of bread. I sometime get few shilling from two or three picture-men, who draw me. It is call model. Anyting for honest bread. I must not be proud. I cannot make above 6s. a week of tom-tom in street. Dere is, well as I know, about fifty of my contreemen playing and begging in streets of London. Dose who sweep crossing are Malay; some Bengal. Many are imposter, and spoil spectacle man. My contreemen live in lodging-house; often many are plenty blackguard lodging-houses, and dere respectable man is always insult. I have room for myself dis tree mont, and cost me tree shilling and six pennies a week; it is not own furniture; dey burn my cole, coal, and candle too. My wife would make work wid needle, but dere is no work for her, poor ting. She servant when I marry her. De little boy make jump in my contree's way wen I play tom-tom – he too little to dance – he six year. Most of my contreemen in street have come as Lascar, and not go back for bosen, and bosen mate, and flog. So dey stay for beg, or sweep, or anyting. Dey are never pickpocket dat I ever hear of.''

I now come to the class of players on the harp and hurdy-gurdy, imitators of farm-yards on the fiddle, performers on bells, and on the bass viol. Among these the Blind Musicians will mostly be found.

A poor, feeble, half-witted looking man, with the appearance of far greater age than he represented himself (a common case with the very poor), told me of his sufferings in the streets. He was wretchedly clad, his clothes being old, patched, and greasy. He is well known in London, being frequently seen with a crowd of boys at his heels, who amuse themselves in playing all kinds of tricks upon him:

"I play the harp in the streets," he said, "and have done so for the last two years, and should be very glad to give it up. My brother lives with me, we're both bachelors, and he's so dreadful lame, he can do nothing. He is a coach body-maker to his business. I was born blind, and was brought up to music, but my sight was restored by Dr. Ware, the old gentleman, in Bridge-street, Blackfriars, when I was nine years old, but it's a near sight now. I'm 49 in August. When I was young I taught the harp and the pianoforte, but that very soon fell off, and I have been teaching on or off these many years – I don't know how many. I had three guineas a quarter for teaching the harp at one time, and two guineas for the piano. My brother and I have 1s. and a loaf a piece from the parish, and the 2s. pays the rent. Mine's not a bad trade now, but its bad in the streets. I've been torn to pieces; I'm torn to pieces every day I go out in the streets, and I'd be glad to get rid of the streets for 5s. a week. The streets are full of ruffians. The boys are ruffians.

The men in the streets too are ruffians, and encourage the boys. The police protect me as much as they can. I should be killed every week but for them; they're very good people. I've known poor women of the town drive the boys away from me, or try to drive them. It's terrible persecution I suffer — terrible persecution. The boys push me down and hurt me badly, and my harp too. They yell and make noises so, that I can't be heard, nor my harp. The boys have cut off my harp-strings, three of them, the other day, which cost me 6½d. or 7d. I tell them it's a shame, but I might as well speak to the stones. I never go out that they miss me. I don't make more than 3s. a week in the streets, if I make that."

One of the long-remembered street performers in London is a blind women, led by a female. She came to me scrupulously clean, and very tidily dressed; she was accompanied by her usual attendant in the streets, who was almost as clean and tidy as herself. Her countenance is cheerful, and her manners those of a well-contented old woman. She plays on a an old hurdy-gurdy, or an instrument of that description, which she calls a cymbal. It has a battered, heavy look with it, and is grievously harsh and out of tune. She said:

"I have been 43 years a public performer. My parents died when I was a child, and I was put into the poor-house, and left it before I was twenty, to earn my own living. The parish paid for my learning music, and bought me an instrument, and so started me in life, God bless them. I started with a cymbal, which some call a hurdy-gurdy, and have been playing it ever since; it's not the same instrument as I carry now, but I've had this one fifteen years last August. I have been blind since I was nine weeks old. When I started on my own account, a woman forty-one years of age, who had been in Bloomsbury poor-house with me, came out to lead me. We shared alike. She died, and I had several after that who didn't do me justice, for they didn't give me all the money. Forty years ago the two of us would get 6s. a day; now sometimes we can only make 2s. a day for the two of us on an average the summer through, and 1s. 6d. in winter. I have my regular rounds. My Monday's round is Marylebone; my Tuesday's is Kentish-town — they call me Mrs. Tuesday there — the people say, 'Ah, here's Mrs. Tuesday come;' Wednesday is Kensington way generally; Thursday is Brixton and that way; Friday, Hackney round, and Saturday is Pimlico way. In some rounds I have friends who have given me a trifle every week (or nearly so) for twenty years."

A quiet-looking man, half-blind, and wrapped in a large old faded, black cotton great coat, made the following statement, having first given me some specimens of his art:

"I imitate all the animals of the farm-yard on my fiddle. I imitate the bull, the calf, the dog, the cock, the hen when's she laid an egg, the peacock, and the ass. I have done this in the streets for nearly twelve years. I was brought up as a musician at my own desire. When a young man (I am now 53) I used to go out to play at parties, doing middling until my sight failed me. I then did the farm-yard on the fiddle for a living. Though I had never heard of such a thing before, by constant practice I made myself perfect. I studied from nature. I never was in a farm-yard in my life, but I went and listened to the poultry anywhere in town that I could meet with them, and I then imitated them on my instrument. The Smithfield cattle gave me the study for the bull and the calf. My peacock I got at the Belvidere-gardens in Islington. The ass is common, and so is the dog, and them I studied anywhere. It took me a month, not more, if so much, to acquire what I thought a sufficient skill in my undertaking, and then I started it in the streets. It was liked the very first time I tried it. I never say what animal I am going to give. I leave that to the judgment of the listeners. They could always tell what it was. I can make 12s. a week this year though. I play it in public houses as well as in the streets. My pitches are all over London, and I don't know that one is better than another. Working people are my best friends. Thursday and Friday are my worst days; Monday and Saturday my best, when I reckon 2s. 6d. a handsome taking. I am the only man who does the farm-yard.''

A hale-looking blind man, with a cheerful look, poorly but not squalidly dressed, gave me the subjoined narrative. He was led by a strong, healthy-looking lad of 15, his step-son:

"I have been blind since within a month of my birth," he said, "and have been twenty-three years a street performer. My parents were poor, but they managed to have me taught music. I am 55 years old. I was one of a street band in my youth, and could make my 15s. a week at it. I didn't like the band, for if you are steady yourself, you can't get others to be steady, and so no good can be done. I next started a piano in the streets; that was twenty-three years ago. I bought a chaise big enough for an invalid, and having had the body removed, my piano was fitted on the springs and the axle-tree. I carried a seat, and could play the instrument either sitting or standing, and so I travelled through London with it. It did pretty well; in the summer I took never less than 20s., and I have taken 40s. on rare occasions in a week; but the small takings in the winter would reduce my yearly average to 15s. a week at the utmost. I played the piano, more or less, until within these three or four years. I started the bells that I play now, as near as I can recollect, some eighteen years ago. When I first played them I had my fourteen bells arranged on a rail, and tapped them with my two leather hammers held in my hands in the usual way. I thought next I could introduce some novelty into the performance. The novelty I speak of was to play the violin with the bells. I had hammers fixed on a rail, so as each bell had its particular hammer; these hammers were connected with cords to a pedal acting with a spring to bring itself up, and so by playing the pedal with my feet, I had full command of the bells, and made them accompany the violin, so that I could give any tune almost with the power of a band. It was always my delight in my leisure moments, and is a good deal so still, to study improvements such as I have described. The bells and violin together brought me in about the same as the piano. I played the violoncello with my feet also, on a plan of my own and the violin in my hand. I had the violoncello on a frame on the ground, so arranged that I could move the bow with my foot in harmony with the violin in my hands. The last thing I have introduced is the playing four accordions with my feet. The accordions are fixed in a frame, and I make them accompany the violin. Of all my plans, the piano and the bells and violin did the best, and are the best still for a standard. I can only average 12s. a week take the year through, which is very little for two."

I had the following narrative from a stout, blind woman, with a very grave and even meditative look, fifty-six years old, dressed in a clean cotton gown, the pattern of which was almost washed out. She was led by a very fine dog (a Scotch colley, she described it), a chain being affixed to the dog's collar. A boy, poor and destitute, she said, barefooted and wearing a greasy ragged jacket, with his bare skin showing through many rents, accompanied her when I saw her. The boy had been with her a month, she supporting him. She said:—

"I have been blind twelve years. I was a servant in my youth, and in 1824 married a journey-man cabinet-maker. I went blind from an inflammation two years before my husband died. We had five children all dead now — the last died six years ago; and at my husband's death I was left almost destitute. I used to sell a few laces in the street, but couldn't clear 2s. 6d. a week by it. I had a little help from the parish, but very rarely; and at last I could get nothing but an order for the house. A neighbour, a tradesman, then taught me at his leisure to play the violin, but I'm not a great performer. I wish I was. I began to play in the streets five years ago. I get halfpennies for charity, not for my music. Some days I pick up 2s., some days only 6d., and on wet days nothing. I've often had to pledge my fiddle for 2s. — I could never get more on it, and sometimes not that. When my fiddle was in pledge I used to sell matches and laces in the streets, and have had to borrow 1½d. to lay in a stock. I've sometimes taken 4d. in eight hours. My chief places when I've only the dog to lead me are Regent-street and Portland-place, and really people are very kind and careful in guiding and directing me — even cabmen — may God bless them."

A stout, hale-looking blind man, dressed very decently in coloured clothes, and scrupulously clean, gave me, the following details:

"I am one of the three blind Scotchmen who go about the streets in company, playing the violoncello, clarionet, and flute. We are really Highlanders, and can all speak Gaelic; but a good many London Highlandmen are Irish. I have been 30 years in the streets of London; one of my mates has been 40 years (he's 69); the other has been 30 years. I became partially blind, through an inflammation, when I was 14, and was stone blind when I was 22. Before I was totally blind I came to London, travelling up with the help of my bag-pipes, guided by a little boy. I settled in London, finding it a big place, where a man could do well (at that time), and I took a turn every now and then into the country. I could make 14s. a week, winter and summer through, 30 years ago, by playing in the streets. Now I can't make 6s. a week, take winter and summer. I met my two mates, who are both blind men – both came to England for the same reason as I did – in my journeyings in London, and at last we agreed to go together – that's twenty years ago. We've been together, on and off, ever since. Sometimes one of us will take a turn round the coast of Kent, and another round the coast of Devon; and then join again in London, or meet by accident. We have always agreed very well, and never fought. We – I mean the street blind – tried to maintain a burying and sick club of our own; but we were always too poor. We live in rooms. I don't know one blind musician who lives in a lodging-house. I myself know a dozen blind men now performing in the streets of London; these are not all exactly blind, but about as bad – the most are stone blind. The blind musicians are chiefly married men. I don't know one who lives with a woman unmarried. The loss of sight changes a man. He doesn't think of women, and women don't think of him. We are of a religious turn, too, generally. I am a Roman Catholic; but the other Scotch blind men here are Presbyterians. The Scotch in London are our good friends, because they give us a little sum altogether, perhaps; but the English working people are our main support; it is by them we live, and I always found them kind and liberal, the most liberal in the world as I know. Through Marylebone is our best round, and Saturday night our best time. We play all three together. 'Johhny Cope' is our best-liked tune. I think the blind Scotchmen don't come to play in London now. I can remember many blind Scotch musicians or pipers in London: they're all dead now. The trade's dead too; it is so. When we thought of forming the blind club there was never more than a dozen members. These were two basket-makers, one mat-maker, four violin players, myself, and my two mates, which was the number when it dropped for want of funds; that's now fifteen years ago. We were to pay 1s. a month, and sick members were to have 5s. a week when they'd paid two years. Our other rules were the same as other clubs, I believe. The blind musicians now in London are we three. C——, a Jew, who plays the violin; R——, an Englishman, who plays the violin elegantly; W——, a harp-player; T——, violin again; H——, violin (but he plays more in public-houses); R——, the flute; M'——, bagpipes; C——, bagpipes; K——, violin: that's all I know myself. There's a good many blind who play at the sailors' dances, Wapping and Deptford way. We seldom hire children to lead us in the streets; we have plenty of our own, generally. I have five. Our wives are generally women that have their eyesight; but some blind men – I know one couple – marry blind women."

The *Street Vocalists* are almost as large a body as the street musicians. It will be seen that there are fifty Ethiopian serenaders, and above 250 who live by ballad singing alone. In my present letter I shall deal with the Ethiopian Serenaders and the better class of Ballad Singers:

Two young men, who are of the former class, gave the following account. Both were dressed like decent mechanics, with perfectly clean faces, except that a little of the professional black remained at the root of the hairs on the forehead.

"We are niggers," said one man, "as it's commonly called; that is negro melodists. Nigger bands vary from four to seven, and have numbered as many as nine; *our* band is now six. We all share alike. I (said the same man) was the first who started the niggers in the streets about four years ago. I took the hint from the performance of Pell and the others at the St. James's. When I first started in the streets I had five performers, four and myself. There were the banjo-player, the bones, fiddle, and tambourine. We were regularly full-dressed in fashionable black coats and trowsers, open white waistcoats, pumps (bluchers some had, just as they could spring them), and wigs to imitate the real negro head of hair. Large white wrists or cuffs came out after. It was rather a venturesome 'spec, the street niggers, for I had to find all the clothes at first start, as I set the school a-going. Perhaps it cost me 6s. a head all round; all second-hand dress except the wigs, and each man made his own wig out of horse-hair died black, and sewn with black thread on to the skin of an old silk hat. Well, we first started at the top of the Liverpool-road, but it was no great success, as we weren't quite up in our parts, and didn't play exactly into one another's hands. None of us were perfect, we'd had so few rehearsals. One of us had been a street singer before, another a street-fiddler, another had sung nigger-songs in public-houses, the fourth was a mud-lark, and I had been a street singer. I was brought up to no trade regularly. When my father died I was left on the world, and I worked in Marylebone stone-yard, and afterwards sung about the streets, or shifted as I could. I first sung in the streets just before the Queen's coronation – and a hard life it was. But, to tell the truth, I didn't like the thoughts of hard labour – bringing a man in so little too – that's where it is; and as soon as I could make any sort of living in the streets, with singing and such like, I got to like it. The first debew, as I may say, of the niggers brought us in about 10s. among us, besides paying for our dinner and a pint of beer a piece. We were forced to be steady you see, sir, as we didn't know how it would answer. We sang from eleven in the morning till half-past ten at night, summer time. We kept on, day after day, not rehearsing, but practising in the streets, for reheasing in private was of little use; voices are as different in private rooms and the public streets as is chalk from cheese. We got more confidence as we went along. To be sure we all had cheek enough to start with, but this was a fresh line of business. Times mended as we got better at our work. Last year was the best year I've known. We start generally about ten, and play till it's dark, in fine weather. We averaged £1 a week last year. The evenings are the best time. Regent-street, and Oxford-street, and the greater part of St. James's are our best places. The gentry are our best customers, but we get more from gentlemen than from ladies. The City is good, I fancy, but they won't let us work it: it's only the lower parts, Whitechapel and Smithfield ways, that we have a chance in. Business and nigger songs don't go well together. The first four days of the week are pretty much alike for our business. Friday is bad, and so is Saturday, until night comes, and we then get money from the working people. The markets, such as Cleveland-street, Fitzroy-square (Tottenham-court-road's no good at any time), Carnaby-market, Mewport-market, Great Marylebone-street, and the Edgware-road, are good Saturday nights. Oxford-street is middling. The New Cut is as bad a place as can be. When we started, the songs, we knew was 'Old Mr. Coon,' 'Going, ober de Mountain,' 'Dandy Jim of Caroline,' 'Rowley Bowly, O,' and 'Old Johnny Booker.' We stuck to them a twelvemonth. The 'Buffalo Gals' was best liked. The 'bones' – we've real bones, rib-of-beef bones; but some have ebony bones, which sound better than rib bones – they tell best in 'Going ober de Mountain,' for there's a symphony between every line. It's rather difficult to play the bones well; it requires hard practice, and it brings the skin off, and some men have tried it, but with so little success that they broke their bones and flung them away. The banjo is the hardest to learn of the lot.

We have kept changing our songs all along; but some of the old ones are still going. The other favourites are, or were, 'Lucy Neale,' 'O, Susannah,' 'Uncle Ned,' 'Stop that Knocking,' 'Ginger Blue,' and 'Black-eyed Suseannah.' Things are not so good as they were. We can average £1 a-piece now in the week, but it's summer-time, and we can't make that in bad weather. Then, there's so many of us. There's the Somers-town 'mob' now in London; the King-street, the four St. Giles's mobs, the East End (but they're white Niggers), the two Westminster mobs, the Marylebone and the Whitechapel. We interfere with one another's beats sometimes, for we have no arrangement with each other, only we don't pitch near the others when they're at work. The ten mobs now in London will have fifty men in them at least; and there's plenty of stragglers, who are not regular niggers; there's so many dodges now to pick up a living air, sir. The Marylebone and Whitechapel lots play at nights in penny theatres. I have played at the Hay-market in 'the New Planet,' but there's no demand for us now at the theatres, except such as the Pavilion. There are all sorts of characters in the different schools, but I don't know any runaway gentleman, or any gentleman of any kind among us; not one; we're more of a poorer sort, if not to say a ragged sort, for some are without shoes or stockings. The 'niggers' that I know have been errand-boys, street-singers, turf-cutters, coalheavers, chandlers, paviours, mudlarks, tailors, shoemakers, tinmen, bricklayers' labourers, and people who have had no line in particular but their wits. I know of no connection with pickpockets, and don't believe there is any, though pickpockets go round the mobs; but the police fling it in our teeth that we're connected with pickpockets. It's a great injury to us is such a notion. A good many of the niggers – both of us here likes a little drop – drink as hard as they can, and a good many live with women of the town. A few are married. Some niggers are Irish; there's Scotch niggers too. I don't know a Welsh one, but one of the street nigger singers *is* a real black, an African."

An experienced street vocalist, of the better kind, upon whose statements I satisfied myself that every reliance might be placed, described to me the present condition of his calling. He was accompanied by his wife: –

"I have been in the profession of a vocalist," he said, "full twenty-five years. Before that I was a concert singer. I was not brought up to the profession; I was a shipping agent, but I married a concert-singer, and then followed the profession. I was young, and a little stage-struck." ("Rather," said his wife smiling, "he was struck with those who were on the stage"); "and so I abandoned the ship-agency. I have tried my fortune on the stage as a singer, and can't say but what I have succeeded. In fact, my wife and I have taken more than any two singers that have ever appeared in the humble way. We have been street vocalists for twenty-five years. We sing solos, duets, and glees, and only at night. When we started, the class of songs was very different to what it is now. We were styled 'the royal glee singers.' 'Cherry ripe,' 'Meet me by moonlight,' 'Sweet home,' were popular then. Haynes Bailey's ballads were popular, and much of Bishop's music, as, indeed, it is still. Barnett's or Lee's music, however, is now more approved in the concert-rooms than Bishop's. Our plan was and is to inquire at gentlemen's houses if they wished to hear glee, or solo singing, and to sing in the street, or in the halls, as well as at parties. When we first commenced we have made £3 and £3 10s. in a night this way; but that was on extraordinary occasions, and £3 a week might be the average earnings, take the year through. These earnings continued eight or ten years, and then fell off. Other amusements attracted attention. Now, my wife, my daughter, and I may make 25s. a week by open-air singing. Concert singing is extra, and the best payment is a crown per head a night for low-priced concerts. The inferior vocalists get 4s., 3s., 2s. 6d., and some as low as 2s. Very many who sing at the concerts have received a high musical education; but the profession is so overstocked, that excellent singers are compelled to take poor engagements." The better sort of cheap concert singers, the man and wife both agreed in stating, were a well-conducted body of people, often struggling for a very poor maintenance, the women rarely being improper characters. "But now (said the husband) John Bull's taste is inclined to the brutal and filthy. Some of the 'character songs,' such as 'Sam Hall,' 'Jack Sheppard,' and others, are so indelicate that a respectable man ought not to take his wife and daughters to see them. The men who sing character songs are the worst class of singers, both as regards character and skill; they are generally loose fellows; some are what is called 'fancy men;' persons supported, wholly or partly, by women of the town. I attempted once to give concerts without these low character-singings, but it did not succeed, for I was alone in the attempt. I believe there are not more than half-a-dozen street vocalists of the same class as ourselves. They are respecable persons; and certainly open-air singing, as we practise it, is more respectable than popular concert singing as now carried on. No one would be allowed to sing such songs in the streets. The 'character' concerts are attended, generally, by mechanics and their families; there are more males than females among the audiences.''

LETTER LVI
Thursday, June 13, 1850.

In the present Letter I shall conclude my account of the Street Performers and Showmen. The classes that are still undescribed are the lower class of street singers – the street artists – the writers without hands – the blind readers – and the street exhibition keepers. I shall begin with the Street Singers.

Concerning the ordinary street ballad-singers, I received the following account from one of the class: –

"I am what may be termed a regular street ballad-singer – either sentimental or comic, sir, for I can take both branches. I have been, as near as I can guess, about five and twenty year at the business. My mother died when I was thirteen years old, and in consequence of a step-mother, home became too hot to hold me, and I turned into the streets on account of the harsh treatment I met with. My father had given me no education, and all I know now I have picked up in the streets. Well, at thirteen years I turned into the London streets, houseless, friendless. My father was a picture-frame gilder. I was never taught any business by him – neither his own nor any other. I never received any benefit from him that I know. Well, then sir, there was I, a boy of thirteen – friendless, houseless, untaught, and without any means of getting a living – loose in the streets of London. At first I slept anywhere. Sometimes I passed the night in the Old Covent-garden Market; at others, in shutter-boxes; and at others, on door-steps near my father's house. I lived at this time upon the refuse that I picked up in the streets – cabbage stumps out of the market, orange peel, and the like. Well, sir, I was green then, and one of the Stamp-office spies got me to sell some of the *"Poor Man's Guardians"* (an unstamped paper of that time), so that his fellow-spy might take me up. This he did, and I had a month at Coldbath-fields for the business. After I had been in prison I got in a measure hardened to the frowns of the world, and didn't care what company I kept, or what I did for a living. I wouldn't have to fancy though that I did anything dishonest. I mean I wasn't particular as to what I turned my hand to for a living, or where I lodged. I went to live in Church-lane, St. Giles's, at a threepenny house, and having a tidy voice of my own, I was there taught to go out ballad singing, and I have stuck to the business ever since. I was going on for the fifteen when I first took to it. The first thing I did was to lead at glee singing. I took the air, and two others, old hands, did the second and the bass. We used to sing the "Red Cross Knight," "Hail Smiling Morn," and harmonize "The Wolf," and other popular songs. Excepting when we needed money, we rarely went out till the evening. Then our pitches were in quiet streets or squares, where we saw, by the lights at the windows, that some party was going on. Wedding parties was very good, in general quite a harvest. Public-houses we did little at, and then it was always with the parlour company; the tap-room people have no taste for glee singing. At times we took from 9s. to 10s. of an evening – the three of us. I am speaking of the business as it was about two or three and twenty years ago. Now glee singing is seldom practised in the streets of London. It is chiefly confined to the provinces at present. In London, concerts are so cheap now-a-days that no one will stop to listen to the street glee singers; so most of 'the schools' or sets have gone to sing at the cheap concerts held at the public-houses. Many of the glee singers have given up the business, and taken to the street Ethiopians instead. The street glee singers had been some of them brought up to a trade, though some had not. Few were so unfortunate as me – to have none at all. The two that I was with had been a ladies' shoemaker and a paper-hanger. Others that I knew had been blacksmiths, carpenters, linen-drapers' shopmen, bakers, French polishers, pastrycooks, and such like. They mostly left their business and took to glee singing when they were young. The most that I knew were from nineteen to twenty-two years old. They had, in general, been a little racketty, and had got stage-struck or concert struck at public-houses. They had got praised for their voices, and so their vanity led them to take to it for a living when they got hard-up. Twenty years ago there must have been at the east and west end at least fourteen different sets, good and bad, and in each set there was an average three singers; now I don't think there is one set at work in London streets. After I had been three years glee singing in the streets, I took up with the ballad business, and found it more lucrative than the glee line. Sometimes I could take 5s. in the day, and not work heavily for it either – but at other times I couldn't take enough to pay my lodging. When any popular song came up that was our harvest – "Alice Gray,' 'the Sea,' 'Bridal Ring,' 'We met,' 'the Tartar Drum' (in which I was well known), 'The Banks of the Blue Moselle,' and such like – not forgetting 'The Mistletoe Bough;' these were all great things to the ballad singers. We looked at the bill of fare for the different concert rooms, and then went round the neighbourhood where these songs were being sung, because the airs being well known, you see it eased the way for us. The very best sentimental song that ever I had in my life, and which lasted me off and on for two years, was Byron's 'Isle of Beauty.' I could get a meal quicker with that than with any other. The 'Mistletoe Bough' got me many a Christmas dinner. We always works it at that time. It would puzzle any man, even the most exactest, to tell what they could make by ballad-singing in the street. Some nights it would be wet, and I should be hoarse, and then I'd take nothing. I should think that, take one week with another, my earnings were barely more than 10s. a week – 12s. a week, on the average, I think, would be the very outside. Street ballad-singers never go out in costume. It is generally supposed that some who appear without shoes, and wretchedly clad, are made up for the purpose of exciting charity; but this the regular street ballad-singer never does. He is too independent to rank himself with the beggars. He *earns* his money, he fancies, and does not ask charity. Some of the ballad-singers may perhaps be called beggars, or rather pensioners – that is the term we give them; but these are of the worst description of singers, and have money given to them neither for their singing nor songs, but in pity for their age and infirmities. Of these there are about six in London. Of the regular ballad-singers, sentimental and comic, there are not less than 250 in and about London. Occasionally the number is greatly increased by an influx from the country. I should say that throughout England, Wales, and Scotland, there is not less than 700 who live solely by ballad singing, and selling ballads and song books. In London the ballad-singers generally work in couples – especially the comic singers. The sentimental more commonly go alone; but there are very few in London who are merely sentimental ballad-singers – not more than a dozen at the very outside. The rest sing whatever comes up. The tunes are mostly picked up from the street bands, and sometimes from the cheap concerts, or from the gallery of the theatre, where the street ballad-singers very often go, for the express purpose of learning the airs. They are mostly utterly ignorant of music, and some of them get their money by the noise they make, by being paid to move on. There is a house in the Blackfriars road where the people has been ill for these last sixteen years, and where the street ballad-singer always goes, because he is sure of getting twopence there to move on. Some, too, make a point of beginning their songs outside of those houses where straw is laid down in front. Where the knockers are done up in an old glove the ballad-singer is sure to strike up. The comic songs that are popular in the street are never indecent, but are very often political. They are generally sung by two persons, one repeating the two first lines of a verse, and the other the two last. The street ballads are printed and published chiefly in the Seven Dials. There are four ballad publishers in that quarter and three at the East-end. Many ballads are written expressly for the Seven Dials press, especially the Newgate and the political ones, as well as those upon any topic of the day. There are five known authors for the Dials press, and they are all street ballad-singers. I am one of these myself. The little knowledge I have, I have picked up bit by bit, so that I hardly know how I have come by it. I certainly knew my letters before I left home, and I have got the rest off the dead walls and out of the ballads and papers I have been selling. I write most of the Newgate ballads now for the printers in the Dials, and, indeed, anything that turns up. I get a shilling for a 'copy of verses written by the wretched culprit the night previous to his execution.' I wrote Courvoisier's sorrowful lamentation. I called it 'A Woice from the Gaol.' I wrote a pathetic ballad on the respite of Annette Meyers. I did the helegy, too, on Rush's execution. It was supposed, like the rest, to be written by the culprit himself, and was particular penitent. I didn't write that to order − I knew they would want a copy of verses from the culprit. The publisher read it over, and said, 'That's the thing for the street public.' I only got 1s. for Rush. Indeed, they are all the same price, no matter how popular they may be. I wrote the life of Manning in verse. Besides these I have written the lament of Calcraft the Hangman on the decline of his trade, and many political songs. But song and Newgate ballad writing for the Dials is very poor work. I've got five times as much for writing a squib for a rag-shop as for a ballad that has taken me double the time."

I now come to the street artists. These include the artists in coloured chalks upon the pavements, the black profile-cutters, and the blind paper-cutters.

A spare sad-looking man, very poorly dressed, gave me the following statement. He is well-known by his coloured drawings upon the flag stones:

"I was usher in a school for three years, and had a paralytic stroke, which lost me my employment, and was soon the cause of great poverty. I was fond of drawing, and colouring drawings, when a child, using sixpenny boxes of colours, or the best my parents could procure me, but I never had lessons. I am a self-taught man. When I was reduced to distress, and indeed to starvation, I thought of trying some mode of living, and remembering having seen a man draw mackerel on the flags in the streets of Bristol twenty years ago, I thought I would try what I could do that way. I first tried my hand in the New Kent-road, attempting a likeness of Napoleon, and it was passable, though I can do much better now. I made half-a-crown the first day. I saw a statement in one of your letters that I was making £1 a day, and was giving fourteen pence for a shilling. I never did. On the contrary, I've had a pint of beer given to me by publicans for supplying them with copper. It doesn't hurt me, so that you needn't contradict it unless you like. *The Morning Chronicle* letters about us are often talked over in the lodging-houses. It's fourteen or fifteen years since I started in the New Kent-road, and I've followed up 'screeving,' as it's sometimes called, or drawing in coloured chalks on the flag stones, until now. I improved with practice. It paid me well; but in wet weather I have made nothing, and have had to run into debt. A good day's work I reckoned 8s. − or 10s. a very good day's work. I should be glad to get it now. I have made 15s. in a day on an extraordinary occasion, but never more, except at Greenwich Fair, where I've practised these fourteen years. I don't suppose I ever cleared £1 a week all the year round at screeving. For £1 a week I would honestly work my hardest. I have a wife and two children. I would draw trucks or be a copying clerk, or do anything for £1 a week to get out of the streets. Or I would like regular employment as a painter in crayons. Of all my paintings the Christ's heads paid the best, but very little better than the Napoleon's heads. The Waterloo-bridge road was a favourite spot of mine for a pitch. Easton-square is another. These two were my best I never chalked 'starving' on the flags, or anything of that kind. There are two imitators of me, but they do badly. I don't do as well as I did ten years ago, but I'm making 15s. a week all the year through.

A cheerful blind man, well known to all crossing Waterloo or Hungerford Bridges, gave me the following account of his figure cutting:

"I had the measles when I was seven, and became blind, but my sight was restored by Dr. Jeffrey, at Old St. George's Hospital. After that I had several relapses into total blindness in consequence of colds, and since 1840 I have been quite blind, excepting that I can partially distinguish the sun and the gas lights, and such like, with the left eye only. I am now 31, and was brought up to house painting. When I was last attacked with blindness I was obliged to go St. Martin's workhouse, where I underwent thirteen operations in two years. When I came out of the workhouse I played the German flute in the street, but it was only a noise, not music, sir. Then I sold boot-laces and tapes in the street, and averaged 5s. a week by it – certainly not more. Next I made little wooden tobacco stoppers in the street, in the shape of legs – they're called 'legs.' The first day I started in that line – it was in Tottenham-court-road – I was quite elated, for I made half-a-crown. I next tried it by St. Clement's Church, but I found that I cut my hands so with the knives and files, that I had to give it up, and I then took up with the trade of cutting out profiles of animals and birds, and grotesque human figures in card. I established myself soon after I began this trade by the Victoria-gate, Bayswater – that was the best pitch I ever had. One day I took 15s., and I averaged 30s. a week for six weeks. At last the inspector of police ordered me off. After that I was shoved about by the police, such crowds gathered round me, until I at length got leave to carry on my business by Waterloo-bridge – that's seven years ago. I remained there till the opening of Hungerford-bridge, in May, 1845. I sit there cold or fine, winter or summer, every day but Sunday, or if I'm ill. I often hear odd remarks from people crossing the bridge. In winter time, when I've been cold and hungry, and so poor that I couldn't get my clothes properly mended, one has said, 'Look at the poor blind man, there;' and another (and oft enough, too) has answered, 'Poor blind man! he has better clothes and more money than you or me; it's all done to excite pity.' I can generally tell a gentleman's or lady's voice, if they're the real thing. I can tell a purse-proud man's voice, too. He says, in a domineering, hectoring way, as an ancient Roman might speak to his slave, 'Ah, ha! my good fellow, how do you sell these things?' Since January last I may have averaged 8s. a week; that's the outside. The working and the middling classes are my best friends. I know of no other man in my particular line, and I've often inquired concerning any.''

The next in order are the writers without hands, and the readers without eyes.

A man of 61, born in the crippled state he described, tall, and with an intelligent look and good manners, gave me this account:

"I was born without hands, merely the elbow of the right arm and the joint of wrist of the left. I have rounded stumps. I was born without feet also, merely the ankle and heel, just as if my feet were cut off close within the instep. My father was a farmer in Cavan county, Ireland, and gave me a fair education. He had me taught to write. I'll show you how, sir. (Here he put on a pair of spectacles, using his stumps, and then holding the pen on one stump, by means of the other he moved the two together, and so wrote his name in an old-fashioned hand.) I was taught by an ordinary schoolmaster. I served an apprenticeship of seven years to a turner, near Cavan, and could work well at the turning, but couldn't chop the wood very well. I handled my tools as I've shown you I do my pen. I came to London in 1814, having a prospect of getting a situation in the India-house, but I didn't get it, and waited for eighteen months until my funds and my father's help were exhausted, and I then took to making fancy screens, flower vases, and hand-racks in the streets. I did very well at them, making 15s. to 20s. a week in the summer, and not half that, perhaps not much more than a third, in the winter. I continue this work still when my health permits, and I now make handsome ornaments, flower vases, &c., for the quality, and have to work before them frequently to satisfy them. I could do very well but for ill health. I charge from 5s. to 8s. for hand-screens, and from 7s. 6d. to 15s. for flower vases. Some of the quality pay me handsomely – some are very near. I have done little work in the streets this way, except in very fine weather. Sometimes I write tickets in the street at a halfpenny each. The police never interfere unless the thoroughfare is obstructed badly. My most frequent writing is 'Naked came I into the world, and naked shall I return.' 'The Lord giveth and the Lord taketh away. Blessed be the name of the Lord.' To that I add my name, the date sometimes, and a memorandum that it was the writing of a man born without hands or feet. When I'm not disturbed I do pretty well, getting 1s. 6d. a day, but that's an extra day. The boys are a great worry to me. Working-people are my only friends at the writing, and women the best. My best pitches are Tottenham-court-road and the West-end thoroughfares. There's three men I know who write without hands. They're in the country chiefly, travelling. One man writes with his toes, but chiefly in the public-houses or with showmen. I consider that I am the only man in the world who is a handicraftsman without hands or feet. I am married, and have a grown-up family; two of my sons are in America, one in Australia, one a sailor, the others are emigrants on the coast of Africa, and one a cabinet maker in London — all fine fellows, well made. I had fifteen in all. My father and mother, too, were a handsome well-made couple.''

An intelligent man gave me the following account of his experience as a *blind reader*. He was poorly dressed, but clean, and had not a vulgar look.

"My father died when I was ten years old, and my mother in the coronation year, 1838. I am now in my thirty-eighth year. I was a clerk in various offices. I was not born blind, but lost my sight four years ago, in consequence of aneurism. I was a fortnight in the Ophthalmic Hospital, and was an out-patient for three months. I am a married man with one child, and we did as well as we could, but that was very badly, until every bit of furniture (and I had a house full of good furniture up to time) went. At last I thought I might earn a little by reading in the street. The Society for the Indigent Blind gave me the Gospel of St. John, after Mr. Freer's system, the price being 8s.; and a brother-in-law supplied me with the Gospel of St. Luke, which costs 9s. In Mr. Freer's system the regular alphabet letters are not used, but there are raised characters, 34 in number, including long and short vowels, and these characters express sounds, and a sound may comprise a short syllable. I learned to read by this system in four lessons. I first read in public in Mornington-crescent. For the first fortnight or three weeks I took from 2s. 6d. to 2s. 9d. a day — one day I took 3s. My receipts then fell to something less than 18d. a day, and have been gradually falling ever since. Since the 1st of January, this year, I haven't averaged more than 2s. 6d. a week by my street reading and writing. My wife earns 3s. or 4s. a week with her needle, slaving for a 'sweater' to a shirtmaker. I have never read anywhere but in Easton-square and Mornington crescent. On Whit Monday I made 2s. 0½d., and on Whit-Tuesday, 2s. 0½d., and that I assure you I reckon really good holiday earnings, and I read until I was hoarse with it. Once at Mornington-crescent, I counted, as closely as I could, just out of curiosity, and to wile away the time, above 2,000 persons, who passed and repassed without giving me a halfpenny. The working people are my best friends, most decidedly. I am tired of the streets, besides being half starved. There are now five or six blind men about London, who read in the streets. We can read nothing but the Scriptures, as 'blind printing' — so it's sometimes called — has only been used in the Scriptures. I write also in the streets as well as read. I use Wedgwood's manifold writer. I write verses from Scripture. There are no teaching necessary for this. I trace the letters from my knowledge of them when I could see. I believe I am the only blind man who writes so in the streets.''

After the street artists, readers, and writers, come the street exhibition men. These include the exhibitors of peep-shows, happy families, &c.

First of the peep-shows. Concerning these I received the subjoined narrative from a man of considerable experience in the "profession":

"Being a cripple I am obliged to exhibit a small peep-show. I lost the use of this arm ever since I was three months old. My mother died when I was ten years old, and after that my father took up with an Irishwoman, and turned me and my youngest sister (she was two years younger than me) out into the streets. My father had originally been a dyer, but was working at the fiddle-string business then. My youngest sister got employment at my father's trade, but I couldn't get no work because of my crippled arm. I walked about till I fell down in the streets for want. At last, a man, who had a sweetmeat-shop, took pity on me. His wife made the sweetmeats, and minded the shop while he went out a juggling in the streets, in the Ramo Samee line. He told me as how, if I would go round the country with him and sell a few prints while he was a juggling in the public-houses, he'd find me in wittles, and pay my lodging. I joined him and stopped with him two or three year. After that I went to work for a werry large waste paper dealer. He used to buy up all the old back numbers of the cheap periodicals and penny publications, and send me out with them to sell at a farden a piece. He used to give me 4d. out of every shilling, and I done very well with that, till the periodicals came so low and so many on 'em, that they wouldn't sell at all. Sometimes I could make 15s. on a Saturday night and a Sunday morning a-selling the odd numbers of periodicals, such as 'Tales of the Wars,' 'Lives of the Pirates,' 'Lives of the Highwaymen,' &c. I've often sold as many as 2,000 numbers on a Saturday night, in the New Cut, and the most of them was works about thieves and highwaymen and pirates. Besides me there was three others at the same business. Altogether, I dare say my master alone used to get rid of 10,000 copies of such works on a Saturday night and Sunday morning. Our principal customers was young men. My master made a good bit of money at it. He had been about 18 years in the business, and had begun with 2s. 6d. I was with him 15 year on and off, and at the best time. I used to earn my 30s. a week full at that time. But then I was foolish, and didn't take care of my money. When I was at the 'odd number business' I bought a peep-show. I gave £2 10s. for it. I had it second-hand. I was persuaded to buy it. A person as has got only one hand, you see, isn't like other folks, and the people said, it would always bring me a meal of victuals, and keep me from starving. The peep-shows was a doing very well then (that's about five or six years back), when the theaytres was all a shilling to go into them whole price, but now there's many at threepence and twopence, and a good lot at a penny. Before the theayters lowered, a peep-showman could make sure of his 3s. or 4s. a day, at the least, in fine weather, and on a Saturday night about double that money. At a fair he could take his 15s. to a £1 a day. Then there was about nine or ten peep-shows in London. These were all back-shows. There are two kinds of peep-shows, which we call 'back-shows' and 'caravan-shows.' The caravan-shows are much larger than the others, and are drawn by a horse or a donkey. They have a green baize curtain at the back, which shuts out them as don't pay. The showmen usually live in these caravans with their families. Often there will be a man, his wife, and three or four children living in one of these shows. These caravans mostly go into the country, and very seldom are seen in town. They exhibit principally at fairs and feasts or wakes in country villages. They generally go out of London between March and April, because some fairs begin at that time, but many wait for the fairs at May. Then they work their way right round, from willage to town. They tell one another what part they're a-going to, and they never interfere with one another's rounds. If a new hand comes into the business they're werry civil, and tells him what places to work. The carawans comes to London about October, after the fairs is over. The scenes of them carawan shows is mostly upon recent battles and murders. Anything in that way of late occurrence suits them. Theattical plays ain't no good for country towns, 'cause they don't understand such things there. People is werry fond of the battles in the country, but a murder wot is well known is worth more than all the fights. There was more took with Rush's murder than there has been even by the battle of Waterloo itself. Some of the carawan shows does werry well. Their average taking is 30s. a week or the summer months. At some fairs they'll take 5*l.* in three days. They have been about town as long as ever we can recollect. I should say there is full 50 of these carawan shows throughout the country. Some never comes into London at all. There is about a dozen that comes to London regular every winter. The business in general goes from family to family. The cost of a carawan show, second-hand is 40*l.* – that's without the glasses, and them runs from 10s. to 1*l.* a piece, because they're large. Why, I've knowed the front of a peep-show, with the glasses, cost £60; the front was mahogany, and had 36 glasses, with gilt carved mouldings round each on 'em. The scenes will cost about £6, if done by the best artist, and £3 if done by a common hand. The back-shows are peep-shows that stand on trussels, and are so small as to admit of being carried on the back. The scenery is about 18 inches to 2 foot in length, and about 15 inches high. They have been introduced about 15 or 16 years. The man as first brought 'em up was named Billy T——; he was lame of one leg, and used to exhibit little automaton figures in the New-cut. On their first coming out, the oldest backshowman as I know on has told me they could take their 15s. a day. But now we can't do more than 7s. a week, run Saturday and all the other days together – and that's through the theayters being so low. It's a regular starving life now. We has to put up with the hinsults of people so. The back-shows generally exhibits plays of different kinds wot been performed at the theayters lately. I've got many different plays to my show. I only hexhibit one at a time. There's 'Halonzer the Brave and the Fair Himogen.' 'The

Dog of Montargis and the Forest of Bondy,' 'Hyder Halley, or the Lyons of Mysore,' 'The Forty Thieves' (that never done no good to me), 'The Devil and Doctor Faustus;' and at Christmas time we exhibits pantomimes. I has some battle scenes as well. I've 'Napoleon's Return from Helba,' 'Napoleon at Waterloo,' 'The Death of Lord Nelson,' and also 'The Queen embarking to start for Scotland, from the Dockyard at Voolich.' We takes more from children than grown people in London, and more from grown people than children in the country. You see grown people has such remarks made upon them while they're a-peeping through in London, as it makes it bad for us here. Lately, I have been hardly able to get a living, you may say. Some days I've taken 6d., others 8d., and sometimes 1s. – that's what I call a good day for any of the week days. On a Saturday it runs from 2s. to 2s. 6d. Of the week days, Monday or Tuesday is the best. If there's a fair on near London, such as Greenwich, we can go and take 3s. and 4s., or 5s. a day, so long as it lasts. But, after that, we comes back to the old business, and that's bad enough; for, after you've paid 1s. 6d. a week rent, and 6d. a week stand for your peep-show, and come to buy a bit of coal, why all one can get is a bit of bread and a cup of tea to live upon. As for meat, we don't see it from one month's end to the other. My old woman, when she is at work, only gets five fardens a pair for making a pair of drawers to send out for the conwicts, and three halfpence for a shirt; and out of that she has to find her own thread. There are from six to eight scenes in each of the plays that I shows; and if the scenes are a bit short, why I puts in a couple of battle-scenes; or I make up a pannerrammer for 'em. The children *will* have so much for the money now. I charge a halfpenny for a hentire performance. There is characters and all – and I explains what they are supposed to be a talking about. There's about six back-shows in London. I don't think there's more. It don't pay now to get up a new play. We works the old ones over and over again, and sometimes we buys a fresh one of another showman if we can rise the money – the price is 2s. and 2s. 6d. I've been obligated to get rid on about twelve of my plays to get a bit of victuals at home. Formerly we used to give a hartist 1s. to go in the pit and sketch off the scenes and figures of any new play that was a doing well and we thought 'ud take, and arter that we used to give him from 1s. 6d. to 2s. for drawing and painting each scene, and 1d. and 1½d. each for the figures, according to the size. Each play costs us from 15s. to £1 for the inside scenes and figures, and the outside painting as well. The outside painting in general consists of the most attractive part of the performance. The New-cut is no good at all now on a Saturday night; that's through the cheap penny hexhibitions there. Tottenham-court-road a'nt much account either. The street markets is the best of a Saturday night. I'm often obliged to take bottles instead of money, and they don't fetch more than 3d. a dozen. Sometimes I take four dozen of bottles in a day. I lets 'em see a play for a bottle, and often two wants to see for one large bottle. The children is dreadful for cheapening things down. In the summer I goes out of London for a month at a stretch. In the country I works my battle pieces. They're most pleased there with my Lord Nelson's death at the battle of Trafalgar. 'That there is,' I tell 'em, 'a fine painting representing Lord Nelson at the battle of Trafalgar. In the centre is Lord Nelson in his last dying moments, supported by Captain Hardy and the chaplin. On the left is the hexplosion of one of the enemy's ships by fire. That represents a fine painting, representing the death of Lord Nelson at the battle of Trafalgar, wot was fought on the 12th of October, 1805.' I've got five glasses, they cost about 5s. a piece when new, and is about 3½ inches across, with a 3 foot focus.''

"Happy Families," or assemblages of animals of diverse habits and propensities living amicably, or at least quietly, in one cage, are so well known as to need no further description here. Concerning them I received the following account:—

"I have been three years connected with Happy Families, living by such connection. These exhibitions were first started at Coventry, sixteen years ago, by a man who was my teacher. He was a stocking-weaver, and a fancier of animals and birds, having a good many in his place: hawks, owls, pigeons, starlings, cats, dogs, mice, rats, guinea-pigs, jack-daws, fowls, ravens, and monkeys. He used to to keep them separate and for his own amusement, or would train them for sale, teaching the dogs tricks and such like. He found his animals agree so well together, that he had a notion – and a snake-charmer, an old Indian, used to advise him on the subject – that he could show in public animals and birds, supposed to be one another's enemies and victims, living in quiet together. He did show them in public, beginning with cats, rats, and pigeons in one cage,. and then kept adding by degrees all the other creatures I have mentioned. He did very well at Coventry, but I don't know what he took. His way of training the animals is a secret which he has taught me. It's principally done, however, I may tell you, by continued kindness and petting, and studying the nature of the creatures. Hundreds have tried their hands at happy families and have failed. The cat has killed the mice, the hawks have killed the birds, the dogs the rats, and even the cats, the rats the birds, and even one another; indeed, it was anything but a Happy Family. By our system we never have a mishap, and have had animals eight or nine years in the cage – until they've died of age, indeed. In our present cage we have 54 birds and wild animals, and of 17 different kinds; 3 cats, 2 dogs (a terrier and a spaniel), 2 monkeys, 2 magpies, 2 jackdaws, 2 jays, 10 starlings (some of them talk), 6 pigeons, 2 hawks, 2 barn fowls, 1 screech owl, 5 common-sewer rats, 5 white rats (a novelty), 8 guinea pigs, 2 rabbits (1 wild and 1 tame), 1 hedgehog, and 1 tortoise. Of all these the rat is the most difficult animal to make a member of a 'Happy Family.' Among birds, the hawk. The easiest trained animal is a monkey; and the easiest trained bird, a pigeon. They live together in their cages all night, and sleep in a stable unattended by any one. They were once thirty-six hours, as a trial, without food — that was in Cambridge; and no creature was injured, but they were very peckish, especially the birds of prey. I wouldn't allow it to be tried (it was for a scientific gentleman) any longer, and I fed them well to begin upon. There are now in London five Happy Families, all belonging to two families of men. Mine, that is the one I have the care of, is the strongest, 54 creatures; the others will average 40 each, or 214 birds and beasts in Happy Families. Our only regular places now are Waterloo-bridge and the National Gallery. The expense of keeping my 54 is 12s. a week; and in a good week — indeed the best week — we take 30s., and in a bad week sometimes not 8s. It's only a poor trade, though there are more good weeks than bad; but the weather has so much to do with it. The middle class of society are our best supporters. When the Happy Family — only one — was first in London, fourteen years ago, the proprietor took £1 a day on Waterloo-bridge, and only showed in the summer. The second Happy Family was started eight years ago, and did as well for a short time as the first. Now there are too many Happy Families. There are none in the country.''

LETTER LVII.
Thursday, June 20, 1850.

I now return to treat of the condition and earnings of the London Artizans.

The most convenient and systematic arrangement of the several classes of handicrafts is, as I have before said, according to the materials operated upon; and, comfortably with this classification, I find that there are twelve different kinds of *skilled* workmen: — 1. The workers in wool, silk, cotton, and the other textile materials. 2. The workers in skin, hair, &c. 3. The workers in woollen, silk, cotton, and leather manufactures. 4. The workers in wood, ivory, &c. 5. The workers in osier, cane, reed, rush, and straw. 6. The workers in brick and stone. 7. The workers in glass and earthenware. 8. The workers in metal. 9. The workers in paper. 10. The workers at printing. 11. The workers connected with the Fine Arts (as drawing, painting, music, &c.) 12. The manufacturers of chemicals.

This, I believe, exhausts the whole of the arts and manufactures. Every kind of artisan, mechanic, or handicraftsman, therefore, is included in one or other of the above orders of skilled labourers. Of many of these I have already treated at considerable length; and I shall proceed to inquire into the condition and earnings of the others as time and occasion may serve. At present I purpose devoting a few letters to the *workers in wood*.

These form a very considerable class, and include many handicrafts which the division of labour has long rendered distinct. Among the most important are carpenters and joiners, cabinet makers, chair makers, coach makers, wheelwrights, shipbuilders, coopers, sawyers, and turners — numbering, in London alone, upwards of 40,000 operatives and 3,500 masters. The numerical strength of the whole of the metropolitan workers in wood, at the time of taking the last census, amounted to 52,262; but of these, according to the "Post Office Directory," a considerable number (nearly 5,000) are masters — so that, deducting these, and allowing at the same time for the increase of population since 1841, it may be safely said that the entire number of working men in London connected with the fashioning of timber, is upwards of 50,000.

In my next letter I shall give a statement of the number of operatives and masters connected with each of the several handicrafts appertaining to this branch of art; at present I shall confine myself to the supply of the material.

The use of an article of such general application as timber exhibits forcibly the social and industrial progress of a people. It is of even more importance to a nation than iron or coal, being one of the principal materials used in the construction of houses, furniture, ships, boats, carts, and carriages. For each of these a different kind of wood is generally used, derived mostly from a different soil. Our houses are made principally of pine, our furniture of mahogany, our ships of oak, and our carts of ash. Most of these woods are imported from abroad; for, owing to the deficiency of our home supplies, the main part of the timber used for "framing" and "Finishing" the houses in which we live, or for constructing the beadsteads on which we sleep, the chairs on which we sit, and the tables at which we eat, originally grew in some far-distant forest. The ships that we sail in, and the carts in which our goods are carried, are, however, chiefly of home produce.

Concerning the several uses to which the different kinds of wood are applied, I have obtained the following account from one of the most intelligent men belonging to the trade in the metropolis. The timber which takes precedence in point of importance over all others in this maritime country is the English oak, of which our ships are principally constructed. English oak supplies the best quality of wood, Baltic oak the next, while the American oak is the poorest of all. The number of English oak logs employed in the building of a vessel of 1,000 tons burden, including all the frame and floor timbers, is 864. African oak and teak logs, to the number of 90, supply the materials for the beams, and the same quality of wood is used for the shelves, water-way, keelson, &c., for which purposes 56 logs are consumed; the planking inside and out, which is also of teak and African oak, requires not less than 926 planks; the average number of planks cut from each teak or African oak log being three. To form the keel, elm is used, and six logs supply the quantity required. Of Dantzic three and four inch deals, 500 are laid down to form the decks. The masts are of teak-wood, Danzic, or red fir wood. When the mast is in three pieces, it is dowelled and hooped together. English oak logs are not now cut for planking, hence for every 1,000 ton ship nearly 1,500 logs or trees are consumed. Oak timber, in addition to the uses of ship-builders, is used largely for furniture, staves, the framework of machinery, and – in some parts of the country – for gates and palings. It resists decay, or the depredations of insects, longer than most other woods, and an oak cabinet, before iron and fireproof safest depositories for deeds or valuable property. When York Minster was burnt the old oaken beams of the roof which escaped destruction were found perfectly sound. Some had grown nearly black; while others, when cut up for souvenirs, presented hardly a darker hue than that of new oakwood. Oak, in olden times, was also largely used for the frames of pictures, mirrors, and for the ornamental carved work of cathedrals and churches.

The bark of the oak supplies an important article for one of our manufactures – viz., leather. Sir Humphry Davy prepared a table, showing the quantity of extractive matter and tan in 100 parts of several substances used by tanners. The white inner bark of young oak gives 77 parts; and the coloured or middle bark, 19. The entire bark of the oak gives 29; that of the elm 13, and that of the common willow 11. Elm, a close-grained and long-enduring wood, is used for coffins. No other material, it is believed is employed in London, but in the country the cheaper coffins are sometimes made of deal. Elm is also employed largely for wheelers' work. Ash supplies the material for carts, barrows, handles for tools, and oars. Beech is made into chairs, bedsteads, shoemakers' lasts and trees, saddle-trees, and for other articles, where a particular shape, and the retention of that shape, are desirable. It is also worked largely by tool-makers. Box is used by turners, and (as it is the closest-grained wood of any) by wood-engravers, the best and largest blocks being brought from Turkey. Yew is little used now comparatively, but it has been made into presses, and (in some country places) into coffins. Walnut is the wood of which gun-stocks are made, and within the last few years it has come into use for articles of furniture. It is an exceedingly knotty wood, and was formerly considered so difficult to work that a walnut-tree cabinet, a century ago, was as valuable as curious. Fir and pines (deal) are the material of which scaffoldings, masts, ladders, flooring, roofing, doors, window-frames, and shop-fronts are constructed. Larch is used for buildings in the country. For the last ten years it has been in extensive demand, too, for railway sleepers. The once unproductive hills which, as well in Scotland as in Cumberland and Westmorland, have (many of them within the present century) been covered with larch plantations, have thus supplied a cheap and plentiful kind of timber for a purpose never dreamed of when the trees were planted. The wood of the apple and pear trees is used for butter-moulds and similar purposes. Sycamore is required sometimes for cutting boards for saddlers, bootmakers, and others who use fine-edged knives, and who must have a wood on which leather or any material may be cut without the edge of the knife being turned. Lime, however, is now accounted superior for such requirements, as chesnut was once. Maple (chiefly foreign) is used for furniture, and of late has been extensively wrought into picture frames. Birch (chiefly foreign) is employed in the manufacture of furniture, and is sometimes stained or dyed so as to resemble mahogany or rosewood. Birch bark communicates the peculiar and agreeable fragrance which distinguishes Russia leather. Willow may be cut the thinnest of any wood, so as to retain strength, and it is therefore used in making sieves, as well as by some toymakers, who also use, occasionally, alder, fir, and soft woods, working them wet. Of holly the Tonbridge ware is made (articles somewhat similar have been made of cherry tree), and it is employed for "stringing;" it is often dyed, and being white and fine grained, it would be dyed more largely to resemble ebony or the costlier foreign woods, but the small size of the tree unfits it for that purpose. Of the foreign woods, mahogany furnishes the grand staple of the better description of furniture. Coach panels and the spokes of the wheels of the best kind of work are also constructed of mahogany, the other portions of the wood-work of wheels being usually ash. Honduras mahogany is used somewhat extensively in ship-building. Lance-wood is worked into gig-shafts, and is much used for the best kind of gig whips, and for walking-sticks. Of rosewood, satinwood, and sandalwood dressing-cases, ladies' work-boxes, writing desks, tea-caddies, and similar ornamental articles of furniture are made. Cedar is ocassionally used for the like purposes, and altogether in the manufacture of pencils. It is worked too into the sides of drawers, for which its pleasant odour recommends it. Ebony and lignum vitae are used by turners, and are made into bowls, pestles, &c.

As to the quantity of timber of all kinds used in this country, it is difficult to arrive at very accurate results. "Much uncertainty," says Mr. Porter (Progress of the Nation, p. 588), "must always attend upon computations affecting the consumption of articles which, like timber, are partly furnished from our own soil, and respecting the home production of which we are without any means of calculating." It will, however, be seen from the above statement that the three principal uses to which timber is applied are the building and furnishing of houses, the construction of ships, and the making of coffins. Concerning the quantity of timber annually consumed in this manner there exist facts sufficient to enable us to arrive at a proximate conclusion. In order to do this I shall endeavour to show, first, the quantity of timber used every year in building and furnishing the houses of this country.

The number of houses in the United Kingdom at different periods can be readily obtained from the Population Returns. From these we gather the following results: —

In 1801, the number of inhabited houses in England and Wales was 1,575,923
1811 1,797,504
1821 2,088,156
1831 2,481,544
1841 2,943,939

Hence we find, that from 1801—11, the annual increase in the number of houses in England and Wales was 22,168; from 1811—21 it was 29,065; from 1821—31 it was 39,338; from 1831—41 it was 46,239; and assuming the increase during the last ten years to have been in the same ratio, we shall find that from 1841 to 1850 there have been very nearly 55,00 houses built annually throughout the kingdom, or sufficient to form one continuous row from London to Liverpool. Now it appears, from the returns obtained under the Property tax Act, that the gross rental of the houses and other buildings in England and Wales amounted in 1842−43 to upwards of thirty-five and a half millions sterling. The number of houses at that period was (allowing for the yearly increase) 2,990,178, which would give an average rental of very nearly £12 per house. It may therefore be asserted that there are 55,000 houses of an average rental of £12, built every year throughout the kingdom. To build a £12 house in the country, I am credibly informed, rather more than three loads of timber are required for the roofing, joists, &c., and about seven loads for the flooring, staircases, windows, and other parts. A load of timber, upon an average, is the produce of two trees; consequently, as there are ten loads of timber, twenty trees are used in the building of each £12 house in England and Wales; and as it has been shown that there are 55,000 such houses built every year, it follows that no less than 550,000 loads of timber, or, 1,100,000 trees are annually consumed by us in this manner. Calculating, then, that each of these trees in their native woods occupied respectively the hundredth part of an acre − or in other words, stood between twenty and twenty-one feet apart − it follows that 11,000 acres of woodlqand must be cleared every year to supply the timber for building the houses in England and Wales. To give the reader, however, a more definite idea of the extent of ground required for this purpose alone, it may be said that, in the course of every four years, we "use up" in the construction of our new buildings a forest equal in size to the whole of the metropolis, extending from Poplar in the East to Kingston in the west, and from Stoke Newington in the north to Camberwell in the south.

But each of these houses requires to be furnished; and I find, from inquiries among the trade, that the furniture appertaining to a twelve pound house may be said to consist on an average of thirty-six chairs, six tables, four bedsteads, four wash-hand stands, four chests of drawers, and one wardrobe or press. The quantity of timber requisite for making these articles I am informed by an experienced and inteligent tradesman is as follows: − The tables take upon an average one twelve foot deal each, and the chairs half a deal each; the bedsteads one deal each, and the wash-hand stands half the quantity; the chests of drawers two deals each, and the press the same amount. To make the whole of the furniture above enumerated, therefore, forty 12-foot deals would be required; thirty such deals make one load of timber, and a load of timber is equivalent to two trees; hence, allowing for other wooden articles of domestic use, as wash-tubs, stools, clothes-horses, &c., it may be asserted that one load and a half of timber, or three trees, are used upon average in furnishing each house in England and Wales. There are 55,000 new houses built every year; consequently 165,000 trees are required to make the furniture for them.

The timber required every year for the construction of the new houses in the metropolis is of course considerably less than the above, but still it is so vast as to make us wonder how the supply can possibly be maintained. According to the last census, the number of houses in London in the year 1831 was 196,666; in 1841 it was 225,531. This gives an annual increase of 2,886 houses. But an official return laid before the House of Commons in the course of last year tells us that the number of houses built within the metropolitan police district since the 1st of January, 1839, is 64,058, which gives an average annual increase during the last ten years of no less than 6,405, or very nearly double what it was in the preceding period. It also tells us that the number of new streets that have been formed since that time has been 1,652, which is at the rate of 165 every year, and that the gross length of those made since 1839 is no less than 200 miles − that is to say, there have been built in London during the last ten years a row of houses, with an average frontage of 16½ feet each, as long as the ancient Watling-street, which extended direct from London to Chester. At this rate we build every year in the metropolis houses sufficient to form one continuous line to Windsor. By the returns obtained under the Property and Income Tax Acts, the total annual value of the houses in London in 1842−43 was as follows:−

	Gross Rental.
London	£1,369,515
Inns of Court	107,527
Westminster	2,176,516
Middlesex	5,579,872
	£9,233,430

At that period the number of houses in the metropolis (allowing for the annual increase) was 231,936, which gives very nearly £40 for the average annual rental per house. I am informed that a £10 house in the country is equivalent to a £30 house in London − or, in other words, that the same quantity of materials and labour is required for the construction of the one as the other. Since, then, a £30 London house needs nine loads of timber for the construction of the roof, floors, partitions staircases, doors, window-frames, &c., it may be safely asserted that a £40 house required twelve loads for the same purpose, and consequently that each of the metropolitan houses consumes upon an average as much wood as is the produce of 24 trees. Hence the total number of trees used every year in building the new houses in London alone will amount to 153,720; and supposing these trees to occupy the same ground as before, and to run 100 to the acre, it follows that there are 1,537 acres of woodland annually consumed in this manner; that is to say, that the trees which are used every year in building the new streets of London, are sufficient to form a forest half as large again as the city of Bath.

The timber used in the construction of the new ships that are annually launched throughout the kingdom forms, likewise, a considerable item in the annual consumption. According to the returns for the last ten years, I find that the average number of vessels built every year in this country amounts to 944, the average burden of each being 145 tons. In M'Culloch's statistics of the British empire there is a statement of the number of loads of timber required for building ships of different tonnage, and according to this estimate, a ship of 161 tons will take 186 loads of timber. Hence, a ship of 145 tons burden would use 167 loads; and supposing two of such loads to be the produce of three trees, each of the ships annually built would require upon an average 250 trees for their construction; and since there are in round numbers 950 ships built every year, it follows that there are 237,500 trees used every year in the construction of the merchant vessels of this kingdom – which is equal to a forest of 2,375 acres.

The timber annually consumed in the construction of coffins also comes to a very large amount. The average number of deaths throughout the United Kingdom every year for the last ten years has been 376,093 – hence precisely that number of coffins must have been annually made. Each coffin, I am credibly informed, takes upon an average 56 feet superficial measure of one-inch elm board. An elm tree contains upon an average about 600 superficial feet of such board, so that one tree would make about 10 average-size coffins; consequently there would be 37,609 elm trees used annually in the interment of the deceased; and assuming these trees, like the rest, to run 100 to the acre, it follows that we annually consume in the burial of our dead a plantation of elms exactly equal in size to the "City of London within the walls."

We have now to inquire whence these immense supplies are derived; and this part of the subject necessarily divides itself into two branches – viz., the resources of this country, and the amount obtained from foreign lands.

Concerning the quanity and value of the timber of this island, the following is the best information to be obtained. The principal woodland counties in England are Kent, Sussex, Surrey, Hants, Worcester, Chester, with parts of Oxford, Northampton, Berks, Leicester, Nottingham, &c. In general the western counties are better wooded than the eastern, and the southern than the northern. In some of the southern and in the greater number of the south-eastern and western counties there are large stocks of timber in hedges and in pasture grounds, and the woods and plantations are in many places very considerable. The trees that are said to be indigenous to Great Britain are the oak (two species), the elm (five species), the beech, the ash, the maple, sycamore, hornbeam, lime (three species, according to Smith), the Spanish chestnut (?), the alder, birch, poplar (four species), and the Scotch fir. Of these the oak, beech, birch, and Scotch fir grow in vast forests, almost to the exclusion of other trees. The finest forests of beech are unquestionably to be seen in the southern parts of England; that tree flourishing to an extraordinary degree in the chalk and deep clay soils of Sussex and some of the neighbouring counties. The Scotch fir *(pinus sylvestris)* constitutes noble forests among the mountainous districts of North Britain, filling the valleys, and occasionally ascending to the height of 2,500 feet upon the hills, and exhibiting individual specimens of extraordinary size and beauty. Oak is found in the greatest perfection in the Weald of Kent, Sussex, and Surrey. It is also found in great excellence in hedge-rows, in Cheshire, Hereford, Monmouth, Flint, and many other parts of England and Wales. In 1792 the Surveyor-General of the Woods and Forests reported that there was a great and rapidly decreasing deficiency in the supply of oak, and he concluded by recommending that 100,000 acres in the royal forests and elsewhere should be planted with this tree. In accordance with this recommendation various enclosures have been made at different periods since that time, and now the entire extent of the royal forests enclosed and bearing oak is estimated at from 50,000 to 60,000 acres. The following table, extracted from the Fourth Report of the Commissioners of Woods and Forests (p. 27), shows the extent of the different royal forests, as well as of the number of acres in each, enclosed and appropriated to the growth of timber for the navy:

Royal Forests	Acres in each forest	Acres enclosed for the growth of timber
New Forest	66,942	6,000
Dean Forest	23,015	11,000
Alice Holt Forest	1,892	1,892
Woolmer Forest	5,945	1,700
Bere Forest	1,417	1,417
Whittlewood Forest	5,424	3,895
Salcey Forest	1,847	1,121
Whichwood Forest	3,709	1,841
Waltham Forest	3,278	..
Windsor Forest	4,402	4,402
Delamere Forest	3,847	3,847
Parkhurst Forest	900	900
Acres	122,622	38,015
Lands in Kent, Gloucester, Derby, Durham, &c., belonging to the Crown, enclosed, and planted with oak		6,612
Enclosures thrown open, and enclosed woods of spontaneous growth belonging to the Crown, estimated at		7,000
Lands in New, Dean, and Woolmer Forests, that may be planted		11,000
Total		62,627

According to the above table, the royal forests occupy altogether 122,622 acres of ground, of which not quite one-third are enclosed and appropriated to the growth of timber for the navy. This, with other Crown lands planted with oak, makes the entire space of ground devoted to the cultivation of this one tree in England, amount to upwards of 50,000 acres.

There are, however, no means of forming anything like an accurate estimate of the total quantity of woodland in England, or the value of the timber thereon. Dr. Beeke, in his "Observations on the Income-tax," says, that an estate is in general considered as having less than its proportion of growing trees of all ages, if their value do not amount to nearly two years of the clear rent. On this hypothesis, the total value of the timber in this country would be nearly £80,000,000 – the gross rental of England and Wales, in 1842-43, as determined by the assessments under the Property and Income-tax Acts, being £40,176,086, the total number of acres 4,752,000, and the average rent per statute acre, 18s. 6¾d. Mr. M'Culloch doubts, however, whether the supply of timber in the kingdom, at present, is so large as it was in 1800, when Dr. Beeke's tract was published. "Perhaps we should not be far from the truth," he says, "if we estimated the present value of the timber of England and Wales at from £40,000,000 to £50,000,000, and its yearly product at from £1,300,000 to £2,000,000. The annual income from woods is said to be "4 per cent on their value, after deducting the cost of repairs."

In the General Report of Scotland (vol. ii, page 321), the total extent of woodland in that country was estimated at 913,695 English acres, of which 501,469 were natural woods, and 462,226 plantations. If this estimate may be relied on (says Mr. M'Culloch), the total woodland must now considerably exceed one million acres. The largest and most valuable woods are in Perthshire, Aberdeenshire, Ross-shire, and Inverness-shire.

Respecting the quantity of foreign timber annually used in this country, there is little difficulty in arriving at a correct estimate. The returns given in the Trade and Navigation accounts furnish us with accurate calculations upon this point. The principal places from which our supplies of foreign timber are derived are British North America, and the shores of the Baltic. The timber trade of British America, the value of which at the beginning of the present century did not exceed £32,000, surpassed all others in magnitude a few years ago. It was favoured principally by the duty upon timber imported from British possessions, as compared with that brought from the Baltic and other foreign parts. The Canadian timber is obtained chiefly from the immense forests on the shores of the great interior lakes. The trees are cut down during the winter, partly by American axemen, who are peculiarly skilful; and the business is attended with great hardship, both from the work itself and the inclemency of the season. The trees, when felled, are put together into immense rafts, which often cover acres, and on them are raised small huts – the residence of the woodsmen and their families. Ten or twelve square sails are set up, and the rafts are navigated to Quebec, through many dangers, in which nearly a third of them are said to be lost. Those which are brought safe to their destination are ranged along the river in front of Quebec, forming a line four or five miles in extent, till they are taken down and exported in the shape of timber, deals, and staves. In 1830, the Canada merchants estimated the capital invested in this trade at £1,250,000. The value of the timber exported in 1831 was reckoned by Mr. Bliss at £1,038,000 sterling. The Canadian timber, however, is allowed by all parties to be of very inferior quality to that of the Baltic. Dr. William Howeison, in his account of the forest trees and timber trade of Russia, says, while speaking of the value of the forest trees to the Russians – "They furnish them with fir timber of the finest kind, possessing the most durable and dense texture, and in the most profuse abundance, with no trouble but that of cutting down." The most common species of wood in the immense tracts of forests extending over the northern parts of the Russian empire, consists, he tells us, for the most part, of the pine tribe. In some places the pine trees grow to a great height and size. The greater the intensity of the cold the firmer and more dense does the timber become. "The timbers that we took in at Memel, in my last voyage," I was told by a seaman belonging to a Baltic vessel, "were floated alongside on immense rafts; some of them came hundreds of miles down the rivers. There are vast forests there, and they'll last for centuries to come. The first that I saw I thought was more like a black cloud than anything else. The rough timber is cut in windmills, built for the purpose; and the deals are cut and squared in them. I have seen scores of windmills on the Russian coast, and in the Gulf of Finland. Some of the windmills I have seen keep twenty saws continually going." The committee of the House of Lords observe, in their first report on the foreign trade of the country, that the North American timber is more soft, less durable, and every description of it more liable to dry-rot than timber of the north of Europe. "On the whole," they say, "it is stated by one of the commissioners of his Majesty's navy – the most distinguished for practical knowledge, experience, and skill – that the timber of Canada, both oak and fir, does not possess, for the purpose of ship-building, more than half the durability of wood of the same description. The result of its application to other purposes of building," they add, "is described by timber-merchants and carpenters to be nearly similar (p. 4)." In his evidence before the committee, Sir Robert Seppings said, "About the year 1796 there were a certain number of frigates built of the fir of the Baltic, and their average durability was about eight years. About the year 1812 there were a considerable number of frigates built, also of fir, but of the growth of North America, and their average durability was not half that time." Mr. Copland, an extensive builder and timber-merchant, also stated, in his evidence before the same committee, that the bulk of timber imported from America is very inferior in quality to the Baltic timber, being much softer in its nature, not so durable, and particularly liable to dry-rot; indeed, it is not allowed to be used by any professional man under Government," he said; "nor is it ever used in the best buildings in London. It is only speculators that are reduced to use it, from the price of it being much lower than the Baltic timber, on account of the difference in the duty. If you were to lay two planks of American timber upon each other, they would, to a certain extent, have the dry-rot, almost invariably, in the course of a twelvemonth."

The greater part of the mahogany imported into this country comes from Honduras, where there are thick forests containing this and the logwood tree. On this coast the English have stipulated for a right to settle. They are established on the river Belise, which is navigable for 200 miles up the country. The mahogany trees are very thinly scattered through the forests, and are cut down by gangs of negroes, preceded by what is called "the finder," who mounts the tops of the highest trees, and finds out where a mahogany tree stands. The chief expense is in the conveyance of the trunks to the coast.

Before entering into a statement as to the exact quantity of foreign timber introduced into this kingdom, it is necessary that I should explain certain customs and technicalities of the trade.

The foreign timber trade is divided into two classes – hewn and sawn timber, called in the trade "timber" and "deals." By "timber" is meant that which is merely hewn and brought to this country, squared ready for use, and fit for house or ship building. This consists of American red pine, yellow pine, elm, ash, oak, and birch. The teak trade is of recent date, and seems to be an exception to this classification. Mahogany and dye woods, again, are not styled timber. The deals are sawn for the carpenters', or joiners', use. They are sawn in Canada and the other countries from which they are imported, and where immense steam-mills have been erected for that purpose. The advantage to the trader, in having this process effected abroad rather than in England, seems to be that no refuse matter forms a part of the cargo. Were the pine brought in logs, the bark and the unevenness of the tree would add greatly to the freight for what was valueless; but, being cut into different lengths, widths, and thicknesses, it admits of more compact stowage.

When the timber is sawn it has different names applied to it, according as it is cut into pieces of different lengths, widths, or thicknesses. If cut into pieces above 6 foot long and under 2½ inches thick, it is termed *battens or deals,* according as they are respectively under or over 7 inches wide; if cut into pieces under 6 foot long, it is called either batten ends or deal ends, according as they are under or over 7 inches in width; while, if cut into pieces of the same length and width as the deals, but under 4 inches in thickness, they are termed *planks,* and when 1½ inch thick, the right name is *boards.* A batten, then, is strictly a narrow deal; a batten end a short batten; and a deal end a short deal. A *board,* on the other hand, is merely a thin plank. Firewood consists of hewn timber ends, and deal ends, not more than 18 inches long, and each of these must be twice split before leaving the ship, so that it may not be converted to other uses.

The table on page 39 showing the quantity of hardwoods and timber imported into the United Kingdom, during the last ten years, has been constructed from the Trade and Navigation Accounts.

On reference to the table on page 39, it will be seen that the principal kinds of hardwood and timber imported into this country are mahogany, "hewn logs of fir, eight inches square and upwards," sawn deals, and deal ends. The average quantity of mahogany imported every year appears to be 30,000 tons, and that of the hewn and sawn timber between 1,500,000 and 2,000,000 loads − a load being 50 cubic feet. Of this nearly the whole is consumed in the United Kingdom, only a small proportion − not half per cent. of the whole − going out of the country.

As a ready means, however, of obtaining a concise summary of the facts detailed in the above table, I avail myself of the annual returns given in the valuable circular of Messrs. Churchill and Sim, the eminent wood-brokers (to whom I beg thus publicly to tender my thanks), especially as the reader will bι ∾nabled by this means to arrive at the relative quantities of foreign and colonial timber that have been introduced since 1844.

	Colonial Timber and Deals in Loads.		Foreign Timber and Deals in Loads.		Total Loads.
1844	941,221	......	544,136	......	1,485,357
1845	1,281,974	......	676,752	......	1,958,726
1846	1,221,096	......	809,024	......	2,030,110
1847	1,084,000	......	776,000	......	1,860,000
1848	1,102,254	......	701,080	......	1,803,334
1849	1,072,000	......	580,000	......	1,652,000

Hence it appears that the colonial timber constitutes nearly two-thirds, and the foreign about one-third, of the entire quantity imported. If we assume the whole of the timber brought into this country to represent 100, the proportions contributed by Russia, Prussia, Sweden, Norway, and British North America, which are the principal places from which our supply is derived, will be as follows:− Russia 13.2 per cent., Prussia 12.7 per cent., Sweden 6.8 per cent., Norway 5.5 per cent., of the whole, and British North America 61.8 per cent. of the entire quantity imported.

I now come to consider the value of the timber imported into this country. Concerning the worth of the supplies derived annually from abroad, the Government returns hardly enable us to come to any definite result, for they are calculated at the *official* rates of valuation which were fixed in 1695, and these have consequently, long ceased to be any test of the *real* value of commodities.

QUANTITIES OF HARD WOODS AND TIMBER IMPORTED INTO THE UNITED KINGDOM DURING THE FOLLOWING YEARS:

		1839	1840	1841	1842	1843	1844	1845	1846	1847	1848	1849
HARD WOODS												
Box wood	Tons	496	1,609	2,405	1,082	2,779	1,328	1,377	889	1,306	1,124	No returns
Cedar (under 8-inch square)	"	3,144	2,697	1,381	819	2,722	3,340	4,631	5,593	1,671	741	..
Mahogany	"	25,859	23,115	19,502	16,938	20,284	25,622	38,350	41,689	34,009	31,668	29,021
Rosewood	"	1,738	1,585	2,491	1,115	3,262	4,337	1,196	3,417	998	1,949	No returns
TIMBER, viz.:												
Batten and batten ends	Gt. Hds.	20,118	19,449	19,546	8,797							
Deal and deal ends	"	80,647	73,669	73,866	36,042							
Masts above 6 in. and under 8 in. diameter	Numbers	17,188	17,102	15,259	5,543							
Ditto above 8 in. and under 12 in.	"	5,263	5,932	4,854	2,164							
Ditto 12 in. and upwards	"	9,308	7,264	*7,446	*3,460							
Oak planks	"	3,558	7,012	*2,577	*2,172							
Staves	Gt. Hds.	81,020	96,849	92,069	35,797							
Fir 8 in. square and upwards	Loads	623,265	692,498	654,111	231,386							
Oak	"	50,752	59,136	44,372	11,317							
Unenumerated	"	51,676	65,529	63,687	17,200							
Wainscot logs	"	2,644	2,827	1,501	1,125							
TIMBER, entered since Oct. 10, 1842, viz.:												
Sawn or split	Loads				159,044	609,693	727,456	881,643	775,833	861,755	864,593	811,120
By tale: Battens and batten ends, boards, deals, deal ends, and planks	Gt. Hds.				195	318	246	130	77	44	110	25
Not sawn or split	Loads				220,209	767,952	757,901	1,077,084	1,249,106	1,031,067	928,741	821,594
Staves	"				17,147	57,594	73,255	86,011	79,648	62,681	54,306	79,882

*These are counted in loads.

VALUE OF THE HARD WOODS, TIMBER, DEALS, AND STAVES
IMPORTED INTO GREAT BRITAIN, CALCULATED AT THE OFFICIAL
RATES OF VALUATION.

Year.	Mahogany	Rosewood	Timber sawn or split.	Timber, not sawn or split.	Staves.	Total.
	£	£	£	£	£	£
1841	223,605	33,289	145,206	772,312	65,274	1,239,686
1842	172,588	52,447	128,739	724,118	61,737	1,139,629
1843	140,098	27,222	90,511	457,364	33,157	748,352
1844	175,872	68,496	119,568	665,690	39,147	1,068,773
1845	219,416	25,115	145,539	763,286	51,380	1,144,736
1846	342,618	92,389	179,495	980,721	57,537	1,662,760
1847	352,536	71,760	158,066	1,158,862	54,689	1,795,913
1848	304,618	21,088	186,122	980,597	46,589	1,539,014
1849	292,436	41,847	183,659	851,879	38,472	1,498,293

As a guide to the *real* value of the several kinds of wood imported into this
country, I shall now give an account of the prices that foreign timber and
deals have obtained in the London market for the last six years. These are
collected from the circulars of Messrs. Churchill and Sim, who have kindly
supplied me with copies of their annual statements since the year 1844. By
these means we shall be enabled to arrive at a brief history of the timber
trade; which becomes especially valuable when viewed in connection with
the account of the duties given below.

The Wood trade in the year 1844 commenced with large stocks and lower
prices than had been previously known; almost every article was below the
cost of importation. The great feature of the season was the Swedish wood
trade – the supply of fir timber thence having been larger than had ever
been known, and the price below all other Baltic timber or Quebec red pine.
The importations from Canada were extensive, though less considerable
than in 1843. In the foreign trade, Norway deals maintained their general
character, and realised a steady price throughout the year, the importation
not having been excessive. The Russian trade from St. Petersburg and
Archangel was rather less than in the previous year. In 1845, the importation
of wood was greater than that of 1841, the ships being of heavier tonnage.
From Russia, moreover, the supply was rather under the average, in
consequence of the advanced cost in shipping, price, and freight. Quebec
oak and elm timber rose high towards the close of the season, but ash timber
was scarcely saleable. Staves from the Baltic were imported more extensively than in former years, owing to the total remission of duty. In this year,
railway sleepers of Quebec pine timber were extensively imported from the
colonies, chiefly on contract. In 1846 the increased importation of foreign
timber in London was the chief feature of the season. From Russia the
supply of deals was rather less than usual, and remunerative rates were

obtained at the latter part of the year for fresh St. Petersburg and Archangel deals. The trade in Norway deals was also much reduced. The consumption of East India teak rendered it a growing trade, especially as the supply of African teak was difficult to procure. The leading feature in the foreign timber trade of 1847 was an increased supply of Dantzic fir. In 1848 abundant supplies were received from Sweden, the trade from the ports within the Baltic being the leading feature in the foreign importation of that year. The supply from Prussia was less than in the preceding year, on account of the suspension of the trade during the Danish embargo. East India teak became an established trade, the wood being much esteemed. In 1849 the importation from Canada was very large, the deals exceeding the supply of 1848; the staves being double, while the timber remained the same. The trade with Norway was small, and the sales very difficult. The Finland supply of deals and battens was larger than in 1848. East India teak was brought in freely. Quebec red pine had again to contend with "low-priced" timber from the Baltic, the import cost being too high to be realised for a single cargo. Inferior deals and battens were likewise imported on account of the restriction of the trade between Norway and France. Firewood continued to constitute a large portion of the freights from Norway; and the ports of Sweden, in the Gulf of Bothnia, increased their supply of timber to this country. On the whole, the wood trade of 1849 was carried on with loss to Canada, and without profit to New Brunswick. it was adverse to Norway in quality, to Russia in price, and favourable only to the timber of Sweden, the deals of Russia, and the staves of all countries. Such is a brief history of the foreign timber trade for the last six years.

The next part of the subject that presents itself is the amount of duty imposed upon the different kinds of timber and hard woods, as well as the revenue derived from the importation of wood. In the Trade and Navigation Accounts the different kinds of woods are divided into two classes, viz., hard woods and timber. The hard woods there enumerated, as formerly subject to duty, are boxwood, cedar, mahogany, and rosewood; while under the denomination of "timber" are given deals and dead ends, battens and batten ends, masts, staves, fir, oak, wainscot logs, &c. Since the 10th of October, 1842, the several kinds of "timber" have been differently arranged, and now they are divided into "timber or wood sawn or split," and into "timber or wood not sawn or split, or otherwise dressed, except hewn." The rates of duty levied on the hard woods were, in 1839, from 20s. to 80s. per ton, if imported from British possessions; and from 100s. to 200s., if from foreign parts. The largest amount of duty, namely, 200s., was upon rosewood. The duty upon mahogany was as high as 100s. per ton, if brought from foreign parts, and 80s. from British possessions; while that on cedar and boxwood was 10s. and 20s. from British possessions, and 50s. and 100s. from foreign parts. The duty on hard woods continued the same until the 9th of July, 1842, when it was considerably diminished; and on the 19th of March, 1845, all hard woods were allowed to be introduced into England *free*.

The rates of duty levied on "timber" were, in 1839, as follows: For battens, according to their size, from 20s. to 40s. per 120, if imported from British possessions; and from 200s. to 400s. per 120, when imported from foreign parts. Batten ends were rated at from 7s. 6d. to 15s. per 120, from British possessions; and from 60s. to 120s. from foreign parts. For deals, the duty ranged, according to their size, from 40s. to 200s. per 120 from British possessions; and from 330s. to 880s. from foreign parts. Deal ends were charged from 15s. to 30s. per 120, if brought from British possessions; and from 120s. to 240s., if from foreign parts. The impost upon masts was, in proportion to their diameter, from 1s. 6d. to 4s. each, from British possessions; and from 8s. to 22s. from foreign parts. Oak planks, per load, were 15s., from British possessions; and 80s., from foreign parts. Staves, according to their length, from 2s. to 10s. per 120 from British possessions, and from 23s. to 96s. from foreign parts. Fir was 10s. per load, from British possessions, and 55s. per load from foreign parts; and oak the same. Wainscot logs of British produce were 12s., and of foreign 55s. per load; while other unenumerated kinds of timber were 5s., if from British possessions; and 28s., if from foreign parts. On May 15, 1840, a slight increase took place in the duties on all the above classes of timber, with the exception of staves, the shortest kind of deals, and the smaller description of masts, which were allowed to remain the same. After this, the duties continued unaltered until October 10, 1842, when an entirely different arrangement was made. Timber was then, as I before stated, divided into "sawn or split," and *"not* sawn or split." The duty on the former class was 2s. per load, if from British possessions, and 38s. if from foreign parts; while that on the latter was 1s., when imported from British possessions, and 30s. from foreign parts.

The duty on staves of British produce was fixed at 2s. per load, while the foreign were 28s. The duty on battens and batten ends, per 120, was at the same time changed to 36s. 7d. British, and 256s. foreign; and that on boards, deals, deal ends, and planks, to 58s. 8d. British, and 497s. foreign. In 1843 the duty on battens and batten ends, and on boards, deals, deal ends, and planks, was slightly decreased. The duty on staves remained unaltered, as did the duty on timber coming from British possessions, whether "sawn or split," or "not sawn or split;" while that coming from foreign parts was somewhat reduced if "sawn or split," and increased if "not sawn or split." No further alteration took place (with the exception of staves under 72 inches long, which became free on the 19th of March, 1845) until April 5, 1847. Then the duty on timber sawn or split, and not sawn or split, if imported from foreign possessions, was considerably decreased. That brought from British possessions, however, remained unaltered. The duty on battens and batten ends, boards, deals, deal ends, and planks, whether from British possessions, or foreign parts, were likewise greatly reduced. Foreign staves also underwent a slight reduction per load. On the 5th of April, 1848, a further change took place; the duty on timber sawn or split was reduced to 20s. per load, if coming from foreign parts; and that on foreign timber not sawn or split to 15s. per load. The duty on timber of British produce remained unchanged, as did that upon staves coming from British possessions; while on those coming from foreign parts it was decreased to 18s. Battens and batten ends, and boards, deals, and planks, were also reduced. Upon battens and batten ends, if imported from British possessions, the impost was 18s. 6d. per load; and from foreign parts, 129s. Upon boards, deals, and planks, it was 29s. 10d., if of British growth; and 251s. 4d., if brought from foreign parts.

The duty at the present time stands thus: – Upon "timber sawn or split" it is 2s. per load, if brought from British possessions; and 20s. per load, if from other parts. Upon battens and batten-ends boards, deals, deal-ends, and planks, the impost is the same, while timber not sawn or split is charged at the rate of 1s. per load British, and 15s. foreign. Staves of all kinds are free.

The net revenue derived from the receipt of the duties above enumerated has been as follows:

Year.	Hard Woods.	Timber.	Total.
1839	£63,144	£1,540,200	£1,603,344
1840	60,966	1,662,770	1,723,736
1841	55,712	1,438,331	1,494,043
1842	18,783	917,601*	936,384
1843	15,447	643,980	659,427
1844	16,969	901,078	918,047
1845	2,540§	1,431,737	1,434,277
1846	Free.	1,109,060	1,109,060
1847	...	974,299	974,299
1848	...	721,659	721,659

* The duty was altered on the 10th October of this year: the duty collected before that date in the same year was 766,803*l.*, and after it 210,798*l.*

§ The duty was taken off hard woods on the 19th March in this year.

The next point that it becomes necessary to ascertain, in order to take a comprehensive view of all the parties engaged in the wood trade, is the number of hands engaged in bringing the foreign timber to this country. This is easily ascertained from the Government reports.

The following table, which has been constructed from the official returns, shows the number and the average tonnage and crew of the vessels that entered the ports of the United Kingdom from the different countries whence our foreign timber and deals are derived.

TABLE, EXHIBITING THE NUMBER AND AVERAGE TONNAGE OF VESSELS (BRITISH AND FOREIGN) TRADING FROM THE BALTIC AND BRITISH NORTH AMERICAN COLONIES THAT ENTERED THE PORTS OF THE UNITED KINGDOM IN 1848.

	BRITISH.			FOREIGN.		
	Ships.	Average Tonnage	Average Crew	Ships.	Average Tonnage	Average Crew
British North American Colonies ..	2,270	380	14	—	—	—
Russia	2,274	214	9	228	267	15
Prussia	1,343	150	6	671	193	8
Sweden	136	134	6	539	183	8
Norway	34	58	6	928	153	8

But the whole of these vessels do not bring wood cargoes only. The proportions of those coming from the several countries above mentioned, I am informed, by Mr. Taylor, of the West India Dock, may be estimated as follows: – Of the Russian and Prussian vessels, two-thirds are laden with timber; of the Swedish vessels only one-third, while the whole of the ships coming from Norway and British North America seldom or never bring any other cargo. Hence the number of seamen – British and foreign – engaged in the carrying of timber to the country may be said to be as follows: – Employed in the North American timber trade, 31,906; British seamen; in the trade from Russia, 13,644 British seamen and 2,880 foreigners; in that from Prussia, 5,376 British, and 3,584 foreigners; in that from Sweden, 270 British and 1,440 foreigners; and in that from Norway, 204 British seamen, and 7,424 foreigners. From this, then, it would appear that the timber trade of the Baltic and the British North American colonies gives employment to no less than 51,400 British seamen, and 15,328 foreigners, or, in all, to 66,728 mariners.

Besides the seamen engaged in "carrying" the foreign timber, there are the labourers employed at the several ports and docks throughout the kingdom to discharge the cargoes of the timber ships, and the raftmen and porters to sort, pile, and stow. This class may fairly be estimated at some few thousands. The men who are engaged in the working or fashioning of the wood itself constitute a very large portion of the community, and one of the most intelligent and respectable classes among the artisans. Of these the carpenters and joiners are by far the most numerous. In Great Britain they amount to nearly 180,000 individuals. In 1841 their number was 162,977; and, allowing them to have increased at the rate of 10 per cent. since that period, their precise number at present would be 179,274. The cabinet-makers, at the time of taking the last census, were, in round numbers, 30,000; the sawyers 29,500; the wheelwrights, 26,000; the shipbuilders, ship-carpenters and shipwrights, 20,500; the coopers, 18,000; the coachmakers, 12,500; the turners, 7,000; and the hair-makers, 5,000; and over and above these there were upwards of 30,000 individuals engaged in other descriptions of wood work, such as pattern and clog making, boat and barge building, block, mast, and oar making, lath rending and making, bobbin making, &c. &c. These altogether give a sum total of nearly 330,000 individuals; so that, allowing for the increase of population since 1841, it may be safely stated that the workers in wood throughout Great Britain at the present time are at least 350,000 in number; and, adding to these the 50,000 seamen engaged in the foreign timber trade, as well as the dock labourers and porters connected therewith, we arrive at the conclusion that there are at present in Great Britain between four and five hundred thousand working men, or nearly one fortieth part of the entire population, connected with the wood trade of this country. This agrees in a great measure with the opinions of the operatives themselves, who estimate their body at half a million strong.

The above is as comprehensive a view of the timber trade of this country generally as it is possible to give in this brief space. Concerning the trade of the metropolis in particular, it is my intention to be more explicit. But this I must reserve for my next letter.

LETTER LVIII.
Thursday, June 27, 1850.

In my last Letter I gave an account of the supply and consumption of timber throughout the country generally. In the present I shall confine myself to the importations of the condition of the labourers connected with the foreign and colonial timber trade.

The quantity of colonial and foreign timber that has been brought into the Port of London since the year 1843 has been as follows:

Imported into London	1844.	1845.	1846.
Colonial Deals and Battens (in pieces)	2,025,000	2,349,000	2,355,000
Foreign ditto (in ditto)	2,130,000	2,290,000	1,242,000
Total pieces	4,155,000	4,639,000	3,597,000
Colonial Timber (in loads)	57,200	55,800	53,600
Foreign ditto (in ditto)	58,200	68,100	86,000
Total loads	115,400	123,900	139,600
	1847.	1848.	1849.
Colonial Deals and Battens (in pieces)	3,339,000	2,740,000	2,722,000
Foreign ditto (in ditto)	1,996,000	2,044,000	1,903,000
Total pieces	5,335,000	4,784,000	4,625,000
Colonial Timber (in loads)	49,600	38,300	38,600
Foreign ditto (in ditto)	79,100	69,000	61,400
Total loads	128,700	107,300	100,000

The consumption of the metropolis has been little less than the quantity imported. In the six years above enumerated, the total importation of foreign and colonial deals and battens was 27,135,000 pieces, of which 26,695,573 were consumed in London; and the total importation of foreign and colonial timber was 714,900 loads of which 644,224 were consumed. This gives an average annual importation of 4,522,500 deals and battens, of which only73,238 have been sent out of the country every year. Of timber, the average annual importation was 119,159 loads, and the average annual exportation only 11,779 loads.

The number of wood-laden ships that have entered the Port of London since 1840, together with the countries whence they came, is given below. By this we shall perceive that our trade with Norway in this respect has sunk to exactly one-half of what it was ten years back; while that with Sweden and Finland has been very nearly doubled in the same time. The timber ships from the Prussian ports have increased little less than one-third, while those from Russia have decreased in the same proportion. The trade with Quebec and Montreal also appears to be much greater than it was in 1840; though, compared with 1841, there has been a considerable falling off; that of New Brunswick and Nova Scotia remains very nearly the same as it was at the beginning of the decennial period. Altogether the great change appears to have been the decline of the Norwegian and Russian timber trade, and the increase of that with Sweden and Prussia. It is also worthy of notice that, notwithstanding the increase of population, the number of wood-laden ships entering the Port of London every year has not materially increased within the last ten years.

THE NUMBER OF CARGOES OF TIMBER, DEALS AND BATTENS IMPORTED INTO LONDON IN THE FOLLOWING YEARS:—

....	1840	1841	1842	1843	1844	1845	1846	1847	1848	1849
Christiana and Sannesund .	49	50	47	27	36·	27	22	32	39	23
Other Ports of Norway	52	43	38	36	49	39	17	28	25	27
Gothenburg	61	64	49	59	59	66	30	67	55	41
Swedish Ports and Finland .	85	84	85	102	90	149	103	101	138	154
Russian Ports	181	108	130	119	163	115	146	91	113	136
Prussian Ports	70	70	52	104	143	124	100	187	108	100
Quebec and Montreal	168	224	188	230	206	206	166	216	179	196
New Brunswick and Novia Scotia	104	97	62	134	90	102	127	145	108	105
Sierra Leone, Moulmein, &c.	16	20	29	31	5	10	20	21	13	20
....	786	760	681	842	841	838	740	868	778	790

The next step in our inquiry is what becomes of the 800 "wood-laden" ships that annually enter the Port of London? Whither do they go to be unladen — to what docks or places of "special security" are they consigned to be discharged, and to have their cargoes delivered or bonded?

For this purpose there are five docks, three of which lie on the Surrey side of the river. These three are the Commercial Docks, the Grand Surrey Canal Dock, and the East Country Dock, and they are almost contiguous to each other — the Surrey Canal Dock lying immediately alongside the Commercial, and the East Country at the upper end of it. They are situated in, and indeed occupy nearly the whole of, that small cape of land which is formed by the bending of the river between the Pool and Limehouse Reach. The docks on the Middlesex side of the river, which are used for the reception and unlading of timber ships, are the West India and the "Regent's Dock," or the entrance to the Regent's Canal.

The number of wood-laden ships that have entered the three principal docks for the last ten years is given below. I am informed by Mr. Jones, of the Commercial Docks, that for every ship above 100 tons, six men are required to sort and pile away. Rafting from ships of the above burden requires one or two men daily, according to circumstances.

THE NUMBER OF WOOD-LADEN SHIPS WHICH ENTERED THE DIFFERENT DOCKS UNDERMENTIONED, IN THE FOLLOWING YEARS:—

Year.	West India Docks.		Commercial Docks.		Grand Surrey Docks.	
	Vessels.	Tons.	Vessels.	Tons.	Vessels.	Tons.
1840	155	62,024	211	65,809	135	40,447
1841	201	82,196	215	70,438	114	34,594
1842	136	54,931	250	87,124	100	29,596
1843	169	71,211	368	121,846	108	31,299
1844	121	53,581	480	142,223	173	48,896
1845	149	70,514	424	137,047	155	43,211
1846	182	88,308	351	111,189	195	50,908
1847	228	124,114	423	143,966	226	62,433
1848	138	76,650	412	132,406	195	53,423
1849	138	67,860	410	136,329	212	58,780
Total	1,617	751,389	3,544	1,148,377	1,613	453,587
Average number of ships per year, and ther average tonnage	161	4,464	354	321	161	281

The foreign and colonial timber trade is, then, confined to five of the seven docks belonging to the port of London. Of these five, three — the Commercial, the Grand Surrey Canal, and the East Country — ae situate on the Surrey side of the river, occupying altogether an area of 172½ acres, of which 100½ are water, and 72 land, and offering accommodation and protection for no less than 678 vessels. Here the principal part of the timber and deal trade is carried on — the Commercial receiving the greatest number of wood-laden vessels — perhaps greater than any other dock in the world. These together with that portion of the West India Dock which is devoted to the same purpose, make the entire extent of the timber docks attached to the port of London about 250 acres, of which upwards of 140 are water — a space sufficient to give berths to no less than 940 ships.

I now come to speak of the condition and earnings of the labourers connected with the "timber" and "hardwood" trade. Of these it appears there are 1,000 men casually employed at all the timber docks, of whom only 132 obtain work all the year round. How the 900 casual "deal porters" and "rafters" live during the six months of the year that the "slack season" usually lasts in the timber trade, is another of the great mysteries of London life. As not a sixpence of their earnings is saved in the "brisk season," their fate in the winter is to suffer privations and afflictions which they only know.

I shall begin with the state of the Dock labourers employed at the Furniture and Hard Wood Trade. This trade is confined mainly, of not solely, to the West India Dock.

Concerning this branch of the wood trade, I give below the statement of a man who has worked at it for many years, and in doing so I wish to draw attention to the latter part of the narrative, as a proof of what I have repeatedly asserted respecting the regard exhibited by the authorities of the West India Dock, and in particular by Mr. Knight, the superintendent, for the welfare of all the men, whether directly or even *indirectly* employed by them.

This *indirect* employment of workmen, however, is the great bane of the industrious classes. Whether the middleman goes by the name of sweater, chamber-master, lumper, or contractor, it is this trading operative who is the great means of reducing the wages of his fellow-working men. To make a profit out of the employment of his brother operatives he must obtain a lower-class labour. He cares nothing about the quality of the work, so long as the workman can get through it somehow, and will labour at a cheap rate. Hence it becomes a *business* with him to hunt out the lowest grades of working-men – the drunken, the dishonest, the idle, the vagabond, and the unskilful – because these, being unable to obtain employment at the regular wages of the sober, honest, industrious, and skilful portion of the trade, he can obtain their labour at a lower rate than what is usually paid. "Boy labour or thief labour," said a middleman on a large scale, as I showed in a former letter, "what do I care, so long as I can get my work done cheap?" I have already shown that the wives of the sweaters not only parade the streets of London on the look-out for youths raw from the country, but that they make periodical trips to the poorest provinces of Ireland, in order to obtain workmen at the lowest possible rate. I have shown, moreover, that foreigners are annually imported from the Continent for the same purpose, and that among the chamber-masters in the shoe trade, the child market at Bethnal-green, as well as the workhouses, are continually ransacked for the means of obtaining a cheaper kind of labour. All my investigations go to prove that it is chiefly by means of this middleman system that the wages of the working men are reduced. This contractor – this trading operative – uses the most degraded of the class as a means of underselling the worthy and skilful labourers, and of ultimately dragging the better down to the abasement of the worst. If *men* cannot subsist on lower prices, then he takes apprentices, or hires children; or if workmen of character and worth refuse to work at less than the ordinary rate, then he seeks out the moral refuse of the trade – those whom none else will employ; or else he flies to the workhouse and the gaol to find labour meet for his purpose. Backed by this cheap and refuse labour, he offers his work at lower prices, and so keeps on reducing the wages of his brethren, until all sink in poverty, wretchedness, and vice. I am, therefore, the more anxious to impress upon the minds of those gentlemen who are actuated by a sincere regard for the interest and comforts of the men in their employ the evils of such a system; for, however, great may be the saving of trouble effected by it, unless it be strictly watched (as I must confess it is at the West India and Commercial Docks), it can only be maintained by the employment of a cheaper and worse-class labourer, and therefore must result in the degradation of the workmen. I have said thus much because I find this contract system the general practice at all the wood docks, and because I am convinced that the gentlemen to whom the management of those docks is entrusted – Mr. Knight, Mr. Jones, and Mr. Cannan – have the welfare of the men in their employ sincerely at heart. Of the evils of *lumping*, or discharging wood ships by *contract*, I have already treated at considerable length. Under that system, it will be remembered, I showed that the contractor, who is commonly a publican, makes his profit not by cheapening the labourer, but by intoxicating him. Like the contractor for ballast, he gets his money out of the drunkenness of the workmen, and by this means is enabled to undersell the dock proprietors – or, in other words, to discharge the wood-laden ships at a less rate than they could possibly afford to do by the fair and honourable employment of their men. Of the effects of this system – the drunkenness of the men – the starvation of the wives – the squalor and ignorance of the children – the wretchedness and desolation of the homes – I have already treated at some length; and it will be seen at the end of the present letter, that in those docks where the supervision that is maintained at the West Indias and Commercial is not kept up, the labourers are reduced to almost the same state of poverty and destitution.

But to return. A man living in a small room, in a poor neighbourhood, but in a tidy apartment, and with a well-kept little garden at the back, gave me the following account of his earnings and labour in the *Mahogany Department of the West India Docks*:

"I have worked in the West India Docks for eleven years, and for the last half of that time in the mahogany part of the wood-yard. Before that, I was eleven years in the merchant service as able seaman. But I got married, and thought I could do better in the docks, for, after all, what is £18 a year, supposing I had the luck to be at sea for nine months every year, at £2 a month? What is £18 a year, sir, to keep a wife and family on, as well as a man himself, when he's ashore? At the West India Dock we unload the mahogany, or logwood, or fancy woods, from the ships, and pile them wherever they're ordered. We work in gangs of six or seven, with a master at the head of the gang. The logs are got out of the hold with a purchase and a jigger, and heaved ashore by a crane on to a truck, and we drag the truck to the place to stow the timber. In the wood-yards a machine lifts the timber up, by us men turning handles to work the machine, and puts it into its place in the warehouse. We are paid 2s. 6d. a day, working from eight to four. If only employed for four hours – and we're not set to work for less than four hours – we have 1s. 4d. If I could get 2s. 6d. a day all the year through I'd be a happy man, but I can't. Me, and such as me, earns 10s., 11s., or as far as 15s. a week when we are wanted. But, take the year through, I make between 9s. and 10s. a week. Out of that I have to keep a wife and four children. I've lost one child, and my wife can get little or nothing most times to do with her needle, and if she does get work, what can she make at five farthings or three-halfpence a shirt for the slop-shops? My eldest child, however, does make 1s. or 1s. 6d. a week. I live on bread and butter, with a drop of beer now and then, six days out of the seven. On Sundays we has mostly a shilling's worth of meat – bullock's head generally. Sometimes our work is very hard with heavy lifting. A weakly man's no use, and I've wondered how I have the strength I have on bread and butter. We are all paid in the dock, and there's nobody allowed to get the men to drink or to traffic with them anyhow, but in a fair regular way. There's plenty hang about every day, who would work a day's work for 2s. There's a good many Irish. I don't know that there's any foreigners, without it be on the sugar-side. Sometimes 100 men are employed in our part of the business. To-day there was from 40 to 50 at work, and 100 more was to be had if they'd been wanted. Jobs often come in in a lump – all at once or none at all; very often with the wind. We run backwards and forwards to the sugar-side or the Surrey Dock as we expect to be wanted. We don't know what the foremen of the gangs get, but the company won't allow them to underpay us, and I've nothing to complain about either of them or the company, though we're bad off. The foreman can pick his men. Many of us has to go to the parish. Once I earned only 3s. in three weeks. Our best time is from June or July, continuing on for two, three, four, or five months as happens. We live half the year, and starve the t'other. There's very few teetotallers among us. Men want beer if they live on bread and butter. There's many, I know, lives on a meal a day, and that's bread and butter. There's no drunkards among our men. We're mostly married men with families. Most poor men is married, I think. Poor as I am, a wife and family's something to cling to, like.''

I now come to the Timber and Deal trade. The labourers connected with this portion of the trade are rafters or raftsmen, and deal or stave porters; these are either "permanently" or "casually" employed. I shall give an account of each, as well as of the system pursued at each of the docks – beginning with the Commercial, because it does the most extensive business in this branch of the wood trade; and here let me acknowledge the obligations I am under to Mr. Jones, the intelligent and courteous superintendent, for much valuable information.

The Working Lumpers, as I before explained, are the labourers employed to discharge all wood-laden vessels except foreign ships, which are discharged by their own crews. The vessels unladen by the lumpers are discharged sometimes in the dock, and sometimes (when too heavily laden) in the river. The cargoes of wood-laden vessels are termed either landed or rafted goods. The landed goods are deals, battens, sleepers, wainscot logs, and, indeed, all but hewn timber, which is "rafted." When a vessel is unladen in the river, the landed goods are discharged by lumpers, who also load the lighters; whereas, in the dock, the lumpers discharge them into the company's barges, which are loaded by them as well. With smaller vessels, however, which occasionally go alongside, the lumpers discharge directly to the shore, where the "goods" are received by the company's porters. The lumpers never work upon shore. Of the porters working on shore, there are two kinds, viz., deal and stave porters, whose duty it is to receive the landed goods, and to pile and sort them, either along the quay or in the bonding ground, if duty has to be paid upon them.

The hewn timber or rafted goods the lumpers thrust through the port-hole in the water; and there the raftman receives them, puts them into lengths and sizes, and then arranges them in floats – there being 18 pieces to a float. If the ship is discharged in the river, the rafter floats the timber to the docks, and then to the "ponds" of the company. If however, the ship is discharged in dock, then the raftman floats the timber only from the main dock to the ponds.

The Rafters are all freemen, for otherwise they could not work on the river. They must have served seven years to a waterman, and they are obliged to pay 3s. a year to the Watermen's Company for their license. There are 16 or 17 rafters (all preferable men) employed by the Commercial Dock Company, and in busy times there are occasionally as many as 40 casual rafters, or "pokers" as they are called (from their poking about the docks for a job). These casual men are not capable of "rafting a ship," nor are the free watermen. They are only employed to float the timber from the ship up to the ponds and stow it, or to attend to deliveries. The skill of the rafter lies in gauging and sorting the timber according to size, quality, and ownership, and making it up into floats. It is only an experienced rafter who can tell the different sizes, qualities, and owners of the timber. This the "pokers," again, cannot float the timber from the river to the ponds. This is owing to two reasons – 1. They are not allowed to do so, on account of not being free watermen; and 2. They are unable to do so from the difficulty of navigation. The pokers work exclusively in the docks. Neither the rafters nor pokers work under contractors; but the deal and stave porters invariably do.

The following statement of a rafter at the Commercial Dock, I had from a prudent, well-behaved, sober man. He was in company with another man, employed in the same capacity at the same docks, and they both belonged to the better class of labouring men: —

"I am a rafter at the Commercial Dock. I have been working a that dock for the last six years in the same capacity, and before that I was rafter at the Surrey Dock for between five and six years. I served my apprenticeship to a waterman. I was bound when I was sixteen. We are not allowed to work till we have served two years. In my apprenticeship I was continually engaged in timber towing, lightering, and at times sculling, but that I did only when the other business was slack. After my time was out I went lightering, and about a dozen years after that I took to rafting. I had been a rafter at the Surrey Canal before then — while I was in my apprenticeship, indeed. I had 18s. a week when I first commenced rafting at the Surrey Canal; but that of course, all went to my master. I was with the Surrey canal about two years as rafter; and then I joined another party, at 30s. a week, in the same capacity. This party rented a wharf of the Surrey Canal Company, and I still worked in the Dock. There I worked longer time — four hours longer. The wages would have been as good at the Surrey Canal at outside work as they were with the second party I joined. The next place that I went to as rafter was the Commercial Dock, where I am now, and have been for the last six years. I am paid by the week. When I work at the dock I have £1 1s. a week; and when I am rafting short-hour ships (*i.e.,* ships at which we work only from eight till four), I get 4s. per day. When I am working long-hour ships (*i.e.,* ships at which the working lasts from six till six), I get 5s. a day. The other rafters employed by the company are paid the same. Our wages have remained the same ever since I have been in the business. All the other men have been lowered — such as carpenters, labourers, watchmen, deal-porters, and the like; but we are not constant men, or else I dare say ours would have been reduced too. They have lowered the wages of the old hands, who have been there for years, 1s. a week. Formerly they had £1 1s., now they get £1. The men are dissatisfied. The wages of the casual dock labourers have been reduced a great deal more than those of the constant men. Three months ago they all had 18s. a week, and now the highest wages paid to the casual labourers is 15s. The reason why the wages of the rafters have not been lowered is, I take it, because we are freemen, and there are not so many to be had who could supply our places. Not one out of a hundred lightermen and watermen are able to raft. We are only emloyed at certain times of the year. Our busy time begins at July, and ends in October. We are fully employed about four months in the year, and get, during that time, from £1 1s. to 30s. a week, or say 25s. upon an average. The rest of our time we fills up as we can. Some of the rafters has boats, and they look out for a job at sculling, but that's poor enough now." "Ah! very poor work, indeed," said an old weather-beaten man, who was present, and had had 40 years' experience at the business. "When I first joined it, it was in the war time," he added, "and then I was scarcely a day idle, and now I can't get work for better than half my time." "For the other eight months," continued the other man, "I should think the rafters upon an average make 5s. a week. Some of them has boats, and some gets a job at timber towing, but some (and that's the greatest number) has nothing at all to turn their hands to excepting the casual dock labour – that is, anything they can chance to get hold of. I don't think those who depend upon the casual labour of the docks, after the fall-season is over (the fall-ships are the last that come), make 5s. a week, take one man with another. I should say, more likely their weekly earnings is about 4s. There are about sixteen rafters at the Commercial Docks, and only one single man among the number. They none of them save any money during the busy season. They are in debt when the brisk time comes, and it takes them all the summer to get clear, which perhaps they does by the time the fall-ships have done, and then of course they begin going on in the old strain again. A rafter's life is merely getting into debt and getting clear of it – that is it – and that is a great part of the life of all the labourers along-shore."

He then produced the following accounts of his earnings for the last year:

1st week	....	£1	1	0		29th	,,	....	1	4	0
2d ,,	....	1	8	0 (a)		30th	,,	....	1	3	0
3d ,,	....	1	4	0		31st	,,	....	1	1	0
4th ,,	....	1	5	6		32d	,,	....	1	6	0
5th ,,	....	0	0	0		33d	,,	....	1	3	0
6th ,,	....	1	1	0		34th	,,	....	1	1	0
7th ,,	....	0	0	0		35th	,,	....	0	14	0
8th ,,	....	1	1	0		36th	,,	....	1	7	0
9th ,,	....	0	0	0		37th	,,	....	2	0	0 (h)
10th ,,	....	1	1	0		38th	,,	....	1	5	0
11th ,,	....	0	4	0 (b)		39th	,,	....	1	0	6
12th ,,	....	1	1	0		40th	,,	....	1	4	0
13th ,,	....	0	4	0 (c)		41st	,,	....	1	10	0
14th ,,	....	0	17	6 ,,		42d	,,	....	1	4	0
15th ,,	....	0	0	0		43d	,,	....	1	10	0
16th ,,	....	0	0	0		44th	,,	....	1	14	0
17th ,,	....	1	1	0		45th	,,	....	1	5	6
18th ,,	....	0	10	0 (d)		46th	,,	....	1	10	0
19th ,,	....	1	4	0		47th	,,	....	0	5	0
20th ,,	....	0	17	6 (e)		48th	,,	....	1	10	0
21st ,,	....	0	13	0 ,,		49th	,,	....	1	10	0
22d ,,	....	0	7	0 ,,		50th	,,	....	1	10	0
23d ,,	....	1	1	0		51st	,,	....	1	7	0
24th ,,	....	0	10	0 (f)		52d	,,	....	1	1	0
25th ,,	....	0	2	6 ,,							
26th ,,	....	0	4	0 ,,				1850			
27th ,,	....	0	1	0 ,,		1st	week	....	1	10	0
28th ,,	....	1	1	0 (g)		2d	,,	....	0	10	6

3d	,,	....	1 1 0	12th	,,	....	0 18 0 (l)
4th	,,	....	0 12 6	13th	,,	....	0 10 0 (m)
5th	,,	....	2 10 6 (i)	14th	,,	....	0 0 0 ,,
6th	,,	....	1 1 0 ,,	15th	,,	....	1 0 0 ,,
7th	,,	....	1 7 0 ,,	16th	,,	....	0 12 0 ,,
8th	,,	....	1 8 0 ,,	17th	,,	....	1 1 0 ,,
9th	,,	....	0 19 0 ,,	18th	,,	....	1 5 0 (n)
10th	,,	....	1 1 0 (j)	19th	,,	....	1 0 0 ,,
11th	,,	....	0 3 0 (k)	20th	,,	....	0 0 0 ,,

(a) Outside work.   (f) Jobbing.   (k) Jobbing.
(b) Jobbing.   (g) Busy time begins.   (l) Dock work.
(c) Jobbing.   (h) Working Sunday and nights.   (m) Jobbing.
(d) Jobbing.   (i) Contract job on river.   (n) Dock work.
(e) Jobbing.   (j) Dock work.

This gives an average, for the seventy-two weeks above cited, of 18s. 6¼d. per week. "Where I get £1," the man continued, after I had copied his accounts, "many don't get 5s. I know many friends on the river, and I get a number of odd jobs which others can't. In the last six years my earnings have been much about the same. But others, I am sure, don't make half what I do. I have earned £1 8s. when I know they have been walking about and not earned a penny. In busy times as many as forty 'pokers' are employed, sometimes for as many as five weeks in the year. They get 3s. 6d. a day, from six to six. After they are out of work they do as best they can. It's impossible to tell how one-half of them live. Half their time they are starving. The wives of the rafters go some of them charing, some are glove-makers, and others dressmakers. None that I know of do slop-work."

I now come to the deal and stave porters. First, as to those employed at the Commercial Docks.

From a man who has an excellent character given of him by his employers I had the following account:

"At our dock," he said, "timber and corn are the principal articles, but they are distinct branches, and have distinct labourers. I am in the deal part. When a foreign timber ship comes into the dock, the timber is heaved out of the port-hole by the crew themselves. The deal ships, too, are sometimes unloaded by the foreigners themselves, but not often; three or four out of a dozen may. Ours is very dangerous work. We pile the deals sometimes 90 deals high — higher at the busiest time — and we walk along planks with no hold, carrying the deals in our hands, and only our firm tread and our eye to depend upon. We work in foggy weather, and never stop for a fog; at least we haven't for eight or nine years, to my knowledge. In that sort of weather accidents are frequent. Last year there was, I believe, about 35 falls but no deaths. If it's a bad accident the deal porters give 6d. a piece on a Saturday night to help the man that's had it. There's no fund for sickness. We work in gangs of five usually, sometimes more. We are paid for carrying 100 of 12 feet deals, 1s. 9d.; 14 feet, 2s. 2d.; 20 and 21 feet, 3s.; 22 feet, 3s. 8d.; and from 24 to 27 feet, 4s. 3d. That's at piecework. We used to have 3d. per 100 more for every sort, but it was reduced three or four months back, or more, may be. In a general way we're paid nothing extra for having to carry the deals beyond an average distance, except for what we call 'long runs;' that's as far, or about as far as the dock extends from the place we start to carry the deals from. One week with another the year through, we make from 12s. to 15s. – the 15s. by men that have the preference when work is slack. We're busiest from July to Christmas. I'm the head of a gang or team of five, and I am only paid as they are; but I have the preference if work is slack, and so have the men in my team. Five men must work at the Commercial, or none at all. We are paid in the dock at the contractor's-office (there are three contractors), at four o'clock every Saturday evening. Drinking is kept down in our dock, and with my contractor drunkards are discharged. The men are all satisfied but for the lowering of their wages. No doubt they can get labour cheaper still; there's so many idlers about. A dozen years back or so they did pay us in a public-house. Our deal porters are generally sober men. The beermen only come into the dock twice a day – ten in the morning and half-past three in the afternoon – and the men never exceed a pint at a time."

An older man in the same employ said:

"I've known deal-portering for twenty years back, and then, at the Commercial Dock, men was paid in a public-house, and there was a good deal of drunkenness. The men weren't compelled to drink, but was expected to. In that point it's far better now. When I was first a deal porter I could make half as much more as I do now. I don't complain of anybody about the dock; it an't their fault; but I do complain uncommon about the times; there's so little work, and so many to snap at it."

From a *stave porter* at the same dock I had the following account:

"We are paid by the piece, and the price varies according to size – from 1s. 6d. to 10s. the 1,000. Quebec staves, 6 feet long by 2 inches thick, and a few inches broad, are 10s. the 1,000, and other sizes are paid in the same proportion, down to 1s. 6d. We pack the bigger staves about our shoulders, resting one stave on another, more like a Jack-in-the-Green than anything else, as our heads comes out in the middle of 'em. Of the biggest, five is a good load, and we pack all sizes alike, folding our arms to hold the smaller staves better. Take it altogether, we make at stave work what the deal porters do at their work; and indeed, we are deal porters when staves isn't in. There's most staves comes to the Surrey Canal Dock."

A man who had worked at the West India Dock as a *deal porter* informed me that the prices paid were the same as were paid by the Commercial and East Country Dock Companies before the reduction, but the supply of labour was uncertain and irregular – chiefly at the spring and fall, and in British American ships. As many as 100 men, however, my informant stated, had been so employed at this dock, making from 15s. to 25s. per week, or as much as 30s. on occasions, and without the drawback of any compulsory or "expected" drinking. Such, as far as I could learn, is the condition of the labourers employed at these timber docks, where the "drinking system" and the payment of men in public-houses are not allowed. Concerning the state of the men employed at the other docks, where the public-house system still continues, I had the following details:

A deal porter at the Surrey Canal Dock stated—

"I have worked a good many years in the Surrey Dock. There were four contractors at the Surrey Canal, but now there's one, and he pays the publican, where we gets our beer, all that's owing to us deal porters, and the publican pays us every Saturday night. I can't say that we are compelled to take beer — certainly not when at our work in the dock; but we're 'expected' to take it when we're waiting. I can't say either that we are discharged if we don't drink; but if we don't we are kept waiting late on a Saturday night on an excuse of the publican's having no change, or something like that; and we feel that somehow or other, if we don't drink, we'll be left in the back-ground. Why don't the superintendent see us paid in the dock? He pays the company's labourers in the dock — they're corn-turners and rafters — and they are paid early, too. We now have 4s. 4d. a day of from eight to four, and 5s. 8d. from six to six. It used to be, till four months back I think, 4s. 10d. and 6s. 4d. In slack times, say six months in the year, we earns from 10s. to 12s. a week; in the brisk times, 30s., and sometimes more, but 30s. is about the average. We are all paid at the public-house. We gathers from after five or so every Saturday night. We are kept now and then till twelve, and after twelve, and it has been Sunday morning before we've got paid. There is more money spent, in course, up to twelve than up to ten. To get away at half-past nine is very early. I should say that half our earnings, except in our best weeks, goes to the publican for drink — more than half oft enough, if it's a bad week all our earnings, or more. When it waxes late, the wives, who've very likely been without Saturday's dinner or tea, will go the publican's for their husbands, and they'll get to scold very likely, and then they'll get beaten very likely. We are chiefly married men with families. Pretty well all the deal porters at the dock are drunkards; so there's misery enough for their families. The publican gives credit two following weeks, and encourages drinking in course, but he does it quietly. He'll advance any man at work 1s. a night in money, besides trusting him for drink. I don't know how many we are — I should say from 50 to 200. In old age or accident, in course, we comes on the parish."

Other men whom I saw corroborated this statement, and some of their wives expressed great indignation at the system pursued in paying the labourers. None of them objected to their husbands having four pints of beer when actually at their work in the dock; it was against the publican's temptations on Saturday and other nights that they bitterly inveighed.

At the earnest entreaty of a deal porter's wife, I called on Saturday evening at the public-house where the men were waiting to be paid. I walked into the tap-room as if I had called casually, and I was then unknown to all the deal porters. The tap-room I found small, dark, dirty, and ill-ventilated. What with the tobacco-smoke and the heat of the weather, the room was most disagreeably close and hot. As well as I could count – for, though it was a bright summer's evening, the smoke and gloom rendered it somewhat difficult – there were twenty-four men in this tap-room, which is fitted up in boxes, and the number completely filled the apartment. In the adjoining room, where was a small bar, there were some six or eight more deal porters, lounging about. These numbers, however, fluctuated, for men kept coming in and going out; but all the time I was there thirty men might be stationery in the two hot, dirty, little rooms. They were strong-looking men enough, and all sunburnt; but amongst them were some with pinched features and white lips. There they sat, each man with his beer before him. There was not the slightest hilarity among them; there was not the least semblance of a convivial Saturday night's gathering. The majority sat in silence. Some dozed – others drank or sipped at their pint measures, as if they must do it, or to while away the time. These deal porters were generally dressed in corduroy, fustian, or strong coarse blue woollen jackets, with trowsers of similar material, open big woollen waistcoats, and with coloured cotton handkerchiefs rolled round some thick substance in the way of a stock, and tied loosely round their necks over a striped cotton or coarse linen shirt.

All had rough bristly beards, intimating that their shaving was confined to the Sunday mornings. With respect to the system pursued at this dock in the payment of the deal porters, it is right that I should state that I heard from many deal porters praises of the superintendent, though certainly not of the contractor or the publican. I am glad to be able to state, however, that it is the determination of the company to attempt – and that, indeed, they are now attempting – the abolition of the system of public-house payment. Mr. M'Cannan, the superintendent of these docks, to whom I am indebted for many favours and courtesies, informs me that an arrangement was once made for the payment of the deal porters in "an old box" (a sort of wooden office) within the dock; but the impatience and struggling of the men who had to wait a little while for their weeks earnings almost demolished the frail timbers of the old box, and the attempt was abandoned. Within the dock the supply of beer is now limited to three times a day, with a "vend" of half-a-pint a man each visit.

A middle-aged man, sun-burnt, and with much of the look of a seaman, gave me an account of his labour as a *deal porter at the East Country Dock*. His room – and he, with his wife and children, had but one – was very sparely furnished, the principal article being a large clean bed. He complained that his poverty compelled him to live in the neighbourhood of some low lodging-houses, which caused all sorts of bad characters to resort to the locality, while cries of "murder" were not uncommon in the night:—

"I have been a deal porter," he said, "nearly 20 years, and for the last few years I have worked at the East Country Dock. Sometimes we work single-handed, sometimes in gangs of two, three, or four. The distance the deals have to be carried has a good deal to do with it, as to the number of the gang. We're paid nothing extra for distance. Mr. —— contracts with the Dock Company to do all the deal portering. There are three gangs regularly employed, each with a master, of foreman, or ganger over them. They have always the preference. If three ships were to unlade on one day, there would be one for each gang, and when more hands are wanted the men of the regular gangs are put over deal porters, such as me, who are not regularly employed, but on the look-out for piece work or a day's work. We reckon when that happens that the ganger's men have 9s. for our 4s. We are paid at a public-house. The house belongs to the company. We pay 4d. a pot for our beer, and we're expected to drink no less than four pints a day. We're not obligated, you understand, sir, but we're expected to drink this; and if we don't do as we're expected, why we're not wanted next time, that's all. But we're only expected to take our regular beer when work's brisk. We're not encouraged to run into debt for drink, and work it out. Indeed, if a man be 1s. or 1s. 6d. in debt to the publican, he can't get credit for a bit of bread and cheese, or a drink of beer. We have good beer, but sometimes we'd rather be without it. But we can't work without some. Many deal porters I know are terrible drunkards. We are paid the same as at the Commercial Dock, and were reduced about the same time. If I had a regular week's work now, and no stop, I could make 26s. – less by 8d. a day, or 4s. a week, for beer. We're not expected to drink any gin. Before wages came down I could have made 30s. Our beer money is stopped out of our earnings by the masters, and paid to the publican. It's very seldom, indeed, we get a regular week's work, and take it the year through I don't clear 12s. a week. To-day there was only sixteen men at work, but sometimes there's eighty. From June to Christmas is the best time. Sometimes we may wait three or four days for a job. The regular pay for the Custom-house hours, from eight to four, is 4s. a day to a deal porter, but there's plenty to do it for what they can catch. Lots of Irish, sir. They'll work for anything, and is underselling all of us, because an Englishman and his family can't live like them. In the winter my family and me starved on 4s. or 5s. a week, but I kept clear of the parish, though plenty of us have to come on the parish. Much in pawn, sir? I have so. Look at my place – it *was* a nice place once. Most of what you may call the regular hands has been brought up as deal porters. I don't know how many you may call regular at our dock; it varies – working and waiting for a turn; but we're no regular turn at work; there's 100 perhaps, or near about it. Ours is very hard and very dangerous work. Last year one man was killed by a fall, and two had broken legs, and two broken thighs, but it was an easy year for accidents. There is no fund to help or to bury us; only the parish. In a bad case were carried to the Dreadnought, or some hospital. We are all of us dissatisfied. I wish I could have 2s. 6d. a day for regular work, and I'd live twenty years longer than I shall now, with nothing to do one day, and tearing my soul out with slaving work at others.''

The result of all my inquiries shows that the deal porters in no wise exaggerated the hardness or the danger of their labour. I saw them at work, walking along planks – some sloping from an elevated pile of timber to one somewhat more elevated, the plank vibrating as two men, carrying a deal, trod slowly, and in measure, along it; and so they proceed from one pile to another, beginning perhaps from the barge, until the deals have been duly deposited. From a distance, when only the diminished thickness of the plank is visible, they appear to be walking on a mere stick. The space so traversed is generally short, but the mode of conveyance seems rude and primitive.

In the foregoing narratives frequent mention has been made of the casual labourers at the timber docks, and I now proceed to give some short account of the condition and earnings of this most wretched class. On the platform surrounding the Commercial Dock basins are a number of men whom I heard described as "idlers," "pokers," and casual labourers." These men are waiting "in hopes of a job," which they rarely obtain until all the known hands have been set to work before them. The casual labourers confine themselves to no particular dock, but resort to the one which they account the most likely to want hands; and some even of the more regularly employed deal porters change their docks occasionally for the same reason. These changes of locality puzzle the regular deal porters in their estimation of the number of hands in their calling at the respective docks. On my visits the casual labourers were less numerous than usual, as the summer is the season when such persons consider that they have "the best chance" in the country. But I saw groups of ten or twenty waiting about the docks – some standing alone, and some straggling in twos or threes as they waited, all looking dull and listless. These men, thus wearisomely waiting, could not be called ragged, for they wore mostly strong canvas or fustian suits – large, and seemingly often washed, jackets predominating; and rents and tatters are far less common in such attire than in wool cloth garments. From a man dressed in a large coarse canvas jacket, with worn corduroy trowsers, and very heavy and very brown laced leather boots, I had the following statement, in a somewhat provincial tone:—

"My father was a small farmer in Dorsetshire. I was middling educated, and may thank the parson for it. I can read the Bible, and spell most of the names there. I was left destitute, and I had to shift for myself; that's nine year ago, I think. I've hungered, and I've ordered my bottle of wine since, sir. I got the wine when railways was all the go, and I was a navvy; but I didn't like wine drinking; I drank it just for the fun of the thing – or, mayhap, because gentlemen drunk it. The port was like rather rough beer, but stronger, certainly. Sherry I only had once or twice, and liked good old ale better. I shifted my quarters every now and then till between two and three years ago, and then I tried my hand in London. At first Mr. —— (a second cousin of my father he was) helped me now and then, and he gave me odd jobs at portering for himself, as he was a grocer, and he got me odd jobs from other people besides. When I was a navvy I should at the best time have had my 50s. a week and more, if it hadn't been for the tommy shops. And I've had my 15s. in portering in London for my cousin, but sometimes I came down to 10s. – and sometimes to 5s. My cousin died sudden, and I was very hard up after that. I made nothing at portering some weeks. I had no one to help me; and in the spring of last year – and very cold it often was – I've walked after ten, eleven, or twelve at night, many a mile to lie down and sleep in any bye-place. I've never stole, but have been hard tempted. I've thought of drowning myself and of hanging myself; but somehow a penny or two came in to stop that. Perhaps I didn't seriously intend it. I begged some times of an evening. I stayed at lodging-houses – for one can't sleep out in bad weather – till I heard from one lodger that he took his turn at the Commercial Docks. He worked at timber, or corn, or anything; and so I went – about the cholera time last year – and waited, and run from one dock to another, because I was new, and hadn't a chance like the old hands. I've had 14s. a week sometimes, and many's the week I've had 3s., and more's the week I've had nothing at all. They've said 'I don't know you.' I've lived on penny loaves – one or two a day – when there was no work; and then I've begged. I don't know what the other people waiting at any of the docks got. I didn't talk to them much, and they didn't talk much to me.''

LETTER LIX.
Thursday, July 4, 1850.

The London Sawyers, though not a numerous body, still require full consideration, as belonging to a trade which has been extensively superseded by machinery.

According to the last census the number of sawyers in Great Britain in 1841 was 29,593; of these 23,360 resided in England, 4,550 in Scotland, 1,508 in Wales, and the remaining 175 in the British Isles. About one-tenth part of the whole of the sawyers in Great Britain were then located in the metropolis, the number in London being 2,978, of whom only 186 were under twenty years of age. Strange to say, one of the sawyers above twenty was a *female!* At the time of taking the previous census the number of the Metropolitan Sawyers above twenty years of age was 2,180; so that, from 1831 to 1841, the London trade had increased 612. Since then, however, I am informed that the number has declined nearly one half. The number of steam saw-mills in the metropolis, in 1841, was 15; at the present moment, they are 68, including those for cutting veneers as well as timber and deals.

The increase and decrease in the number of sawyers in the different parts of the country is a curious and important point to ascertain. By calculations, made from the Government Returns of 1831 and 1841, I find that the greatest addition to the number of sawyers took place in Lanark, where the population, between 1831 and 1841, increased 48 per cent., and the sawyers no less than 230 per cent. – thus making an increase of 182 per cent. over and above that of the population. The next county in rotation is Sutherland, where the sawyers have increased 156 per cent. beyond the population. After this comes Pembroke, showing an increase of 121 per cent.; Radnor and Cardigan, 100 per cent. each; the North Riding of Yorkshire, 87 per cent.; Inverness, 82; Berwick, 76; Renfrew, 75; and Cornwall, 73 per cent. above that of the population. In all of these counties, however, the population increased considerably; whereas in Dumfries, where the population decreased 1 per cent., the number of sawyers at the same time increased as much as 111 per cent., so that the total increase was equal to 112 per cent.

The great decrease in the number of sawyers seems to have occurred in the following counties, that which shows the greatest diminution of all is

Linlithgow, where the population increased 44 per cent., whilst the sawyers decreased 33 per cent. After this comes Caithness; here the sawyers decreased 63 per cent. and the population increased 1 per cent. At Clackmannan the population increased 31 per cent., while the number of sawyers was augmented only 3 per cent.

In Aberdeen, Peebles, and Perth, there was an actual decrease, in each county respectively, of 7, 14, and 18 per cent., on the number of sawyers in 1841, compared with the number in 1831. Whether a comparative increase in the wages of the sawyers took place between 1831 and 1841, in those counties where the hands decreased – or whether there was a corresponding fall in the prices that the men obtained for their work in counties where the sawyers increased – I have no means of determining. Supposing the amount of work to be done to have remained the same, it is clear that, according to the law of "supply and demand," a rise or fall in the wages inversely proportional to the decrease or increase of the hands would have been the necessary result.

England, upon the whole, shows an increase of sawyers to the amount of 23 per cent, above that of the population; Wales, 44 per cent.; and Scotland, 25 per cent. Great Britain altogether gives an increase of 24 per cent.; a decrease in the wages of the sawyers, throughout the country, therefore, should have occurred to an equal extent.

Of sawyers there are four kinds – viz., the hardwood and timber sawyers, the cooper's stave, and the shipwright sawyers. The hardwood sawyers are generally employed in cutting mahogany, rosewood, and all kinds of foreign fancy woods. This work demands the greatest skill in sawing. It requires special nicety in cutting, because the timber is more valuable, and a "bungler" might be the cause of great loss to his employer. A hardwood sawyer can generally turn his hand to timber sawing, but the timber sawyers are seldom able to accomplish the cutting of hard woods. Timber sawyers are mostly engaged in cutting for carpenters and builders. The work of the cooper's stave sawyers consists principally in cutting "doublets" out of the foreign wood. The shipwright sawyers cut the "futtocks" and planks for ships. *Timber sawing*, by manual labour, has been unchanged within the recollection of the oldest man in the trade. One elderly man assured me that his grandfather, a sawyer, had told him that the work was always the same in his day. Two men work in a pit, which is generally 6 feet deep, and 4 feet 6 inches wide. These two men are termed the topman and pitman, according as they work *above* or *in* the pit. The pits are of two kinds, "scaffold" and "sunk" pits; the scaffold pit being raised from the ground, and almost always constructed of timber, while the sunk pit is dug into the earth. The men saw the trunks of trees, as well as the deals brought from the Baltic or Canada, when it is necessary to reduce them in thickness. Nearly all the English trees are roughly sawn in the woods where they are felled. Oaks felled in the Royal forests for building are sawn within the forest itself, a pit being dug as contiguous as possible to the fallen trees. The tree is lopped of its branches, and hewn; or, in other words, shaped or roughly squared with the axe for the readier work of the sawyers. Some of the timber hewers, however, are sufficiently skilful to chop the trees almost as smoothly as if it were planed. Oak is always "rended" (stripped of its bark), for tanning purposes. In some country places it is not an unfrequent thing for sawyers to sink a pit close by the building being erected, and then to saw the timber required for the frame-work of the house. In London, however, at present, this is seldom or never done. The general rule is, that "timber" is sawn at the yards, either by the steam machinery of the merchant, or by the manual labour of the sawyers in his employ. For ship timbers, the entire oak is generally sawn, for one oak is sometimes used for one of the curvilinear planks of the "futtocks" (the part above the keel). Ship timber sawing is confined to the ship-builders' yards; machinery is seldom employed for sawing the timber used by ship or barge builders, which is genrally sawn curved. For planking, and the "straight cuts" in ship building, however, machinery is used. Sometimes two whole oaks are merely squared for the "beams" of the deck. For coopers' work, the timber (oak) comes in "staves" from the Baltic or America, and runs from 2ft. to 9ft. long, with an average of 6 inches wide and 3 inches thick. The thickness of the stave is sawn through to the substance required. "Doublets" (of which I have given an account from a cooper's stave-sawyer) are the most difficult parts of the stafe-sawyer's work. The straight sawn staves, which may be done by machinery, are used for milk and other pails, brewers' vats, and for cabinet work, such as drawer bottoms, &c. The staves are "hewn" abroad, and generally out of the trunks of the inferior trees (rarely out of the branches), and hewn to the sizes most convenient for stowage. The process observed by the shipwrights' or coopers' sawyers is the same as that of the timber and hardwood sawyers; it is all carried on in the pits. These four classes of the trades, with the exception of the cooper's stave sawyers, are greatly reduced in numbers. It is generally considered in the trade that there were five and twenty years ago. Formerly there used to be a great many shipwright sawyers along the banks of the Thames, but now, I am informed, the greater part of the yards are shut up, and many of the sawyers and shipwrights have emigrated to America. The year after the strike in 1833 there were 1,500 sawyers on the books of the union, exclusive of the cooper, staves, and shipwright sawyers; and now there are not more than 320 members belonging to the three district societies. The great decrease in the numbers of the trade is owing to the introduction of machinery. The first steam saw-mill set up in the neighbourhood of London was established at Battersea, about the year 1806 or 1807. It was erected principally for the cutting of veneers, and the trade, though aware that it could not fail to take the work from them, still believed that it never could do so to the extent that it has. "We knew," says my informant, "that the mills could cut the veneers better and thinner than what we could, and more in an inch, which is a great object of course in valuable woods, but still we never expected that steam power would be applied to the cutting of timber and deals. Since that time the mills have gone on increasing gradually, year after year, until now there are twenty regularly at work between Stangate and London-bridge, and no less than sixty-eight altogether, scattered throughout the metropolis."

The trade society of sawyers is divided into six districts. The first of these is the West London, which extends from Back-hill, near Hatton-garden, to Brentford; the second, or City District, reaches from Back-hill to St. George's-in-the-East; while the third, or Surrey District, runs from Dock-head, Bermondsey, to Westminster. These three belong to the general or timber and hardwood sawyers. The fourth district is in connection with the coopers' stave sawyers, and extends from Southwark-bridge to the Commercial Docks on the one side of the river, and to Limehouse on the other. The districts frequented by the shipwright-sawyers are Lime-house and Rotherhithe. Each class (excepting the shipwright-sawyers) has a trade society; and the following table shows the number of members belonging to each society, as well as the "non-society men" in each district, together with the total number and the aggregate total of the London operative sawyers generally:—

	Society Men.	Non-Society Men.	Total Society and Non-society Men in each District.
West London District	60	140	200
City District	150	275	425
Surrey District	20	300	320
Total General Sawyers	230	750	945
Southwark, or Coopers' Stave Sawyers	60	40	100
Limehouse ....,	...	450	450
Rotherhithe	...	100	100
Total Shipwright Sawyers	...	590	550
Aggregate Total of Society and Non-society Men	290	1,305	1,595

The houses of call at which the different societies meet have nothing whatever to do with the obtaining of employment for the men (as in the tailors' trade), but are simply places of meeting to discuss the affairs of the trade. The mode adopted by men wishing to obtain employment is making inquiry at the different yards. Concerning "benefits," or sums given in cases of affliction or distress, there are a few such provisions in connection with the trade societies, though they have no *provident funds,* such as the superannuation and vocation funds of other trades. The way in which assistance is rendered to the sick, and to the widow of a member of the trade societies, is by voluntary subscriptions, obtained either by petition or raffle − from 30s. to £3 being the sum usually collected in this manner, while, in the case of death, £5 is sometimes obtained in the city. The shipwright sawyers have a benefit society, called "The Good Samaritan," to render assistance to each other, in case of accident or death. Here the weekly contributions are 3d., and the "benefits" received from £1 to £10.

The weekly contributions paid by the members of the trade societies, are 2d. in the West London and City districts, and 3d. in the Surrey and Southwark. The chief part of the money thus obtained is devoted to "trade purposes," and the remainder to philanthropic objects. These "trade purposes" consist principally of means adopted to uphold the wages of the trade − and the philanthropic objects, in the payment of small sums to the aged and infirm members, as well as those suffering from accidents. The tramps belonging to country societies are relieved by some of the London bodies. They are usually furnished with a card of the society to which they belong, and duplicates of these cards are kept at one or other of the London district houses. The operative sawyers of the metropolis are in correspondence with almost all the societies throughout the country, and the country societies are likewise in correspondence with each other, especially those in the north of England, where the greatest number of sawyers are located.

A tramp, upon ariving in town and producing the card of his society at one of the London houses of call, receives from the metropolitan society the sum of 5s. The country societies usually give from 1s. to 2s. tramps, and in some cases a supper and a bed. The object of this relief to tramps is to assist a man in getting employment in another town, and the donations are given only to those parties who subscribe to some recognized society throughout the kingdom. Once a year an account of the money thus dispensed to tramps is taken; the delegates of the different country societies meeting annually in the north of England for that purpose. In the case of London, however, the districts meet in "central committee," and then make out a statement of the sum which has been disbursed by them throughout the year; this they forward to the different societies in the country. Of late years the London operative sawyers, I am informed, have been greatly opposed to any active resistance to their employers. The last strike among them took place in the years 1833 and 1834, and since that time they have generally sought to remedy any difference between them and their masters by more conciliatory measures. As an instance of this, I was furnished with copies of some circulars that had been sent round to the leading timber merchants on the occasion of the last disagreement. The tone of these was courteous and manly – neither cringing nor insulting – and spoke volumes for the intellectual and moral advance of the class since the days when Richardson's mill was destroyed by them.

The majority of the London sawyers, I am informed by some of the most intelligent and experienced members of the trade, are countrymen. They are generally the sons of village carpenters or wheelwrights, though some have been "bred and born" in the trade, as they say. As a body of men they are essentially unpolitical. I could not hear of one Chartist among them; and, although suffering greatly from machinery, I found few with what may be called violent or even strong opinions upon the subject. They spoke of the destruction of Richardson's Saw-mill as one of the follies and barbarisms of past days, and were quite alive to the importance of machinery as a means of producing wealth in a community. They also felt satisfied that it was quite out of their power to stop the progress of it. As a body of men I found them especially peaceable, and apparently of very simple and kindly dispositions. They are not what can be called an educated class, but those whom I saw were certainly distinguished for their natural good sense. They are usually believed to be of intemperate habits, and I am informed that in the palmy days of the trade there was good reason for the belief. But since then work has declined, and they have become much more sober. There are many teetotallers now among them; it is supposed that about one in ten has taken the pledge, and one in twenty kept it. The cause of the intemperance of the sawyers, say my informants, was their extremely hard labour, and the thirst produced by their great exertion. Moreover, it was the custom of their employers, until within the last 15 years, to pay the men in public-houses. Since then, however, the sawyers have received their wages at the counting-houses of the timber merchants; and this, in connection with the general advance of intelligence among the body, has gone far to diminish the intemperance of the trade. The coffee-shops, again, I am assured, have added greatly to the sobriety of the operative sawyers. The large reduction which has taken place in the earnings of the sawyers has not been attended with any serious alteration in their habits. As a general rule, neither their wives nor their children "go out to work;" and since the decline of their trade no marked change in this respect has occurred. The majority of the men are certainly beyond the middle age – many that I saw were between sixty and seventy years. Cooper's stave-sawyers, however, are younger men. This is accounted for by the fact that since the decline of the trade of the "general sawyers," very few fresh hands have been brought into the trade, while many of the younger men have emigrated or sought some other employment – whereas the old men have been not only loath to leave to the country, but unable to turn their hand to a new business. The coopers' stave- sawyers, however, have considerably increased in number, owing to the difficulty of machinery to effect their work; hence, many of the other sawyers have taken to this branch. A large number of the general sawyers have been compelled to seek parish relief. Within the Lambeth workhouse alone, I am informed, there are as many as sixteen sawyers, besides others, in the receipt of out-door relief. Formerly there was in connection with each district society a fund for assisting the aged and infirm, but within the last fifteen years this has been done away with; and, as before stated, there are neither benefit nor superannuation funds belonging to two of the trade societies at the present day. The Surrey District Society, however, has recently started a "philanthropic fund" in connection with its trade society. As a rule, however, the men and their families are wholly unprovided for, either in case of sickness, old age, accident, or death, so that in the event of any affliction coming upon them, the parish alone is their refuge. From all I can gather, it appears that the general sawyers have declined in numbers at least two-fifths, and that only one-third of those now remaining can obtain full employment; another third have about three or four days' work in the week, and the other third but one day or two, and often none at all. The slack season with the general and coopers' stave-sawyers commences about a month before, and continues till a month after, Christmas. With the shipwright sawyers, however, the winter is the busiest time.

I shall now give an account of the earnings and condition of each of the different classes of sawyers above described, beginning with those engaged in the cutting of timber and hard wood. After which I purpose describing some of the principal steam saw-mills in London, and showing the amount of manual labour that they have superseded. To this I shall append a statement of two of the most intelligent men in the trade concerning the effect of machinery upon the working classes generally. In doing this I trust I need not remind the reader that the opinions there expressed are those of the *working men* themselves, who have been allowed to state their sentiments, because, suffering severely from machinery, it was considered to be but fair to express their thoughts and feelings upon this subject. It is right I should add, that I have found not one man in the trade opposed to machinery, in the abstract. The main objection of the operatives appear to be, that machinery benefits the capitalist, at the expense of the working man.

From "a pair" of deal or general sawyers, whom I found at their work, I had the following statement. The "pitman" said –

"I have been above thirty years a sawyer and a pitman; that is, the sawyer who works in the pit. We work in pairs – the topman and the pitman. The topman's part is the most difficult certainly, as he directs the saw to do her work (we always call the saw a *she*) according to the line. Every piece of timber is lined (chalked). When I first knew the trade things was much better. Me and my mate could earn between us then, £4 10s. a week easy. Top and pit men is paid alike, and has always been so. Now it is with great difficulty that we can make £3 a week the pair of us; and when we earn £3, we receive only £2 15s., for 1d. out of every shilling is deducted. The employer stops the 1d.; it's called 'pence,' for the finding of tools, all of which the master now provides for us." (Another man gave me a full account of the "pence," and calculated the amount of profit made by it.) "That wasn't the case till machinery got into full operation, twenty years ago, or somewhere thereabout." "I believe" (said the other man, the top sawyer), "the first steam saw-mill was started at the foot of Westminster-bridge by a man named Smart, thirty-five years ago, or so. We thought nothing about that then. Smart sawed deals. Master got harder and harder upon us. Our last strike was in the first year of the cholera, in 1833 I believe. We are paid for a twelve-foot deal 3¼d. a cut. Other deals are paid at the same rate. They do it cheapest at saw-mills, but not the best for working purposes as carpenters can't 'bring it up' so well; that is, it's so well adapted for work, because the machinery can't humour the grain. You see, sir, machinery is a ruining of all of us. Where there was 200 pair of sawyers there's not 50 now. We struck to keep up the prices of that day, which was 3½d. a cut in our yard, but the masters got so many hands in from the country and other cheap ways, even if the fellow knew nothing about a saw before, that we was obliged to give way. Ours is very hard work; the general hours is from six to seven. The year through the utmost we average a man is 25s. a week when the pence is paid. We are obligated to drink beer to keep our strength up, and that to from 6d. to 10d. worth a day; but there's no compulsion in any way as to beer. Some drink more than 10d. worth in a day, but that's more than sufficient. Our men can't afford to be what you may call drunkards (but p'r'aps one can't call them exactly sober men). The lazy fellows somehow – and I don't know how – do manage to get drunk pretty often. The wood we saw now is cut much greener than it used to be, and is worse to manage. We get English wood as it falls – oak, ash, elm, beech, and sycamore – them's the principal; and we have to trim it, knock the knots off and the bark off, but the oak comes to us stripped. For trimming the wood we're poorly paid. For ash, elm, beech, and all trees we have 6s. per 100 feet; the masters agree it's worth 1s. more. A man couldn't make 20s. a week at that, and the 'pence' to be stopped out of it. I've been a top man for more than thirty years – I should say about thirty-five. Top and pit sawyers very seldom change places, only for a make-shift. The top-man, though it's the most difficult part, gets no more than the pit man, not a morsel, and he has to keep the saw in order, and he's answerable for all work to the master. The easiest wood of all to saw is American pine; it gives to the saw easiest. English timber (elm, beech, and sycamore) is the hardest. Oak's another thing; it's difficult to get it ready to fit it for sawing, but not harder to saw than elm. With a log of mahogany the top-man must humour the saw so as to cut to the master's orders, and masters are very exacting. If we vexes 'em, they puts us on spruce deals, which are the hardest deals to cut. We can't make above 2s. 6d. a man a day of it, and they keep us at it as long as they think fit. In spruce deals we have to cut what the saw-mills can't well cut; they can cut it, certainly, but they charge higher; for there's only one cut (two boards) in a spruce fir, and it takes them as much time to cut one cut as to cut ten. I've known, in 1821, when George IV, was crowned, 80 pairs of men in two sawpits, where now there isn't a single one. The pits, all of them I think, is coming to a close, and the business is going to the dogs, or the sawmills, for it's all one. Many sawyers is now glad to go in for labourers to saw-yards, for piling and placing the timber, at 3s. or 4s. a day – perhaps only with two days' work a week – because they can't get employment at sawing. One of our saws – they run from five to seven feet – will cost £1 for five feet, and on to 30s. for seven feet, without the frame, which may cost 10s. The weight of a 7-foot saw is from 60 to 70lbs., for two men to pull up and down all day, at the rate of, say ten strokes, or seventy feet, a minute, or 4,200 feet an hour; and that's, as you say, 42,000 feet in a day of ten hours – so that we lift upwards of half-a-hundred weight nearly eight miles high in our day's work. The resistance of the saw – as it pulls like so many hooks coming down and catching – is not an easy calculation. A scientific man – it's ten years ago, I think – calculated, and reckoned that each down stroke (for the up stroke is only a lift up of the saw, like) was equal to lifting 86lb. My opinion is, and I judge by experience and by lifting weights, that he was right; others think so, too. I don't know what he calculated it for.'' (The man then, at my request, went into another calculation as to weight, of course with my assistance with the figures.) ''A force of 86lbs. is required for each down stroke: 10 in a minute is a force of 430lbs. put out by each man every minute, and that's a power of 25,800lbs. an hour. In a day of ten hours, the whole amount of power is equal to 258,000lbs., or more than 18,428 stone; and divide that by 8, and that'll show how many hundred weights – more than 2,303, or upwards of 115 tons a day. The strength's put out equal by the two sawyers, top and pit, generally; and it ought to be always, when each man does his part properly, and like a workman. Provisions has been cheap for some time, and that's a great thing for working men. If we says a word about better pay, or the grievance of the 'pence,' masters stops our mouths with machinery. A 'pair' of sawyers will do three dozen cuts of 12 feet deals a day, or four dozen of battens. A 'cut' is nine inches through in a deal and seven in a batten. The saw may go in a deal and seven in a batten. The saw may go ahead half an inch a stroke as near as may be. Sawyers is generally healthy men and not short-lived.''

From another Deal Sawyer, who had made it his more particular inquiry, I had the following information concerning the *''pence''* alluded to in the preceding statement:

''Putting on the pence,'' he said, ''was one of the sort of things masters have recourse to when they don't want to seem to reduce men's wages right out. They do it by side-winds. The pence is a great saving to the masters. A good saw, which may cost 20s. at the outside, will last eight months. Suppose a pair of sawyers earn £3 a week between them less the pence (which is a penny out of every shilling), that's 5s. stopped for the saw. And suppose in a yard in regular work, and in a pretty brisk time, they work six months, or 26 weeks, at the same rate, the master then has received £6 10s. for what cost him 20s., and that's a profit of £5 10s. The saw will then last two months longer, which is £2 more profit, or £7 10s. in all. To be sure, there's the frame, which may cost, at the utmost, 10s., but one frame, unless there's an accident, will serve for four or five saws. If you reckon, besides this, 1s. a week for files and other costs of tools (though it's not 1s.), the master's clear profit out of the pence will be £5 15s., or say £5 10s. out of each saw, or 200 per cent. Now, suppose eight frames are kept on the way, as may be the case in some few yards still, then the master will clear £60 in all by the 'pence.' It does not matter as regards the master's profits on the pence, in the long run, whether work be slack or brisk, for when it's slack his saws last all the longer, only he doesn't turn over his £5 10s. profit so quick – that's all.''

A tall hale-looking man, with an appearance of great respectability, gave me the following account of Ship-timber Sawing:

''I have been a sawyer of ship timbers these forty years. I worked a few years in the country, and then I came to London. When I first worked in London we were paid 5s. a day, but we now work by the piece, except on a few things. Piece work came to be the regular system 24 or 25 years ago. We are paid the same prices for our labour as I've ever known, but there's not work enough for us, that's where the times are worse. We – that is the pair of us – are paid for sawing English oak, 7s. for 100 feet. We work topmen and pitmen, as in other pits, and are paid each man alike. Sometimes, by agreement, the topman has 1s. or 2s. extra, on account of having the saw to keep in order. We are paid the same price for Memel oak, but that's little used; it's chiefly English that we has to cut, and we've the same price for Quebec oak, and foreign elm, and for teak. There's a good deal of teak cut now. Africa (African oak) is so hard that we have 10s. 6d. per 100ft. for it. For Dantzic and Quebec firs, such as are used for the planking of ships, we get 4s. 6d. We cut the oak used for building 1,000 ton ships in first, second, and third 'futtocks;' that's for the outward sides of the vessel, such as meet the water over the keel. First futtocks are cut 14 inches thick, and as long of course as the tree runs. Second futtocks are 12 inches thick, and thirds 11 inches. For smaller tonnages the futtocks are cut less thick in proportion, down to six inches, which is the thinnest cut, and is used for building small schooners. The 'floor' bottom of a ship of 1,000 tons is cut 15 inches thick, and for smaller craft in the same way down to six. I now reckon 40s. a man an excellent week's work, but it's not often we make that, for there's more than six months in the year very bad, when oft enough we'll not make half-a-crown a day; so the average for the year now runs between 15s. and 40s., or something less, a week. We have no 'pence' to pay, as in some saw-yards, but we have to find our own tools. Our saws are 6½ to 7 feet long. An average one will cost 19s., but the price varies according to the breadth, and that varies from one to eleven inches, though we use narrow saws most. A saw will last us twelve months, as a general calculation, when it's used three days a week. We sometimes saw circular blocks, just the shape of a wooden trencher, for ship-building, and then we are paid by the day, 5s. and 6s. Machinery ruins the saw trade; and now they've come to saw circular, for shipbuilders' use, by steam machinery, worse luck. As yet there's only one steam-mill for ship-timber sawing, besides the Government one at Woolwich. For little masters in the general trade the steam-mills are an accommodation, as credit's given them, and men, of course, must have their Saturday nights. Accidents are very frequent among us. We have no sick fund, but I belong to a general benefit society, as do some others. The men drink a good deal; our work is hard, and four pints of beer a day is a moderate allowance. We are not paid at a public-house, and have no grievances of that sort to complain of, nor any grievances that I know of; for we're fairly treated between master and man. We are slack now. There's many ships brought here ready built, from America mostly. They don't last so long as English-built ships, and have often to be refastened; but if a merchant can insure what does he care? The teak we are now sawing runs 20ft. to 50ft. long. The English oak goes from 20ft. to 70ft. There's nothing like good English oak, sir — nothing.''

A man whom I found residing with his wife and children in a little place of apparently two rooms made the following statement as to cooper's stave sawing. He lived, with many others of the same class, in one of very many alleys that run from the river side, behind the site of what was once the Globe Theatre, to Guildford-street, Southwark. The alleys are built with the utmost economy of space; some of them are almost too narrow for the passage of a horse. I saw nothing, however, to call filth. Abutting on one of the narrowest of these alleys are high dark wooden palings, from behind which come the smell and lowing of cows, a circumstance rather in contrast with the thick packing of human habitations on all sides:

"I have been twenty years a cooper's stave sawyer," he said. "We use different saws to those of the deal sawyers. They are smaller in the teeth, and only four feet long. A saw and frame will weigh 50lb. on an average, and I reckon that we pull 60lbs. weight every stroke. We make 50 strokes a minute up and down. I'm sure of it. We work very quick. That's 200 feet a minute, or 4,000 yards an hour — about 2¼ miles. We are top-sawyers and pitmen. Both are paid alike, though the topman has the hardest work. When I first knew the business times was much better. I could then earn £2 a week, and my mate the same, comfortably, the year through. Now we can each of us earn 25s. on an average the year through. We are paid by the piece. For 6-foot Dantzic or Memel straight cut staves 1s. 7d. per dozen cuts is paid us. We may have one or two cuts in each stave. For Quebec staves of the same length, or even if not quite so long, 1s. 8d.; Quebec hogsheads, 1s. 4d. They run about five feet; Dantzic hogsheads, about 4 feet, 1s. 2d.; brandy pipes, about 5 feet, 1s. 4d.; barrel straight cuts (for beer barrels), between 3 and 4 feet, 1s.; if we cut them into 'doublets' – and in doublets it's easier work for the cooper, for we thin the stave for his purpose – we have 2d. a dozen extra. The master gets more profit by it, but we have only 2d. a dozen, and other sizes in proportion, up to 4d. These are the principal staves; the others are for vinegar kilderkins and small barrels (9 or 18 gallons), and paid in proportion. We work two or three different sorts of timber, but all of them oak; all foreign, Baltic or American. We saw the staves from the timber as it's brought by the ships; it's cleaved (cleft), or chopped, to our purpose abroad. In the winter of '47-8 we were on strike sixteen weeks, but only me and two mates stood out for that time. They reduced us in the doublets 6d., from 1s. 11d. for the long staves to 1s. 5d., and for straight cuts to 1s. 4d., while others were reduced in the same proportion. We formed a committee among ourselves and got our prices back again, however. We did it in a month, after forming a society, though some stave-yards didn't manage it for six or nine months. The masters gave way when they got busy. Our masters can get their staves sawn cheaper at a steam-mill by 6d. a dozen the bigger ones, the straight cuts; but the machine can't make all the turns wanted in the stave – thank God for that. For straight cuts they are working us out. We haven't many straight cuts now to what we had; less by the working sawyer from 10s. to 15s. a week wages. Some masters – mine's one – don't like to send their staves to a steam-mills for straight cuts, for it the timber for the staves be crooked we can cut them to more advantage to the master than the steam-mills can. We take our money in the counting-house. I have been paid, in another employ, at a public-house, and we were obliged to take our beer from there every day, but when we formed our committee we put a stop to all that bad system. It was time, for some of us had to go home with nothing on a Saturday night. Sawing is very hard work, and requires four pints of beer a day to support a man, but many drink a great deal more. The public-house system made men drunkards – I'm sure it did, sir. I confine myself to four pints, which is enough for me. I know of no teetotallers among us. Accidents are common with sawyers. I've fallen many times, and have been cut all to pieces, so to say, by the saw." (He showed me some scars on his arms.) "We have a sick fund. Take sawyers altogether, they're fond of a drop, but I don't think them rougher than other people when they're in liquor. We are nearly all married men with families. Families seems a sort of gift to poor men, instead of to rich ones. I have known sawyers working at 70 years old, hard work as it is. We live as long as other people, I think. We pay no 'pence,' but have to find our own saws. A saw may cost from 7s. to 10s., and the frame 5s., when a new frame is wanted. A frame will last five or six saws. A saw will last us about five or six months in average use.''

Another man, in the same calling, gave me information confirming all the preceding, and said further:

''The timber sawn by coopers' stave sawyers is sawn as it's brought in from foreign parts, and it's brought in all the different lengths, and breadths, and thicknesses that are required for coopering. I'm of opinion that stave-sawyers are safe from being put to one side, for a good while, anyhow, by steam, in sawing 'doublets.' The timber runs irregular like, and is crooked sometimes. It's chiefly 'cleaved,' as we call it (cleft), with a hatchet, or whatever tools they have in those foreign parts. Out of the centre of one of these staves we saw a portion of wood, beginning almost at a point, and spreading out gradually to 'the bouge, that's the centre, where the *bulge* is the greatest. Then, when the *bouge* is reached, we saw along the other part of the wood, just in the same round inclining form as in the first part cut this way, which is like a quarter of an orange flattened out, is used by coopers for the heads of barrels, the two *equal* sides that are sawn from off the middle parts are the *doublets,* which are in this way ready hollowed and curved in the inner part, for cooper's work. Steam won't easy do that, sir.''

The first steam-mill for the sawing of planks was established (as is mentioned in the statement of a sawyer previously given) about thirty-six years ago, by Mr. Smart, near Westminster-bridge. For perhaps twenty years before that period horses had been employed to supersede men's labour. The principle on which these horse-mills were constructed was not dissimilar to that now in use in the steam saw-mills. The horses then did the work of the engine now — working nine saws at once, but with perhaps only half the motive power of steam as regards velocity. About forty-five years ago a party of sawyers one night walked abruptly into the largest of these horse saw-mills — that of Mr. Richardson, of Limehouse — and with sledge-hammers and crow-bars utterly demolished the whole apparatus, which was the work of but a few minutes. The men did not carry a single fragment away with them after the work of demolition had been done, and they studiously abstained from any other act of violence, and even from any act or words of insult. Their plea was, that these horse-mills would bring them and their families to the parish, by making beasts do the work of men, and that they had a right to protect themselves the best way they could, as no man, they said, merely for his own profit, had any right to inflict ruin upon a large body. So I was assured, and such feelings were at that period not uncommon among the ruder class of labourers. These horse-mills were but little remunerative, and Mr. Richardson did not think it worth his while to replace his machinery. It lay scattered about his yard until within 20 or 30 years ago. Another horse-mill, that of Mr. Lett, was demolished in the same way, not long after, by a party of sawyers; and the other proprietors of such places – there were perhaps about six in all – either discontinued the use of horses through fear, or the working of their mills because less remunerative, and they were gradually done away with. I had these particulars from a very intelligent man, now engaged in the sawing business. They were beyond his own recollection; but he had often heard his father, who passed a long life in the capacity of a sawyer, relate the circumstances. My informant was not altogether positive as to dates – he gave them to the best of his recollection. Yet, without this precipitate violence, horse saw-mills would have been discontinued, "for a very sufficient reason," said my informant, "because they didn't pay, I feel pretty well satisfied. Horses, you see, sir, must eat their oats of a night, or whether they are at work or not, but steam consumes coals only when at work."

Steam saw-mills continued to be gradually established throughout the metropolis until they now number 68 – six at least of the proprietors being also timber merchants. These mills average three "frames" each, a frame holding nine saws. In case all the means of these mills were called into operation at one time, 1,755 saws would be at work. Of these the straight saws make 160 "revolutions," as each up or down motion of the saw is technically called, in a minute, the "revolution" being four feet in length. The circular saws, for cutting deals and timber, describe a diameter of from 18 to 36 inches, 18 inches being the most frequent size, perhaps comprising seven-eighths of the circular saws in the London mills. The "circulars" may number one-tenth of the straight saws, and these "circulars" perform 1,800 revolutions in a minute. Of the space thus traversed I have given some curious particulars from an experienced man. Another gentleman, himself the conductor of a steam saw-mill – and I have to thank him also for other valuable and curious information – took pains, at my request, to calculate the number of sawyers superseded by the application of steam power. These, from the best data, he gives as 750 "pairs," or 1,500 men.

In the course of my inquiries I visited a steam saw-mill. It is situated close upon the river, being, indeed, a wharf as well as a mill. Over head is a lofty roof of thin light-coloured timber, through which the light came with a pleasant yellow hue. A timber frontage, in some parts of the nature of a casement, looks on the river. When the machinery was not at work all was pleasant and quiet, but when eighteen saws were in full operation – that number being employed on my visit – there was anything but quiet. The usual noise of a steam-engine had the addition of the grinding sound of the saws, jumping, as it would seem to any one ignorant of the agency employed, up and down most rapidly – while at intervals, through all this combination of sounds, was heard the ripple of the Thames dashing close up to the river front of the mill, for it was then high water, and a strong breeze was blowing. The steam-engine occupies one corner of the premises, and is partly detached. The wheels and machinery by which the mill is worked are beneath the timber flooring of the yard, the main shaft occupying the centre. The frame is simply nine upright, saws, each four feet in length, moving up and down as the timber is sawn, and at a distance from each other, according to the substance the plank is to be sawn. When the machinery is set a-going, the plank, by means familiar to engineers, is made to adjust itself to the action of the saws, being gradually advanced as each cut has been executed. A frame-worker attends to the due adjustment of the timber, however, as well as to the renewal of the saws when the teeth have become blunted by the rapid and severe friction. The machinery, when viewed at work under the flooring through the trap-doors, presents a very curious appearance. The imperfect light throws many of the wheels into the gloom, the brighter parts flashing to the eye, while the reverberation conveys the notion of extended space and far multiplied machinery.

Two engines, each of 10-horse power — and fewer are never fixed in any mill — cost from £650 to £800; about £700 being perhaps the most usual expense. These engines consume a ton of coals in a day of twelve hours, and a quart of machine oil.

Some further particulars concerning *steam saw-mills* I give in the words of a well-informed and observant man long familiar with their working:

"I have been several years — I can't say precisely how many — acquainted with all the parts of the labour required in a steam saw-mill. I am now a foreman. For the management of two engines, each of 10-horse power, or one of 20, there are, besides the foreman, who overlooks the business generally, five men employed — an engine-driver, a saw-sharpener, two frame-workers, and a labourer. The business of the engine-driver and the saw-sharpener everybody can understand; the frame-worker attends to the frames, replacing the saws when it's necessary, and looking to the deals being in a proper position, and all connected with the frames; and the labourer piles the deals which sawn, and does all the 'odd jobs.' He is paid from 3s. to 4s. a day, and the others from 5s. to 6s. The steam-mill saws go from 8 to 10 'runs' — 9 inches is a run — through 12 feet spruce deals, before they require sharpening; through some deals the saw will go more runs. The best and quickest sharpeners, by far, are men who have been used to work as topmen in sawpits; they are better than cutlers. The men's saws, in the pits, require sharpening rather oftener than steam-mill saws. Their saws have teeth — called 'space' — ⅝ or ¾ apart. Steam-mill saws are closer-toothed, and cut finer, and therefore cleaner. The steam saws are made of inferior steel to those of the pit sawyers; they cost about 5s. a piece. It takes a quarter of an hour to replace the nine saws in a frame when they become blunted.

One saw will last six months. Our saw sharpener does nothing else. The topman uses half-round files for his sharpening; the steam-mill saw sharpeners use round files. In our steam-mills we can't cut staves for coopers; that is, we can cut them straight, of course, but not in doublets, which is the main trade. We can't so well cut elm, oak, or ash, as the sawyers. Indeed, we can only outdo the sawyers altogether in deals; but they're more used for general purposes than all other woods put together — far more. Timber merchants who have their own steam-mills have, for some things, to employ sawyers still. We cut deals at 2s. 6d. a dozen, which, by men's labour, costs 3s. 6d. A twenty-horse power engine will do the work of thirty 'pairs' of sawyers — that's sixty men — in a day, in sawing deals, but only deals. Our saws penetrate one-eighth of an inch each 'revolution.' The pit-sawyers penetrate from a quarter to half an inch, according to the quality of the deals. They have more 'holt' (grasp or purchase) on their saws, and so can work them deeper into the wood. A pair of sawyers would most likely beat one saw worked by steam. Our saw would go twice as quick as theirs, but their cuts would go twice as far as ours. Owing to the 'holt,' the pit sawdust is much coarser than ours. One of our frames will make from 3 to 4 sacks of sawdust in a day; almost twice as much as a pair of sawyers will make in a week. A sack, which is generally sold at 6d., is 4 bushels. Some sawmills — our every now and then — can't dispose of their dust quick enough, and have to burn it. It's chiefly sold to 'dust' public-house tap-rooms, and those sort of places. Of all the single consumers, no doubt Astley's is the greatest. Doll-stuffers use it too, but a single sack will stuff a famous lot of dolls. Very few saw-mills, if any, can be said to be paying. But there's the capital sunk in the machinery, and a small return is better than its standing idle. The work is irregular, and many take long credit. Small orders, too, though they must be done, are anything but a profit. A frame makes ten cuts as easy as one. A circular saw, worked by steam, performs 1,800 revolutions in a minute. Take the usual diameter of 18 inches, and, of course, the saw describes a circumference of 54 inches, or one yard and a half, and does it 1,800 times. So that in a minute one mile and a half is done, with 60 yards to spare; and, not reckoning the 60 yards at all, but supposing there was no stop in the working, 90 miles an hour, which, at no more than 10 hours in a day, is 900 miles. The straight saws perform 160 revolutions, each of 4 feet, in a minute, which gives 213 yards a minute, or within 15 yards of 7¼ miles an hour. Reckon 1,000 of these saws going just now, and that's performing a distance (not minding the fifteen yards) of 7,250 miles an hour. Or, if all the saws were going (1,755), of 12,223¾ miles an hour. Of course, that's supposing there is not stop. The penetration through the timber under these circumstances would be between 22 and 23 miles, at an eighth of an inch each cut.''

Concerning the operation of the steam saw-mills upon the working men,

I had the following statement from two picked men: they were general sawyers. One, who was 55 years old, had been 40 years in the trade; and the other, who was 49, had had 35 years' experience in it. "I can recollect," said the younger, "when I could save more money in a week than I can now earn in the same time. Ah! then, if a man was a goodish sawyer, and out of work, he would have twenty or thirty people after him. Often, when I've been going along London streets, with my saw on my back, a timber-merchant or a cabinet maker would hail me, and cry, 'Halloa, ho, do you want any work, my man?' and often they gave a sum of money for a good sawyer to come and work for them." The elder man said, "My father was a sawyer, and often I've heard him say that the trade was better in his younger days than even it was in mine. He used to speak of what it was seventy year ago; the wages weren't better in his younger days than they were in mine, but the work was — there was fewer hands, you see. I have heard him say that him and his mate has earned one pound a day. He became a timber merchant afterwards, and he's told me that he'd paid a pair of sawyers that he had in his employ £24 in the month. They were veneer sawyers, and that was the finest and best paid work in the trade — now that's *all* gone from us. There an't one regular veneer sawyer left in the trade. All veneers are cut at present by machinery. Thirty years ago, when London wasn't half so big, there was three times as many sawyers as there are now, and one pair in every ten out of these used to cut veneers. In every timber yard the 'first pair' was generally employed cutting veneers. In the neighbourhood where I live, the sawyers are not half so many as they were. At R——'s yard, where they used to keep nine pair, they hasn't more than three, and yet the work's increased to that extent that it would keep twenty saws going where only nine was employed before. At S——'s there used to be nineteen pairs of sawyers constantly at work, and now there's not employment for one pair. I think I have heard my father say that there was as many as 3,000 pairs in the metropolis. Why, not more than twenty year ago one master sawyer used to have as many as five apprentices. In the year '26 it was about as good a time for sawyers as ever it was — there was a good demand for men, and good wages." "I can remember it better," said the oldest of the two; "but, never mind, that's the last time that the trade's been what you may call good. It began to decline between '26 and '27 — just about Fauntleroy's bankruptcy. I remember the saw mills began to get more general from that period. I can't recollect when the horse saw-mills was fust put up. Several cabinet-makers used to have hand-mills of their own, which consisted of circular saws in a bench, and worked by a couple of labourers. One of the horse-mills — I remember it was over about Pedler's acre — was said to kill a horse a day. The first steam-mill that was set up was at Battersea. It was a Frenchman (Brunel) that took out the patent for cutting veneers by steam — that's above forty years ago. The steam-mill had been up two or three years when I first came to London, and that was in 1810. I recollect seeing some shortly after I got to town. They was cut more true than any sawyer could do them, but not half as well as they are done now. The first that was done was eight in the inch, and now they can cut 14, as thin as a wafer, and that's impossible for the best sawyer in the world to do. I have cut as many as eight in the inch myself, but then the wood was very shallow – eight or nine inches deep. The general run of veneers cut by hand was about six in the inch. It wasn't until some five or six years after the first steam saw-mill for veneers was set up that one was erected for deals, and some time after that they were used to cut timber. About 1827, they began to get general, and as fast as the saw-mills have been starting up so we have been going down. We only have the rough work, and what the saw-mills can't or won't do. We get chiefly 'one cuts' to do, because the saw-mills can't do that kind of work so well as we can. A sawyer formerly took apprentices." "I was an apprentice for seven years," said the younger man. "And I worked along with my father," said the other. "It was a rule in our trade that the eldest son was entitled to his father's business. Now I don't see a sawyer in London who has an apprentice. Formerly we would allow no man to work at our trade unless he had been apprenticed or articled for three years; now it's open to any man, and yet none that I know of come into it. Many that I am acquainted with have left it, and many more would be glad to get away from it. I was one of the enumerators at the taking of the last census in the district in which I now live, and now I think there are not more than half as many sawyers as what there were then; the old hands die off, and no young ones fill up their places. Some few sawyers perhaps put their boys to the trade because they haven't the means to apprentice them to anything else, and the boy, you see, by working with his father, will bring in something at the end of the week. All that the two earns then goes to one home. I know many sawyers that have emigrated, and among them have been some of the best workmen, and some of the most intelligent. The trade, we think, will keep dwindling and dwindling every year; but machinery, we think, will never be able to take it all from us. I haven't been at work not a day this week. Some times we are worked to death, and sometimes we are picking our fingers. At the beginning of the week we are often obligated to have extra hands, and at the end of the week we are standing still, may be. There may be some few in large firms who may have constant work; but the most of our trade is idle more than half their time. It puzzles me how they live, some of them. Twenty-six years ago, my average wages was 35s. a week all the year through. I don't think the average wages of our trade, take the good with the bad, are above £1, and formerly it was full double that. Why, twenty years ago we used to have a trade dinner every year, somewhere out of town, and to go up to the tavern – wherever it was – in grand purcession, with bands of music and flags flying (we had a union jack that cost forty odd pound then), and the dinner of the whole of the districts used to come to near upon 50 guineas. After all this I leaves you to judge what our opinion is about machinery. Of course we looks upon it as a curse. We have no chance to compete with a machine; it isn't taxed, you see, as we are. I look upon machinery as an injury to society generally, because if it drives the hands out of our trade they must go into some other, so that working men is continually pressing one upon another. If machinery can cut the wood cheaper than we can, it's a gain to the timber merchant, he is enabled to reduce the price, and so some part of society may be a gainer by it, but we think society loses more than it gets. Supposing a machine to do the work of 100 pair of sawyers, then of course it throws 200 men out of employ; and these 200 men have families, and they are all benefited by the employment of the working man's labour. But in the case of machinery only one man is benefited" (this I found to be the common opinion of the operatives); "the money all goes to him and the others are left to starve, or else for society to support, either as paupers or felons, so that society, in the present state of things, after all, loses more than it gains. We see that as science advances the comfort of the working man declines. We believe machinery to be a blessing if rightly managed. It only works for one class at present, but the time *will* work for all parties." (The carpenters, it will be seen in my next letter, hold the same opinion.) "Let machinery go on increasing as it does, and there will come a time when the labour of the many will be entirely done away with; and then what will society gain when it has to keep the whole of the labouring classes? We can see machinery improving every day, so that there is less work for the people and more paupers. Our bread is being taken out of our mouths, and our children left to starve. I am quite satisfied that those who have nothing but their labour to depend upon get up every morning less independent than they went to bed. The many long heads that are scheming how to deprive men of their work is quite sufficient to bring that about. It's no use emigrating either. Let a working man go where he will, machinery pursues him. In America it's worse for sawyers, if possible, than here. There the sawing is all done by water-mills, and wood is so plentiful and so cheap that if they spoil a bit, it ain't no matter. Working-men is much disheartened at the increase of machinery, when they're a standing at the corner of streets idle and starving and see carts coming out of the yard filled with planks that they ought to have had. You see, sir, when some are injured by any alteration, they gets compensation; but here is our trade cut up altogether, and what compensation do we get? We are left to starve without the least care. I have paid 1s. 10d. for a quartern loaf before now, and I could get it much easier than I can now. When I get up in the morning, I don't know whether I shall be able to earn a 6d. before nightfall. I have been at work ever since I was eight years old, and I'm a pretty good example of what the working man has to look for; and what's the good of it all? Even the machines, some of them, can't hardly raise the price of the coals to get their fire up. When they first set up they had 6d. a foot for cutting veneers, and now they have only 1d. Machinery's very powerful, sir, but competition is much stronger.''

LETTER LX
Thursday, July 11, 1850

The number of carpenters and joiners in Great Britain at the time of taking the last census in 1841, amounted to 162,977. Of this number 128,000 were resident in England, 24,000 in Scotland, 8,000 in Wales, and 2,000 in the British Isles. There are no means of ascertaining the entire number of carpenters and joiners in the kingdom at any previous period, because the census of 1831 (which was the first that took any account of the occupations of the people) gave only the number of handicraftsmen and labourers who were 20 years of age and upwards. If, however, we compare the number of carpenters and joiners of that age who were resident in the different counties in 1831 with those located in the same places ten years afterwards, we shall arrive at many curious results; for by such means we shall be enabled to see how this particular craft has increased or declined in particular parts of the country – and then, by ascertaining the rate of wages in those districts, we shall at the same time learn how far the weekly income of the workman has been influenced by the principle of supply and demand. I regret that, at present, I have no means of making the comparison as regards the wages of the carpenters at the two decennial periods; still, to know the rate of increase in a particular craft is of the utmost importance in all questions of social economy, and I have therefore been at considerable pains in arriving at the following results.

The greatest increase among the carpenters – in comparison with the increase of population – took place in Carnarvonshire, where the trade was augmented no less than 223 per cent. more than the general population of that county. The next greatest increase occurred in Renfrewshire, where the number in the trade rose to 151 per cent. above that of the population; and the next in Merionethshire, in which county the increase was 107 per cent. above the people generally. Then came Lanarkshire, where the carpenters increased 97 per cent.; in Durham, 60 per cent.; Bute, 53 per cent.; and Radnorshire, 47 per cent.; while in Yorkshire the increase of carpenters was 46 per cent. *above* the increase of the population. The following counties show, on the whole, an increase of carpenters, but in a *less* degree than the population: – Linlithgow shows an increase from 1831-41, but in the ratio of 22 per cent. less than that of the population. The population of Sussex increased 14 per cent., whilst the number of carpenters remained nearly the same. The increase of the carpenters in Cardiganshire was 8 per cent. below that of the population. Rutland 7 per cent., Breconshire 8 per cent., Dumbarton 4 per cent., Warwick 2 per cent., and Norfolk 1 per cent.

An actual decrease of the carpenters occurred in the following counties: – In Caithness the population increased 1 per cent., whilst the carpenters decreased 14 per cent., making a difference on the whole of 15 per cent. In Elgin the population was augmented by 2 per cent., while the number of carpenters diminished 9 per cent., making a total decrease of 11 per cent. In Roxburgh the population increased 10 per cent., but the carpenters decreased 8 per cent., or 18 per cent. on the whole. At Kinross, Peebles, and Perth both the poulation and the carpenters have decreased, though the carpenters in a greater degree than the population. The increase of carpenters over and above the increase of the population in the three divisions of Great Britain is as follows: –

England, increase of carpenters, 14 per cent.
Scotland, ditto .... 20 ,,
Wales, ditto .... 37 ,,

The increase of the carpenters in the metropolis has been less than the population; and stands thus: – Increase of population, 32 per cent.; carpenters, 28 per cent.; so that the London carpenters increased at the rate of 4 per cent. less than the general London population.

I refrain from drawing any conclusions as to the increase or decrease in the rate of wages in the counties above-mentioned, because I am without any authentic facts for so doing; and I therefore leave it to others, who are in a position to make the comparison, to show how the weekly income of the carpenters in the several counties above enumerated has been affected by the increase or decrease of their numbers.

It is with the carpenters and joiners of the metropolis that I have specially to deal. These, as I said before, numbered in 1841 as many as 18,321 individuals, of whom 16,965 were males, and 83 females, of 20 years of age and upwards and 1,273 males below that age. But among the 18,000 individuals given in the census of 1841, both masters and working men are included, so that to arrive at a correct estimate as to the number of operatives in the metropolis we must take the number of London carpenters who are in business for themselves (and these, according to the "Post-office Directory," are 1,239), and deducting them from the 18,321 individuals cited in the census, we shall come to the conclusion that there were somewhere about 17,000 operative carpenters resident in the metropolis nine years ago; and, presuming the trade to have increased since that period at the same rate as it did in the ten years previous, it follows that there are at this present time upwards of 20,000 operative carpenters in London.

Numerically considered then, the carpenters rank amongst the most important of the working classes of the metropolis. The domestic servants, the labourers, the boot and shoe makers, the tailors, the dressmakers, and the clerks, alone take precedence of them in this respect.

About three-fourths or four-fifths of the carpenters working in the metropolis, I am informed, are from the country; for it is only within the last fifteen or twenty years that the London masters have taken apprentices. Before that time apprentices were taken – with but a few exceptions – only in the City, and those who served their time there did so solely with the view of "taking up their freedom" afterwards. Large masters in London would not then be troubled with lads, though small jobbing masters generally took one or two. Now, however, there is scarcely a master in London but what has some youths in his employ, and many of the large builders have as many lads and "improvers" as they have men, while some of them have even more. All these are used as a means of reducing the cost of men's labour. "When I first came to town, twenty years ago" (said one of the carpenters whom I saw), "I never knew a lad to be employed in any of the large firms in which I worked." As a proof of this, he told me, he never worked at that time but with one "Cockney," that is to say with a person who had been regularly brought up to the carpenter's business in London. Twenty years ago it was usual for the country carpenters to come up to London immediately after having served their apprenticeship; some did this to better their condition, the wages in town being double what they were in the west of England, and some came up to improve themselves in the business and then to return. At that time one-third at least of the number that came to London would go back into the country to settle after two or three years' practice in town. At the present time, however, it is estimated that not one in twelve who come to town from the country ever return. A great number of country carpenters are still attracted to London under the belief that the wages here maintain their former rate. When they arrive in the metropolis they find out to their cost that they can obtain employment only among the speculative builders and petty masters, where but two-thirds of the regular wages of the trade are given; and when once they take to this kind of work, it becomes impossible for them, unless very prudent indeed, ever to get away from it. This, I am informed, is one of the principal reasons of the over population of the London trade – for the work in the metropolis is now sufficient to give employment only to two-thirds of the hands. Another cause of the trade being over stocked is the reduction of wages that has taken place among those working for the speculative builders and petty masters, for I have before shown that the necessary consequences of under-pay is over-work – that is to say, if the wages of the "non-society" carpenters and joiners have been reduced one-third, then each man will endeavour to do one-third more work in his struggle to obtain the same amount of income as he previously did. Again, it will be found that a new race of employers has sprung up in the metropolis of late years, who are known among the trade as "strapping masters," from the fact of their forcing the men to do double as much work in a day as was formerly expected of them. Hence it is clear, that though the London carpenters have increased 4 per cent. less than the general population of the metropolis, still each of the operatives has been compelled of late years, either by the strapping masters, or a reduction of wages, to get through twice or three times as much work as formerly, and thus the trade has become as overstocked by each hand doing double work, as it would have been if the hands themselves had been doubled.

The carpenters and joiners that work for the low speculating builders are, generally speaking, quite a different class of men to those who are in "society." As a rule, to which, of course, there are many exceptions, they are men of dissipated habits. What little they get I am assured is spent in beer or gin, and they have seldom a second suit to their backs. They are generally to be seen on a Sunday lounging about the suburbs of London with their working clothes on, and their rules sticking from their side pockets – the only difference in their attire being, perhaps, that they have a clean shirt and a clean pair of shoes.

The great majority of the hands that work for the speculating builders are young men who have come up from the country, hoping to better their condition. About one-fourth of these who work for the speculative builders are, it is said, men of depraved and intemperate habits, and have scarcely a tool amongst them. The better class of workmen would rather part with the clothes off their backs and the beds from under them, than make away with their tools; so that it is only in cases of the most abject distress that a skilful joiner seeks to raise money upon the implements of his trade. When this is the case, I am told, it is usual for the operatives in "society' to club together, and lend a person so circumstanced, some one tool and some another, until a sufficient "kit" is raised for him to go to work with.

The majority of carpenters who are settled in London are married men with families, and mostly live in lodgings; many of the working, however, are householders, paying as much as £70 per year rent, and letting off apartments, so as to be wholly or nearly rent free. In London there are several of what may be termed colonies of working carpenters. A great many reside in Lambeth, a large number in Marylebone, in the vicinity of Lisson-grove, and a considerable proportion are to be found in Westminster. This is to be accounted for by the fact that several of the principal firms are established in these quarters. The carpenters who live in lodgings mostly occupy a floor unfurnished, and pay from five to seven shillings rent; but men with large families generally contrive to be house-holders, from the fact that children are usually objected to in respectable lodgings, so that they must either live in some low neighbourhood or else pay an exhorbitant rent for their residences in a better district. The more respectable portion of the carpenters and joiners "will not allow" their wives to do any other work than attend to their domestic and family duties, though some few of the wives of the better class of workmen take in washing or keep small "general shops." The children of the carpenters are mostly well brought up, the fathers educating them to the best of their ability. They are generally sent to day schools. The cause of the carpenters being so anxious about the education of their children lies in the fact that they themselves find the necessity of a knowledge of arithmetic, geometry, and drawing in the different branches of their business. Many of the more skilful carpenters I am informed, are excellent draughtsmen, and well versed in the higher branches of mathematics. A working carpenter seldom sees his children except on a Sunday, for on the week day he leaves home early in the morning, before they are up, and returns from his work after they are in bed. Carpenters often work miles away from their homes, and seldom or never take a meal in their own houses, except on a Sunday. Either they carry their provisions with them to the shop, or else they resort to the coffee-shops, public-houses, and eating-houses for their meals. In the more respectable firms where they are employed, a "labourer" is kept to boil water for them, and fetch them any necessaries they may require, and the meals are generally taken at the "bench-end," under which a cupboard is fitted up for them to keep their provisions in. In those shops where the glue is heated by steam the men will sometimes bring a dumpling or pudding and potatoes with them in the morning, and cook these in a glue-pot which they keep for the purpose. In firms where the glue is dissolved by means of hot plates small tins are provided,on which they cook their steaks, rashers of bacon, red herrings, or anything else that they may desire. These arrangements, I am informed, are of great convenience to the men, and in those shops where such things are not allowed they are mostly driven to the public houses for their food. The men speak very highly indeed of both the Cubitts, in whose establishments the arrangements are especially conducive to the comforts as well as the intellectual improvement of the men. (I shall prepares the work fixes it also. Large houses prefer having different hands for these departments, as the work is better and readier done than way, and the men are kept in the shop instead of every one running away out to fix each article as he makes it. In this manner a great deal of time would be lost. Again, the 'benchman,' or man who works in the shop, has always his chest of tools ready by his side; whereas the fixer requires nothing but a basket, which he takes with him to the job. The duty of a fixer is to put up the sashes, frames, shutters, doors (sometimes the staircases), skirtings, cupboards, recesses, architraves, and mouldings, and lay the floors. The preparers are generally the better workmen."

In a large establishment of the best order the joiners' work is first given out to a surveyor – generally one in the master builder's employ. These surveyors are also called "clerks of the works." In one establishment alone there are about 200 surveyors, clerks, and foremen. The architect is usually independent of these. The business of the surveyor is to take the architect's plans, make drawings in detail from them, and give specifications of the cost of the respective parts. His experience, aided by references to the books of the firm, enables him to do this. A plan is made for every story, and the surveyor has to see that all the architect's provisions for the form and elevation of the building are carried out as regards the joiners' work. The surveyor or foreman also "lays out" the carpenters' work, and gives instructions, plans, and details to guide the carpenter in its execution. In small establishments the master "lays out" both the carpenters' and joiners' work himself.

The trade, commercially speaking, divides itself, like all others of the present day, into two distinct branches, viz., the "honourable" and "dishonourable" masters – that is to say, those who have a regard for the welfare and comforts of their men, and those who care only for themselves and seek to grow rich by underselling their fellow-tradesmen, as well as by under-paying the workmen in their employ. As regards skill, these two branches of course divide themselves again into the substantial and the slop trade. The men belonging to the "honourable" part of the trade are mostly paid by the day – the wages being 5s. for ten hours' work (or sixpence per hour), from six to six, with the allowance of an hour for dinner, and half-an-hour each for breakfast and tea. Sometimes the better class of workmen are paid by the piece, and then the prices are regulated by some trade book, as Skyring's/Carpenters, and others. Generally the operatives object to piece work. Such a mode of payment, they say, induces a man to "scamp" his work; that is, to devote less time and labour to the skilful execution of it than he would were he paid by the day. Again, they urge, that when a man is paid by the piece there is no necessity for the work being done under the eye of the mater or his foreman. So long as it is completed to the satisfaction of the employer, it is no matter where or by whom it is executed. Hence the journeyman is at liberty to hire whoever he pleases to help him with it, or even to do it for him, and as this assistance is sure to be paid by him at a less rate than he himself receives, the system of piece-work thus becomes one of the prime causes of the reduction of wages, while the operative is ultimately transformed by it into the middleman or "sweater,' living on the toil and degradation of his fellow working men. The evil effects of this system have been already fully set forth in these letters while treating of the operative tailors of London; and it will be seen, when I come to treat of the speculative builders, that the same system among the carpenters and joiners seems to be attended with the same pernicious results. There it will be found that all the regulations which are observed to ensure skilled labour are utterly disregarded; the work is scamped and the operative is underpaid, and he not only loses thereby his self-respect and self reliance, but sinks into drunkenness and demoralisation. The workman is, moreover, made the means of carrying out the system which results in his own degradation. The houses of a "building lawyers" or "speculating builders" are let to a general contractor; he sub-lets the work, mostly by the piece, to others, who are usually journeymen, and these sub-contracting journeymen sub-let again to others even lower than themselves. By this process men gradually become mere machines, and lose all the moral and intellectual characteristics which distinguish the skilled artisan. Some masters reduce the wages of their workmen, not by smaller payments, but by exacting a greater quantity of work. They compel those in their employ to "scamp" it – that is, to crowd into ten hours, work which fairly requires for its skilful execution fifteen, or give an account of these in my next letter. In some shops as many as from 200 to 300 men are employed, and one of my informants, who worked in as large a shop as any in London, says that among the 300 benchmen employed at his master's, there were not more than six drunkards, and these men were held in general disrepute among their fellow-work men. Before the men leave their work in the large shops, it is usual for them to change their working clothes for other which they keep in a little cupboard under their bench. Their appearance in the street is as respectable as that of any tradesman.

Such is an account of the social condition of the London carpenters and joiners, gleaned from my own investigation, as well as from information supplied to me by the most intelligent and truthful of the operatives. I shall give a description of the several branches of the trade.

The term carpenter, I am told, is applicable to any one who cuts, fashions, and joins timber for building. Those who do the work of houses are house carpenters, while those who build ships are ship carpenters. Correctly speaking, however, the framer of a building is the *carpenter* and the finisher the *Joiner*: nor, as I learn from the most intelligent of the workmen, can there be an interchange of the labour of these two branches without an inferior degree of skill in the execution of the work being the consequence. "In my opinion," said one experienced carpenter to me, "to have the trade right well done carpenters should never be put to joiners' work, nor joiners to carpenters'. When a man's been long at carpentering, if he's put to joinering he's often too rough and rapid; and a joiner, in the same way, is too fine and finicking-like for carpenters' work. Some men will tell you that they can do one kind of work as well as another; and so they may if they're only middling hands; but the best carpenter is always cleverest and quickest at his own branch, and the best joiner at his."

The carpenter makes and fixes the roof of a building, the skeleton parts of the floors before the boards are laid, and the wood-work for partitions. He prepares and fixes the "girders," which are the large beams that form the main support of the floors; the "binding joists," which are the smaller beams connected with the girders, and on which the floor-boards are laid (by the joiner); and in large houses he also constructs the "ceiling joists," which are a series of still smaller beams, to which the laths for carrying the plaster of the ceiling are attached – indeed, he does all the ponderous part of the wood-work appertaining to a building.

The joiner is generally termed – in contradistinction to the carpenter, who mostly works at the building, and seldom uses a plane – a "shop-hand" or a "benchman," from the fact of most of his work being prepared in the shop, and executed at the bench. Should the carpenter require to smooth the surface of a piece of timber, he rigs up a bench on the premises, on two barrels, as he best can. This, however, is by no means an ordinary occurrence, the rule in the trade being that all which the plane passes over is joiners' work. Joinery is, consequently, of a more finished description, and more subdivided than mere carpentry, though the spirit of competition is fast trenching upon these subdivisions, and thereby upon that peculiar fineness of skill which the confining men to one class of work secures. In large establishments, where the division of labour is still maintained, different hands are employed on the staircases, the window-frames and sashes, the doors, the shutters, the flooring and skirting (for which inferior workmen are usually employed); while the other portions, such as the cupboards, are disposed of in any way most convenient to the master.

In the best descriptions of joiners' work a very high degree of skill is displayed. Let any one look at the delicacy of a window-frame, and then recollect that it is so adjusted by the skill of the workman as to be able to bear a heavy degree of pressure and to resist a great degree of violence, and yet to be light and elegant in its structure, "By keeping men to a particular sort of work," I was told by one of themselves, "it is done finer, firmer, and quicker. For instance, for such exact work as window-sash making a different 'kit' of tools is used to that for other kinds of work, and men kept to such work are readier and handier at it, so that time is gained and fewer mistakes made." In a large shop where many hands are employed the joiners' work is prepared and fitted together, ready for fixing, in the shop; frequently it is even painted there. The workmen engaged in this manner are termed *preparers*, and when their work is completed the *fixers* adjust or "fix" it on the building; and thus, again, a more perfect workmanship is attained. "With small masters," said a fixer to me, "the same joiner as even twenty hours; so that the master obtains an amount of work which has been heretofore recognised as sufficient for a day and a half, or even two days, in one day; or in other words, he gets 7s. 6d. or 10s. worth of work for the 5s. which he pays for the day's labour, while the skill of the operative is deteriorated, with the usual deplorable consequences.

Of the carpenters and joiners now in London 1,770 or about one-tenth of the entire number, are "in society." Their houses of call are almost invariably held in public-houses. The objects of these societies are twofold – the upholding of the wages of their trade, and rendering assistance to the aged, disabled, or unemployed of their own body. The members meet periodically at their respective houses of call and contribute such a sum per week (varying from1½d. to 4d.) as is deemed necessary under the circumstances of the trade and the society. Some of the societies are managed by a check steward and three committee men; others have two auditors instead; others again a president, secretary, steward, check steward, and committee men. The officers are all paid from the funds of the society. As regards the initiation of a new member, he is proposed at one meeting, and, if considered eligible, he is admitted on the following meeting night. The expulsion of a member from society is for the following offences: – If he works under the standard rate of wages; if he goes into the country to work for his employer without having his expenses paid; and (where the society is opposed to the short-hour system) if he works short hours.

The houses of call at which these "societies" are held constitute the labour market (so to speak) of the trade. Each house of call is provided with a book, in which the unemployed members, names are inscribed in rotation, and the secretary attends twice a day to call over the names of those enrolled, and to receive notice from any other member who may be out of work. If a master wants a hand he sends to the house of call, and the first in rotation has the right of engagement. If he do not accept it his name is placed last on the list, and the next in rotation has the opportunity in like manner to accept or refuse the engagement. Now, however, it has become almost a general rule for men to call upon the masters or their foremen to solicit work. Besides what may be called the commercial objects of the society, such as upholding a fair rate of wages, there are others of a philanthropic and provident nature. In some cases they have vacation or winter funds, and in others mutual loan funds and building societies. For loss of tools by fire, security is given, from £5 to the whole amount, and by theft to half those sums. Where they have a winter fund, the unemployed members receive from 10s. to 12s. per week, but these winter funds are now giving way to loan societies and mutual building societies among the working men. Some of these loan societies charge 5 per cent. for moneys advanced upon personal security; other lend it out without the payment of interest, to be refunded by instalments when the borrower gets into employment again. The mutual building societies afford partial employment to members out of work, averaging from three days to a week, according to the number of applicants. These three last mentioned arrangements are provided for from the overplus money of the society, and require no extra contribution. There is one society, which has connected with it a Joint Stock Building Company, and is registered according to Act of Parliament – the whole of the members being connected with it. They contribute 1s. per month, for £5 shares, with the privilege of working out the whole amount of their share. Their unemployed members are "taken on" for a week, at £1 per week, in rotation, until the whole of those who are out of work get their turn, and then "go out and in" in rotation. If a man does not pay his contribution to his trade society for four months, he receives notice from the Secretary, and if he neglects payment for two months after such notice he is liable to be expelled, but extreme rigour is seldom exercise on this head. "Tramps" have not been relieved from the society's funds since the great union in 1834. The men are now generally opposed to strikes. The only thing approximating thereunto is "the short hour system." When trade is falling off, a master, not wishing to discharge his hands, proposes to the men to work so many hours less. In some societies this is not allowed, and their members, under such circumstances, are requested to "come out," and on doing so they receive from 12s. to 15s. a week till other work be obtained. Other societies permit the short-hour system. There are no superannuation funds. One of the secretaries informed me that the constant attendance of the men at their houses of call, which are, as I have said, nearly all public-houses, produced the pernicious effects to be expected; and I would here venture to impress upon the more intelligent members of the trade who are anxious for the social and moral improvement of their fellow workmen the advantage of holding their meetings at some other place.

Concerning trade societies in general, one of the most intelligent working men that I have yet met with made these observations to me:

"The public generally suppose that combinations of working men are a great evil, because they see only one side of the question. Their impressions are that trade societies are instituted *only* to obtain an increase of wages, and that they are necessarily connected with strikes. One of the objects of our 'societies' is certainly to prevent the extortions of the capitalist upon the working men, by maintaining the present rate of wages; but this is only one of their objects. Another object of our combinations is to support the aged, and the sick, and the unemployed. To show you, sir, how the public are benefited by these institutions, I will make a calculation as to the number of men who are kept from the workhouse by such means. Now, supposing there are 100 different trades in London, and that each of these trades have 10 societies in connection with them, then we have 1,000 different trade societies, dispersed throughout the Metropolis. A fair average as to the members belonging to each of these societies would be 100, and that would make a total of 100,000 individuals contributing to, and entitled to receive benefits in case of need from such institutions. I think not more than two per cent of this number ever put by a sixpence out of their earnings as a fund against sickness, accident, or old age; but, to be safe, let us say 5 per cent, or 5,000 out of the 100,000, and then we should have 95,000 working men in London, who, in case of their being unable to work, would have to come upon the parish for relief. In the society to which I belong, and which has 450 members appertaining to it, we paid upwards of £600 to men out of work in the winter. We supported on an average 80 men who were un-employed for 13 weeks, and gave them 12s. a week each. Two-thirds of this number had nothing else to depend upon. But say that each of the trade societies in the metropolis distributes only £100 among 100 men, in the winter (ours, I have told you, gave £600 to 450 while out of employment), and twice that amount among the aged or disabled every year, and this is a very low estimate; and then we have just upon £300,000 per annum given by the working-classes towards the support of their own poor, so that I don't think these trade combinations are quite so injurious to society as capitalists generally imagine. If they do uphold the rate of wages, at least this improved rate is used as a means of benefiting not only their own class, but the public, by keeping down the poor-rates generally.''

I shall now proceed to give the statements of the men employed at the several branches of the "honourable" trade, reserving for my next letter a description of the causes and effects of the cheap or slop trade in connection with the carpenters' business. The following information I received from a highly respectable journeyman carpenter working for the best shops at the best prices:

"I have known the London trade between twenty and thirty years. I came up from Lancashire, where I served an apprenticeship. I have worked all that time entirely at carpentering. No doubt I am a pure carpenter, as you call it, never having worked at anything else. Before I got married, eighteen years ago, I tried to make some odds and ends of furniture for myself, but I couldn't manage them at all to please myself, except in the frame of a bedstead, so I got a cabinet maker to finish my chairs and tables for me." (My informant then described the nature of the carpenter's work, and expressed an opinion that to have it executed in the first style a workman should do nothing else.) "I have always had 5s. a day, and in busy times and long days have made 33s. and 35s. a week, by working over time. I have always been able to keep my family, my wife and two children, comfort-ably, and without my wife's having to do anything but the house work and washing. One of my children is now a nurse-maid in a gentleman's family, and the other is about old enough to go and learn some trade. Certainly, I shan't put him to my own trade, for, though I get on well enough in it, it's different for new hands, for scamping masters get more hold every day. There's very few masters in my line will take apprentices; but I could set him on as the son of a journeyman. If I'd come to London now, instead of when

I did, I might have got work quite as readily perhaps — for I didn't get it within a month when I did come; but then I was among friends; but I should have had to work for inferior wages, and scamping spoils a man's craft. He's not much fit for first-rate work after that. I am better off now than ever I was, because I earn the same, and all my expenses, except rent, are lower. I have a trifle in the savings bank. But then, you'll understand, sir, I'm a sort of exception, because I've had regular work, twelve months in the year, for these ten or twelve years, and never less than nine months before that. I know several men who have been forced to scamp it — good hands, too — but driven to it to keep their families. What can a man do if 21s. a week is better than nothing. I am a society man, and always have been. I consider mine skilled labour, no doubt of it. To put together, and fit, and adjust, and then fix, the roof of a mansion so that it cannot warp or shrink — for if it does the rain's sure to come in through the slates — must be skilled labour, or I don't know what is. Sometimes we make the roof, or rather the parts of it, in the shop, and cart it to the building to fix. We principally work at the building, however. There's no rule; it all depends upon weather and convenience. The foreman generally know on what work to put the men so as best to suit, but in no shop I've been it has there been a fixed and regular division of the carpenters into one set as roofers, and another for the other work. Our work is more dangerous than the joiners, as we have to work more on scaffolding, and to mount ladders; but I can't say that accidents are frequent among us. If there's an accident at a building by a fall, it's mostly the labourers. I'm satisfied that the carpenters on the best sort of work are as well conducted and as intelligent as any class of mechanics. With scamping masters character is no recommendation, or very little. A very good hand I know was sometime out of work, and applied to a scamping master, and said, 'Mr. —— would vouch for his being a good workman and a sober man.' 'D—n your soberness,' was answered to him, 'what do I care for that? What I want is plenty of work done.' Men get not to care for their characters when they come to be knocked about by such masters. I myself know three men, at least, that were sober and respectable when in good work: they're scamping it now, and drink all they can get. One of them's a married man, and his wife has to go out washing, and his family's in rags.

We find our own tools, and a first-rate kit of carpenters tools, with duplicates and everything proper, may cost new, and at first hand, on to £30; but perhaps not very many have more than £15 worth, and some have to get on as well as they can with from £5 to £10 worth, or less than £5; but then, of course, they must keep renewing them. It's generally all up with a carpenter if he's popped his tools, and has to get them from his uncle's when he wants them. If they are in heavy, he hardly ever gets a fair start with them all again. I never knew one do it, and I have known very industrious men forced to pledge almost all their kit. We use saws a good deal, and sharpening them is a great cost to us. Wear and tear of tools I reckon at well on to 2s. a week. That's for six days' regular work. In the winter there's mostly a slack, as building, of course, ain't so freely carried on in heavy rain, and frost and snow, and dark short days. Some carpenters have nine months of it, and not a few either have six months' work of it in a year; others just what they can catch.''

A very intelligent man gave me the following information as *to the best description of joiners' work:*

"I have been twelve years a journeyman joiner in London. I consider a joiner a man who works in a building, and usually at a bench, at everything the plane goes over, such as doors, windows, sashes and frames, closets, skirting, flooring; but that's generally sawn and planed at the mills, and we merely lay it − in fact, the joiner is the preparer, fixer, and finisher of a building. The other work is the carpenter's, such as the roof, &c. I have been ten years in one shop, in the honourable trade, where we have as good wages and as good usage as in any shop, and where between 400 and 500 hands in all branches are employed. The wages paid us are 5s. a day for ten hours, from six in the morning to half-past five. Half an hour is allowed for breakfast, an hour for dinner, and half an hour for tea, but that is generally waived, and so we leave work at half-past five. For over-hours we are paid at the same rate, 6d. an hour, unless it be after ten at night, when we have 9d. an hour. On Sunday double time is allowed − that is, 1s. an hour, as is the case in repairing Somerset-house, the Admiralty, and other Government offices, where Sunday labour is resorted to not to interrupt business. I never knew any man to object to work on a Sunday. I would not if I felt it to be a matter of necessity. If it was not a necessity I would object. In our firm over-hours are not frequent, but in some few shops the men now work until eight o'clock. The trade is greatly opposed to over-time, because it keeps many men out of employment, but sometimes it is unavoidable. We prepare the doors, &c., which we make in the workshops (I speak of large and honourable firms), and then take them to the building to be fixed. In each workshop there is a foreman, whose business it is to see that the work is properly done. In a very busy time in our firm he has an assistant, and does not work himself. He overlooks all the men, whether forty-six benches, as in our shop, which is a double shop, or in an establishment where there may be only eight or ten; but smaller masters, or jobbing or speculative builders, frequently act as their own foremen, having sometimes 'a leading hand,' who works like the other men, but may have 2s. a week extra. He 'sets out' the work, and works himself when not so employed. We have no control − I mean our society has none − over the number of apprentices, or rather boys or youths a master chooses to take. Some take an unconscionable number. At ——'s they had to every one man five or six boys or youths, not apprenticed, but learning the trade. That firm's knocked in the head now, but the same system prevails, though not so extensively. In our shop we have only one apprentice and three other boys (one is my son). We never think now, though it was the case, of requiring seven years' apprenticeship for admission into our society. The men's sons had always an exemption from this rule. One of the great evils of the trade, as regards working joiners, is the system of the masters having 'improvers.' These are young men, generally out of their time, who want 'improvement' in their business, and who often come recommended from the country, where the master joiners have many customers; or they are connected with friends of the master, and so are put on. These 'improvers' are paid from 18s. to 24s. a week, of course superseding experienced hands at the regular wages. 'Improvers' are very seldom worth the money they receive; indeed, their object is to learn their business perfectly. The foreman don't trust them with the finest and nicest work of work, such as the frame, the sash, and their staircase, unless he sees they have great capabilities; so that after all, seven-eighths of them don't 'improve' much, but the public don't know good work from bad, and in consequence it appears cheap; and so wages get dragged down, and good hands are superseded. We seldom in our firm work by contract, but it's coming on; it's forced on the master – but then our work is very superior. Competition is ruining fine work, what you may call skilled labour, for there's not the time allowed to do it. Now, for a contract for a large building, honourable masters, treating and paying their men fairly, will take it say at £20,000. Another firm will undertake it at £14,000 or £15,000 (just look at the *Builder* about that). To make up the difference, they must use – the cheap contractors must – inferior timber, put together anyway, inferior and under-paid workmen, 'improvers,' and boys. The clerk of the works sees to the safety of the building; some are easy, and pretty easily managed; others are very strict. All Government work is done by contract, and at the lowest rates – slop wages generally. The Woods and Forests allow 28s. a week, and if an 'honourable' master gets the job he has to pay 30s., as society men won't work under. The new Houses of Parliament are, however, an exception to this rule. The best hands are in society. I have regular work, and have nothing to complain of that way; but for all that I would like to leave the country, for there's worse times coming."

From another joiner, to whom I was referred as one of the most intelligent me in the trade, I had the following statement:

"I have known the London trade for twenty-one years. When I first knew the trade wages were the same as they are now, 5s. a day. Indeed, older men have told me that there has been no change in the rate of our wages for between thirty and forty years. About sixteen or eighteen years ago 5s. 6d. a day was gained generally throughout the trade – at least from all the principal employers; but then the advance was acquired through a strike, which did more harm than good by creating ill-feeling between masters and men, and from the time lost and the expenses incurred in completing the strike. The 5s. 6d. a day didn't continue, as well as I can recollect, above a twelvemonth, not generally, though some few hands kept it longer, but masters kept giving new hands 5s. a day, and so got ride of the 5s. 6d. gradually. The strike was more, or as much, from party spirit as from a real regard for the interests of the journeymen's trade. Before the strike the very superior hands could command 6s. a day, but that's not the case now. Twenty-one years ago it wasn't so easy or so cheap to get to London as it is now, and men came then really for improvement, and went back to their own country places; now they come here and stick here longer than they used to so, especially the west of England men. Wages are lower in Somersetshire, Devon, and Dorset, than in any other part of England. As you go north wages are better. The joiners wages in those three counties are only 14s. or 15s. a week – it's an extraordinary man who gets 16s. there. They're handy men, many of them, when they come to London. There are so many apprentices taken in those counties, who, when out of their time, *must* find another market for their labour. When they come to London they don't undersell, unless occasionally, the regular hands, and respectable masters don't expect it. 5s. a day is a very low rate of wages, when the expense of tools is considered. Ours is one of the worst paid trades in the universe. My tools now would cost me £30 replacing, and no man in a respectable shop can get on with tools less in value than from £20 to £30. The masters find us no tools but extra moulding planes. The wear and tear of our tools is not less than 1s. 6d. a week cost to the workman, and from the loss of chisels and gouges, as well as from their wearing out, and from the expense of saw sharpening. For saws you must find you own files and sharpen them yourself, or pay 4d. for the mere filing of a saw; 6d. if there is anything more required. Our saws require sharpening twice a week on the average. Lead pencils now cost 8d. a dozen, such as twenty years since cost 2s. A pencil may last two months, so it's little matter. I average wear and tear, &c., of tools, at 1s. 6d. a week. I reckon that ten months' work is the year's average of employment, take the trade throughout London. Some have only four months in the year, and it's incredible how they live. There was a time, within these ten years say, when masters would keep a good man on at some inconvenience to themselves, but that's not the case now. Some shops are fairly besieged every Monday morning by men seeking work. It's within the last ten years that the great falling off in our trade has occurred, and it gets worse and worse. This is owing, I am convinced, to the increase of population, and of workmen, and to the decrease of men's labour, through greater use of machinery. Building now is generally a matter of speculation more than a matter of fair and regular trade, and so men seek to get it done in the cheapest instead of the best way. Our book of prices, Skyring's, and he's low enough for doors, gives 10s. 6d. for making a two-inch double-moulded door, but some 'scamping masters,' as we call the slop-masters, give only 5s., so that a man to make his 5s. a day at those prices must do double work, and for longer hours, at a rate that's killing him, or make the door in a very inferior way. I have known men work hard from six in the morning to nine at night, and in winter find their own candles, and not make 5s., or only 5s., then. That's the case now at Notting-hill, but that part is not the worst. Haverstock-hill and by the Brecknock Arms, Camden-town, is now amongst the worst parts of London. St. John's-wood was very bad, but building there's about over now. Some of those houses fetch low prices if they have to be sold a *second time,* the skirtings and doors and other work being so shrunk; but that's an after consideration, for at the time they're run up, the men who build them only look to sell them *once.* Machinery was first brought into competition with us in flooring boards. At first they were only planed by machinery, and the edges cut. I first heard of this planing 21 years ago. The next step was to grove (groove) and tongue the flooring. Formerly, grooves and tongues were made by hand. The joiners thought nothing at first of the planing of these boards by machinery, as only a certain class were put upon sash planing — it was beneath their dignity generally, and I have known men leave a shop rather than do it. Joiners' work is noisy, and they can't talk when carrying it on, and that may account for joiners not being such politicians or thinkers as shoemakers or tailors. The next introduction of machinery, as regards our trade, was the preparation of mouldings for doors, architraves, cornices, and base mouldings; base mouldings are the ornamental tops of the plinth or skirting. Wainscotting is coming into vogue again in some of the better sort of houses — a good deal so of late years, and especially in those in the Gothic style; but machinery affects that less, if anything, than in the general trade. It's almost purely joiners' work. In the trade wainscotting is called 'dadoing.' These are the principal things in which machinery has affected our trade, unless it be in hothouses, the roofs of which are frequently moulded by machinery, which can work ten mouldings where a workman can do one; but it's only the capitalists, the great masters, that are paid by employing the moulding machinery — it won't pay the others. These introductions have injured our trade, because only one-fifth of the workmen are now required in those particular branches. But in one instance machinery has done us good. Mr. ——, invented a very ingenious process for cutting tracing in the Gothic wood-work for churches and chapels. This introduced a taste for these things and a demand for wood carving, and this has been a benefit to the trade. The machine, too, cannot work the tracing right up to the point of a mitre, so that the joiner's work, though apparently superseded by the invention, has actually been increased by it, through the greater demand. But that's a mere trifle to the extent of work and the number of men supplanted by machinery. As the matter is at present carried on, at least one-sixth of the labour of working joiners through London is superseded in this way. It's not the mills that do all this mischief, for in Mr. ——'s, the great builder's, premises one-half of the labour is performed by his own machinery. It's not certain, however, that in our business machinery is so very profitable to the master as in a cotton factory. Machinery, besides, never does such work as moulding so perfectly as we can do it. We often have to trim and refit such mouldings.''

An experienced man gave me the following statement concerning green-house work:

"I have known the hot-house building, and similar branches of the trade – often called 'decorating' – for three or four years, and before that I was a joiner. There is no difference, I have ascertained, in a horticultural joiner's trade, as regards wages, for the last twenty or thirty years. The wages are the same as the joiners', and the same hours. Our work, for gardens, is more a matter of taste than house work, in which certain plans are laid down and must be observed. In hothouses the chief distinctive work is the framing, as the sashes are pure joiners' work. We make also cucumber-frames, summer-houses, conservatories, greenhouses, forcing-houses, lattice and trellice work for the training of climbing plants, and for ornamental purposes – in short, everything connected with gardens. Within these few years, say seven years, there has been a great increase in the demand for this kind of work, especially in greenhouses and conservatories. Not one-tenth of the men employed in this kind of work have been apprenticed to it solely; they are mostly joiners, for men when out of work must turn their hands to anything. Machinery affects our trade, in the preparation of sash bars, which contain the glass. They are chiefly 'stuck,' made by machinery. We can't compete with it. They charge 7s. to 8s. per 100 feet run for bars, finding the material, and having all ready prepared for use. The material, the timber, will cost two-thirds of that sum, and the labour would be, on an average, 3s. 6d. Our work, however, is considerably truer than their's. We can work with our tools to a great nicety, and that can't be done by the machine. None of their mouldings are perfectly regular. If the timber be crooked, the machine works it crooked to the timber, but we don't. Nearly all the mouldings for cucumber boxes and for general purposes are prepared by machinery. The manual labour so superseded is in my opinion one-fifth; and that drives men to undertake any job, and to go in as day workmen, and then look out for another job. Ours is chiefly outdoor work, and is very uncertain, as we can't 'fix' in wet weather. Within seven years iron and metal (composition) roofs, for hothouse and conservatories, have come into rather general use, having a lighter appearance than wood. Perhaps, however, there are nearly twice as many wood as iron or metal roofs made. Metal roofs (they're generally all called so) are fixtures usually. Another system of ventilation is pursued in them, either by a general ventilator at the top of the roof, which is the commonest way, or by perforated glass, the panes then overlapping one another, with an interval between to admit the air. In the wood work, we have sliding frames for ventilation, the upper frame being pulled down over the bottom sash, which is a fixture, the top being then left open for the admission of the air. I have been engaged in constructing hot-houses for nursery grounds and gentlemen's gardens both, from 100 to 150 feet long, for all purposes. The nurserymen have generally the larger hot houses. There is a sort of mania for them now, and more especially since the improved system of heating by hot water came in, within these five or six years. A large-sized boiler, 24 inches diameter, is calculated to heat 1,000 feet run. If for a pinery, this heat is from underneath, in pipes fixed in brick archways, and is forced upwards. If for grapes, the hot-water pipes are laid on the ground, and the same for flowers. Only for pines, or fruits of any kind are the pipes laid underground. The heat may be regulated; it may be concentrated in one part, or may be diffused through a hot-house or any adjacent buildings by means of stop valves, which can be opened or shut at pleasure. This process is better for ripening fruit than sunshine, as it is more regular. We have no society, and I don't know the number in the trade. Our average employment for regular hands is not more than eight or nine months in the year, for those nine months the wages are 30s. in the week. Many, however, get only employment at this work two or three months in the year, and then they look out for any kind of wood work. I know of none regularly doing horticultural work cheaper, but there is slop work got up for the trade, and that can only be done by parties taking less than the regular wages; and that's almost always by inferior workmen. A good hand can get his wages. Slop masters palm off inferior work as the best, and in the long run they'll drag us all down to bad work and bad wages. It's influencing us now. Masters say, 'I can get this done at this or that low rate,' and I have to drive on to meet their views. Masters are beaten oft enough by the slop-masters, and bad men are ruining good ones. Few persons are judges of work. Only to-day a gentleman called wanting a hot-house to be built; he said he could get it done, when the price was named to him, at so much less at ——'s. He was told that one great job which had been done at this cheap slop house had all to be re-done. A great part of the bad work is brought in by slop-masters, but the public themselves, even gentlemen, go about asking prices and cheapening tradesmen in my line, who, to meet the times, must put in, and do put in, inferior materials and use machine labour, even when it's not suitable at al. Gentlemen will offer from £1 to £8 less than a fair price for a hot-house. I have known one who wanted a green-house, call at our place, and state that he could get the fixing done cheaper than we could. He offered for the wood work what was the cost of the material alone. 'There's the duty off timber,' said he, 'and the duty off glass.' He was told that wages were the same, and he replied, 'Well, then, you should reduce them too.' (Hothouses are lower since the duty was taken off glass.) He was then told that to work at his price either the timber-merchant or the working man must be robbed. He replied, 'I'll call to-morrow and tempt you with another guinea, and show you the money, and then I know you'll take it.' He is a man worth £20,000 a year and more, and left his carriage at a distance to pass as a humbler man.''

From a sash-maker, one of the best hands, I received the subjoined narrative:

"I have worked at sash-making ten years, regular. I have done very little else all that time. For nine years I was solely employed at making sashes. In most of the large shops they let the sash-work now to what is termed a task-master, and then he employs his own hands. This is done in many shops where the best prices are paid. The sash-maker in a shop is a party who makes nothing else but the sashes and frames. I have been in London 25 years; sash-making was not a distinct branch of the trade then – it is only since there has been so much contract work, and the master-builders, large and small, have taken to letting the different parts of a house out to different hands, that separate men have been employed for sash-making. By giving the different parts out to different hands, the work, I think, is done in half the time, because a man has all his tools ready and set, and in general work a great deal of time is lost in shifting from one kind of work to another. The tools require to be altered for each class of work. When a man is always doing one job, he can do it almost without noticing his tools. The sash-maker, to whom the work is let, is never paid by the day, but always by the piece; the price is so much per foot for the different kinds of sashes. Common 2-inch or 1½-inch sashes, are about 4½d. per foot (either 'scribed' or 'mitred'); the better kind of deal sashes (which run about 2½ inches) are 6d. the foot. These are the prices in good shops – they may be a halfpenny more or less in different places. The party to whom the sashes are let at these prices is called the taskmaster; and he seldom does anything him-self except setting the work out and superintending. The work itself is done by men whom he employs, and these he always pays by the day. The task-master in good shops generally gives 5s. a day, and I knew one hand who had as much as 6s., but this was an exception rather than the rule. Usually the taskmasters try to cut the workman down as much as possible. Frequently they will give only 28s. a week in the best shops. The taskmaster generally works in the shop of the employer the same as the men, and the employer seldom troubles his head about what he gives those who work under him. A taskmaster will generally have from three to five, and sometimes as many as twenty hands at work for him. The taskmaster will often make 5s. out of the labour of each of the regular sash-makers that he employs under him. I have known one taskmaster to make as much as £10 a week out of ten men that he had working for him. We, of course, could measure the work as well as he could, and calculate what he got out of our labour. The taskmaster system is a very bad one for the working men, or, indeed, any system is bad where one working man is put to make money out of his fellows, for he must either employ cheap or very ready hands to get anything out of the job. It either leads to strapping – that is to making men work unusually hard or else to making them work at unusually low prices. This is one of the reasons why a man cannot find work directly he turns the middle age. Nothing but young strapping hands will do for the taskmasters. The cause of this hurry and scurry, and scramble, and scamping of work, and reducing of wages, is the contract system. First of all, gentlemen and others will have the work done as cheap as possible – the lowest estimate has the preference in contract work. Then masters go to work cutting under one another, just to get the job; and after that why, of course, they must make it up out of the men's muscles and bones. Before this contract system there was no such thing as letting and sub-letting of work, and one journeyman living and preying upon another. When I first came to town, such a thing as piece-work was hardly known, and if a man got a job that way, he was pretty well ousted from society for it – but now piece-work is as common as day-work; so much so, that the usual question among journeymen is whether they have the job by the day or piece. Piece-work is the worst of all things to be introduced into a trade. It has been the great evil, and will be the downfall of our trade; for directly men are paid by the piece, then of course they can employ others to assist them at lower wages than the regular pay, and then begins all kinds of scheming, strapping, and ultimately, starving of the men."

In my next letter I purpose entering more fully into the effects of the contract system.

LETTER LXI
Thursday, July 18, 1850

In my last communication I said that the carpenter's trade divided itself, like many others of the present day, into two distinct branches, viz., the "honourable" and the "dishonourable" masters – that is to say, those who have a regard for the welfare and comforts of their men, and those who care only for themselves, and seek to grow rich by underpaying the workmen in their employ.

I then treated at some length of the "honourable" part of the trade, and I now come in due order to set forth the condition and earnings of the operatives belonging to the "dishonourable" portion of it.

The journeymen in connection with the "honourable" trade amount, as I before stated, to 1,770, so that by far the greater number, or no less than 18,230 of the working carpenters and joiners in the metropolis belong to what is called the "dishonourable" class – that is to say, nearly 2,000 of the London journeymen are "society men," and object to work for less than the recognized wages of the trade, while upwards of 18,000 are unconnected with any of the trade societies, and the majority of them labour for little more than half the regular rates of pay. The "dishonourable" portion of the trade includes many varieties of workmen. In the first place, there are the class called "improvers," or inexperienced hands, who, having learnt their business in the country, come up to town to perfect themselves in the higher branches of the trade, and, while they are so improving themselves, consent to take less wages than the more experienced and skilful operative. These, it will be seen, now constitute a considerable portion of the London trade, and are largely employed by those "enterprising" firms who seek to extend their business merely by underselling their neighbours. Secondly, there are the countrymen, who without any essential view to improvement in their craft, flock to London, from the badly paid parts of the country, in the hope of obtaining higher wages in the metropolis, and who, on their arrival in town, willingly accept a less rate of pay than the superior handicraftsmen. Thirdly, there are what are called the "strapping-shops" – that is to say, establishments where an undue quantity of work is expected from a journeyman in the course of the day. Such shops, though not directly making use of cheap labour (for the wages paid in them are generally of the highest rate), still, by exacting more work, may of course be said, in strictness, to encourage the system now becoming general, of less pay and inferior skill. These strapping establishments sometimes go by the name of "scamping shops," on account of the time allowed for the manufacture of the different articles not being sufficient to admit of good workmanship.

These appear to be the three principal means by which several even of the more honourable firms are now seeking to reduce the "standard rate of wages." The means employed by the dishonourable tradesman are the contract and sub-contract system, adopted by what are called the "speculative builders." It is this contract work, it will be seen, that constitutes the great evil of the carpenters' trade, as well as of many other trades at the present time; and as in those crafts, so in this, we find that the lower the wages are reduced the greater becomes the number of trading operatives or middlemen. For it is when workmen find the difficulty of living by their labour increased that they take to scheming and trading upon the labour of their fellow-operatives. In the slop trade, where the pay is the worst, these creatures abound the most; and so in the carpenters' trade, where the wages are the lowest − as among the speculative builders − there the system of contracting and sub-contracting is found in full force. I shall now proceed to set forth the effects of each of these several causes of low wages *seriatim* − beginning with the means used by the more honourable masters, and concluding with an account of the practices pursued by the speculative builders. First, of the *"strapping"* system. Concerning this I received the following extraordinary account from a man after his heavy day's labour; and never in all my experience have I seen so sad an instance of overwork. The poor fellow was so fatigued that he could hardly rest in his seat. As he spoke he sighed deeply and heavily, and appeared almost spirit-broken with excessive labour:

"I work at what is called a strapping shop," he said, "and have worked at nothing else for these many years past in London. I call 'strapping,' doing as much work as a human being or a horse possibly can in a day, and that without any hanging upon the collar, but with the foreman's eyes constantly fixed upon you, from six o'clock in the morning to six o'clock at night. The shop in which I work is for all the world like a prison − the silent system is as strictly carried out there as in a model gaol. If a man was to ask any common question of his neighbour, except it was connected with his trade, he would be discharged there and then. If a journeyman makes the least mistake, he is packed off just the same. A man working at such places is almost always in fear; for the most trifling things he's thrown out of work in an instant. And then the quanity of work that one is forced to get through is positively awful; if he can't do a plenty of it, he don't stop long where I am. No one would think it was possible to get so much out of blood and bones. No slaves work like we do. At some of the strapping shops the foreman keeps continually walking about with his eyes on all the men at once. At others the foreman is perched high up, so that he can have the whole of the men under his eye together. I suppose since I knew the trade that a man does four times the work that he did formerly. I know a man that's done four pairs of sashes in a day, and one is considered to be a good day's labour. What's worse than all, the men are everyone striving one against the other. Each is trying to get through the work quicker than his neighbours. Four or five men are set the same job so that they may be all pitted against one another, and then away they go every one striving his hardest for fear that the others should get finished first. They are all tearing along from the first thing in the morning to the last at night, as hard as they can go, and when the time comes to knock off they are ready to drop. I was hours after I got home last night before I could get a wink of sleep; the soles of my feet were on fire, and my arms ached to that degree that I could hardly lift my hand to my head. Often, too, when we get up of a morning, we are more tired than we went to bed, for we can't sleep many a night; but we mustn't let our employers know it, or else they'd be certain we couldn't do enough for them, and we'd get the sack. So, tired as we may be, we are obliged to look lively somehow or other at the shop of a morning. If we're not beside our bench the very moment the bell's done ringing, our time's docked – they won't give us a single minute out of the hour. If I was working for a fair master, I should do nearly one-third less work than I am now forced to get through, and sometimes a half less; and even to manage that much, I shouldn't be idle a second of my time. It's quite a mystery to me how they do contrive to get so much work out of the men. But they are very clever people. They know how to have the most out of a man, better than any one in the world. They are all picked men in the shop – regular "strappers," and no mistake. The most of them are five foot ten, and fine broad shouldered, strong backed fellows too – if they weren't they would not have them. Bless you, they make no words with the men, they sack them if they're not strong enough to do all they want; and they can pretty soon tell, the very first shaving a man strikes in the shop, what a chap is made of. Some men are done up at such work – quite old men and gray with spectacles on, by the time they are forty. I have seen fine strong men, of six-and-thirty, come in there and be bent double in two or three years. They are most all countrymen at the strapping shops. If they see a great strapping fellow who they think has got some stuff about him that will come out, they will give him a job directly. We are used for all the world like cab or omnibus horses. Directly they've had all the work out of us we are turned off, and I am sure after my day's work is over, my feelings must be very much the same as one of the London cab horses. As for Sunday, it is *literally* a day of rest with us, for the greater part of us lays a bed all day, and even that will hardly take the aches and pains out of our bones and muscles. When I'm done and flung by, of course I must starve.''

After this the reader can readily imagine that "the old hands" have but little chance of employment in a trade where the strapping system is coming into vogue. Concerning the treatment of the elderly workmen, a well-looking man, cleanly, but poorly dressed, gave me the following account:

"I served my apprenticeship in the country as a carpenter, but have been 49 years in London this July. I am now 79. I have worked all the 49 years in London, except six months. Of course I can't work now as well as I could. I was obliged about five years ago to wear spectacles, as my eyesight wasn't as good. I could do the rougher work of carpentering as well as some years before, but then I can't lift heavy weights up aloft as I could. In most shops the moment a man puts the glasses on it's over with him. It wasn't so when I first knew London. Masters then said, 'Let me have an old man, one who knows something.' Now its, 'Let me have a young man, I must have a strong fellow, an old one won't do.' One master discharged two men when he saw them at work in glasses, though the foreman told him they worked as well with them, and as well every way as ever they did, but it was all no use; they went. I used to wear glasses in one employ, and others did the same, and the foreman was a good man to the men as well as to the master; and if the master was coming, he used to sing out 'Take those sashes out of the way,' and so we had time to whip off our glasses, and the master didn't know we were forced to use them; but when he did find it out, by coming into the shop unawares, he discharged two men. I now work at jobbing and repairing in buildings. It's no use my going to ask for work of any master, for if I hadn't my glasses on he'd see from my appearance I was old, and must wear them, and wouldn't hear of giving an old man a job. One master said to me, 'Pooh, you won't do – you were born too soon.' The fact is, they want strong your fellows from the country, that they can sweat plenty of work out of, and these country hands will go to work for 21s. a week, so that the master has a double pull – more work out of him and less to pay for it. The work's inferior, but they don't look much after the quality of the work now. The old men have only the workhouse left. Few of us have saved money. We can't, with families to bring up, on 30s. a week. I know many old men that were in their day good workmen, now in the workhouse. I know six that's now in Marylebone workhouse that I've worked along with myself. I belong to a benefit club, or there would be nothing but the workhouse for me if I lost my jobbing. Old age coming on men in my way is a very great affliction. We try to hide our want of great strength and good sight as long as we can. I did it for two or three years, but it was found out at last, and I had to go. I average about 12s. a week at jobbing; work's so uncertain, or I could make more."

Another old man corroborated this. He had written out a statement of what he thought his grievances, and called upon me with it. It is as follows: "Old carpenters are generally despised by master-builders; the failure of sight and wearing of spectacles is almost a death-blow to many a good old tradesman. And in many cases, masters will not give an elderly man employment at any price; the consequence is, that many have been compelled to go to the parish for relief, or into the workhouse. Employers instruct their foremen to deny a job to men above a certain age. When employers and clerks in their office are compelled to wear spectacles, it is considered with them an honourable badge; but to the poor workman it is a sudden death — he is no longer employed.'' ''That's what I've experienced myself, sir,'' he added. ''I was an apprentice in Bath, and have been 36 years in London. I am now 63, and strong and able to do a good day's work; but the answer always is, if I ask for work, 'You're too old.' I hadn't worn glasses many months before I was discharged from a place I'd been in a long time. We can't be employed at any price. The society rules allow us to work at reduced wages on account of our age. I job about among my friends, but I'm always in debt, for I have a sickly wife to keep and a sick daughter. Some weeks I make 20s., but many weeks I get not a stroke of work, and don't average altogether 12s. a week. There's not a farthing that's to be got by elderly men in general from masters that's had their youth and strength out of them. I'm in no benefit club. I was in two, but both failed. In case I was sick there's nothing but the parish for me and my family. I can't do work enough for a scamping master, or I might get one for one.''

I now come to treat of the system pursued by the speculating builders of the metropolis. Of all the slop-trades that I have yet examined there appear to be greater evils connected with cheap building than with any other. It will be seen that from this the public derive *no benefit whatsoever* — house rent not even being reduced by it, while the journeymen are ground down to the same state of misery and degradation as in all other trades where the slop system flourishes. Of the 18,000 men working for the dishonourable portion of the building trade, it should be remembered that not one belongs to a society, and consequently they have no resource but the parish in case of sickness, accident, or old age. Consequently, as one of the more intelligent journeymen said to me, it is the master alone who, by reducing the wages of the workmen, is benefited, for though the house is built cheaper, the public have not only to pay the same rent, but to support the workmen out of the poor-rates. Moreover, it is by means of this system that the better, the more skilful, and more provident portion of the trade are being dragged down to the same wretched abasement as the unskilful and improvident workmen. In order, however, that I might not be misled by the journeymen, I thought it my duty to call upon some master-builders of the ''honourable trade'' — gentlemen of high character — as well as upon architects of equally high standing. I found the same opinion entertained by them all as to the ruinous effects of the kind of competition existing in their trade to a master who strives to be just to his customers and fair to his men. This competition, I was assured, was the worst in the contracts for building churches, chapels, and public institutions generally. "Honesty is now almost impossible among us," said one master-builder. "It is impossible in cheap contract work, for the competition puts all honourable trade out of the field; high character, and good material, and the best workmanship are of no avail. Capitalists can command any low-priced work, by letting and subletting, and all by the piece. Most of those speculating and contracting people think only how to make money; or they must raise money to stop a gap (a bill perhaps to be met), and they grasp at any offer of an advance of money on account of a building to be erected. Their proceedings are an encouragement to every kind of dishonesty. They fail continually, and they drag good men down with them." Strong as these opinions are, I heard them fully confirmed by men who could not be mistaken in the matter. "Advertise for contract work," said another gentleman, "and you'll soon have a dozen applicants at all sorts of prices; and all tradesmen like myself, who calculate for a contract at a rate to pay the regular wages, and not to leave either the timber-merchant or anybody else in the lurch, and to yield us the smallest possible per centage for our risk and outlay, are regarded as a pack of extortionate men."

The system of contract-work was known forty years ago, or earlier, among the tradesmen employed in the erection of houses of the best class; but it was known as an exception rather than as an established system. It was long before that, however, not unfrequent as regards the erection of public buildings. A customer would then obtain "estimates" of the probable cost from well-known firms, and so ascertain the lowest price at which a private house could be erected. Thirty years back this system had gained a strong hold on all building capitalists, and it has gone on increasing within these 10 or 12, or more years. No mansion is built otherwise than by contract, except in the rare instance of an old connection of an old firm. The introduction of stuccos, cements, &c., within these 25 years, has further encouraged the contract system, by supplying a low-priced exterior for our houses – while the introduction of cheap paper, and of cheaper wood-work, by means of machinery, supplied the materials of a cheap interior; and a tradesman of little skill or probity can speculate in a building where he is not called upon to make heavy outlays for superior stone or timber, and can employ underpaid labour.

Respectable builders, I am informed, have often to submit to the most degrading terms in sending in their offers of contracts – terms which seem to presuppose every mode of knavery on the builder's part. One of the things in which competition is most ruinous, is, I am assured, in "contracting" for the new windows and embellishments, and the "alterations and improvements," required by competitive tradesmen, who are, at the same time, complaining of the unfair competition to which their particular trade is subject.

The employers of builders on contract have not, however, always escaped loss, and heavy loss, by grasping at a low-priced offer. The dry rot is mouldering away many a house built within these ten years, where the situation is damp. To guard against this pest, a master in the "honourable" trade would have built on a body of concrete – a thing never thought of by a scamping master. "Unless," said one architect to me, "some check be given to this dishonest system, the honourable masters must be dragged down towards the level of the others, and the best artisans must sink with them. The low-priced builders of the worst class cannot possibly do their work in any way but by cheating the tradesman and robbing the artisan."

Such are the opinions of the honourable masters in connection with the building trade, as to the ruinous effects of the slop or contract system. I shall now subjoin the statements, first, of the foremen, and lastly, of the workmen in connection with this part of the trade: –

"I am a foreman to speculating builder. My employer is not in a very large way: he has about ten carpenters and joiners. He does not let the work, he employs all the men by the day. The highest wages he gives is 28s. a week; this sum he pays to three of his men. He gives 24s. to three others: and two more have £1 a week. Besides these employs two apprentices. To the oldest of these he gives 15s. a week, and to the youngest 6s. The men who have 28s. are superior hands – such men as at either of the C——'s would get their 6s. a day. The 24s. men are good skilful carpenters, fairly worth 30s.; and those in the receipt of £1 are young men fresh from the country – principally from Devonshire. The wages in the west of England are from 12s. to 15s.; and these low wages send a lot of lads to town every year, in the hope of bettering their condition. They mostly obtain work among the speculating builders. I suppose there are more carpenters in London from Devonshire and Cornwall than from any other counties in England. At least half of the carpenters and joiners employed by the speculating builders here are lads fresh up from the country. Apprentices are not employed by the speculators as a rule. Most of the speculators have no fixed shops. Their work is carried on chiefly in, what we term, camp shops – that is in sheds erected in the field where the building are going on, and that's one reason why apprentices are not generally taken by speculating builders. The speculators find plenty of cheap labour among the country lads. A hand fresh up from the West of England can't get employment at the best of shops, unless he's got some friends, and so, after walking all London, he generally is driven to look for a job among the speculators at low wages. What few good hands are employed by the speculators are kept only to look after the countrymen. As a rule, I think young hands are mostly preferred, because there is more work in them. It is one of the chief evils of the carpenter's trade that as soon as a man turns of forty masters won't keep him on. The master whom I work for pays much better prices than most of the speculators . The average wages of the inferior hands employed in building is about 15s.; that is, I think, one-half of the hands don't receive more than that, and the other half about 24s. But day-pay is the exception with the speculators.The way in which the work is done is mostly by letting and sub-letting. The masters usually prefer to let work, because it takes all the trouble off their hands. They know what they are to get for the job, and of course they let it as much under that figure as they possibly can, all of which is clear gain without the least trouble. How the work is done, or by whom, it's no matter to them, so long as they can makes what they want out of the job, and have no bother about it. Some of our largest builders are taking to this plan, and a party who used to have one of the largest shops in London has within the last three years discharged all the men in his employ (he had 200 at least), and has now merely an office, and none but clerks and accountants in his pay. He has taken to letting his work out instead of doing it at home. The parties to whom the work is let by the speculating builders are generally working men, and these men in their turn look out for other working men, who will take the job cheaper than they will, and so I leave you, sir, and the public to judge what the party who really executes the work gets for his labour, and what is the quality of work that he is likely to put into it. The speculating builder generally employs an overlooker to see that the work is done sufficently well to pass the surveyor. That's all he cares about. Whether it's done by thieves, or drunkards, or boys, it's no matter to him. The overlooker, of course, sees after the first party to whom the work is let, and this party in his turn looks after the several hands that he has sub-let it to. The first man who agrees to the job takes it in the lump, and he again lets it to others in the piece. I have known instances of its having been let again a third time, but this is not usual. The party who takes the job in the lump from the speculator usually employs a foreman, whose duty it is to give out the materials, and to make working drawings. The men to whom it is sub-let only find labour, while the 'lumper,' or first contractor, agrees for both labour and materials. It is usual in contract work, for the first party who takes the job to be bound in a large sum for the due and faithful performance of his contract. He then in his turn finds out a sub-contractor, who is mostly a small builder, who will also bind himself that the work shall be properly executed, and there the binding ceases – those parties to whom the job is afterwards let, or sub-let, employing foremen or overlookers to see that their contract is carried out. The first contractor has scarcely any trouble whatsoever; he merely engages a gentleman, who rides about in a gig, to see that what is done is likely to pass muster. The sub-contractor has a little more trouble; and so it goes on as it gets down and down. Of course I need not tell you that the first contractor, who does the *least* of all, gets the *most* of all; while the poor wretch of a working man, who positively executes the job, is obliged to slave away every hour night after night to get a bare living out of it; and this is the contract system. The public are fleeced by it to an extent that builders alone can know. Work is scamped in such a way that the houses are not safe to live in. Our name for them in the trade is 'bird cages,' and really nine-tenths of the houses built now-a-days are very little stronger. Again, the houses built by the speculators are almost all damp. There is no concrete ever placed at the foundation to make them dry and prevent them from sinking. Further, they are all badly drained. Many of the walls of the houses built by the speculators are much less in thickness than the Building Act requires. I'll tell you how this is done. In a third-rate house the wall should be, according to the Act, two bricks thick at least, and in a second-rate house, two bricks and a half. The speculators build up the third-rates a brick and-a-half thick, and the second-rates only two bricks, and behind this they run up another half brick, so that they can throw that part down immediately after the surveyor has inspected it. Many of the chimney breasts too, are filled up with rubbish, instead of being solid brickwork. The surveyor is frequently hand in hand with the speculator, and can't for the life of him discover any of these defects but you know there's none so blind as those that *won't* see. And yet, notwithstanding all this trickery and swindling, and starving of the workmen, rents in the suburbs do not come down. Who, then, are the gainers by it all? Certainly not the public, for all they get are damp, ill-drained, and unsafe houses, at the same prices as they formerly paid for sound, wholesome, and dry ones. And most certainly the working men gain nothing by it. And what is even worse than all is that the better class of masters are obliged to compete with the worse, and to resort to the same means to keep up with the times, so that if things go on much longer the better class of mechanics must pass away altogether.''

Concerning ground rents, I had the following account from one well acquainted with the tricks of the speculators: –

"The party for whom I am foreman has just taken a large estate, and he contemplates making some thousands of pounds by means of the improved ground rents alone. There are several with him in the speculation, and this is the way in which such affairs are generally managed. A large plot of ground (six or seven meadows, may be) somewhere in the suburbs is selected by the speculators as likely to be an eligible spot for building – that is to say, they think that a few squares, villas, and terraces about that part would be likely to let as soon as run up. Then the speculators go to the freeholder or his solicitor, and offer to take the ground of him on a ninety-nine years' lease at a rent of about £50 a-year per acre, and may be they take as many as fifty acres at this rate. At the same time they make a proviso that the rent shall not commerce until either so many houses are built, or perhaps before a twelvemonth has elapsed. If they didn't do this the enormous rent most likely would swallow them up before they had half got through their job. Well, may be, they erect half or two-thirds of the number of houses that they have stipulated to do before paying rent. These are what we term 'call-birds,' and are done to decoy others to build on the ground. For this purpose a street is frequently cut, the ground turned up on each side, just to show the plan, and the corner house, and three others, perhaps, are built just to let the public see the style of thing that it's going to be. Occasionally a church is begun, for this is found to be a great attraction in a new neighbourhood. Well, when things are sufficiently ripe this way, and the field has been well mapped out into plots, a board is stuck up, advertising 'THIS GROUND TO BE LET, ON BUILDING LEASES.' Several small builders then apply to take a portion of it, sufficient for two or three houses, may be, for which they agree to pay about five guineas a year (they generally make it *guineas* these gentlemen) for the ground-rent of each house. And when the parties who originally took the meadows on lease have got a sufficient number of these plots let off, and the small builders have run up a few of the carcases, they advertise that 'a sale of well-secured rents will take place at the Mart on such a day.' Ground-rents, you must know, are considered to be one of the safest of all investments now-a-days; for if they are not paid, the ground landlord, you see, has the power of seizing the houses; so gentlemen with money are glad to lay it out this way, and there's a more ready sale for ground-rents than for anything else in the building line. There's sure to be strong competition for them, let the sale be whenever it will. Well, let us see now how the case stands. There are fifty acres taken on lease at £50 an acre a year, and that is £2,500 per annum. Upon each of these fifty acres fifty houses can be erected (including villas and streets, taking one with the other upon an average). The ground-rent of each of these houses is (at the least) £5, and this gives for the 2,500 houses that are built upon the whole of the fifty acres £12,500 per annum. Hence you see there is a clear net profit of £10,000 a year made by the transaction. This is not at all an extraordinary case in building speculations.''

The subjoined supplies information concerning some other tricks of the speculators: –

''For the last fifteen months I have been at work on the estate. You had better not say what estate, or I shall be known. My master was a bankrupt some time back. Since his bankruptcy, he has started in business again. His friends have taken him by the hand, and a speculating builder has no need of any capital. The agents and lawyers find whatever cash is required to pay the workmen on the Saturday night, and the builder makes a smash of it for the materials – as a matter of course. I'll tell you, sir, how this dodge is worked. A party of gentlemen who wishes to put their money into some building speculation that seems to promise well, agrees with a builder to find him all the cash to pay the workmen with, provided he will make himself answerable for the material, and for this they agree to give him a share in the profits if the spec turns out well. If, however, it should turn out bad, he is to be the party to go into the *Gazette*, for whatever may be owing. Of course everything is kept snug and secret among 'em, and if the builder goes to pieces, and doesn't let out who was his backers, why, directly he gets his certificate, they don't mind starting him again on the same terms. This is one of the ways in which building is carried on at the present time, on a large scale. The master I'm a speaking of never gives a carpenter or joiner, if they are at day work for him, less than five shillings a day; he takes it out of the timber merchant and brickmaker, instead of the journeymen.''

As regards ''Improvers,'' I had the subjoined information from a very intelligent and trustworthy man:—

''I am a joiner, receiving the regular wages. I am familiar with all the systems carried on as regards 'improvers.' These improvers are frequently the sons of carpenters and joiners, who have been instructed by their parents, and then seek to complete their knowledge of the business without going through a course of apprenticeship. Or they are often the sons of tradesmen in the country, who comes to town for the name of the thing, and that they may put on their signs — 'So and So, from Messrs. ——, London.' A certain class of young men have been apprenticed, but not being perfect in their business, also go as improvers. The wages of improvers vary greatly — from 10s. to 23s. or 24s. a week. They generally have some interest to get into a shop. They know some friend of the master, or something of that kind. Then there can be no doubt that there are such things as *bonuses* to foremen. No doubt the introduction of these improvers is detrimental to the well-doing of the journeymen, who are driven, especially if they are past their prime, to work for lower wages. Masters don't like old men at all. Many masters are partial to improvers, and keep them on when they discharge journeymen. In the scamping (slop) shops, masters best like strong hearty young fellows from the country as improvers — men they can get plenty of work out of. Scamping masters soon discharge their improvers if they lose any of their strength and capability of hard work. Few improvers are kept on, as improvers, after they are twenty-five. Their ages run generally from sixteen to twenty-four. I have never known an improver become a journeyman in the shop in which he worked as an improver. Masters seem to distrust them. In speculating builders' employ there are generally more improvers than journeymen — thrice as many more. Speculating builders keep on only as few as possible journeymen, and those just to keep the work in decent order. Improvers can't be trusted by themselves. With some speculating builders the improver works by the piece, and is then ground down very low in price. A man of 22 will then not make above half wages, 15s., and work more than the regular hours to do that. Improvers find their own tools, the same as journeymen. I believe that

twenty years ago there was not such a thing as a scamping master in London,
Ten years ago one in ten might be scamping masters, and now quite one-
third are so. Take masters altogether at 1,300, and 430 of them are scamping
masters. Some of them are in a very large way, and employ occasionally 200
hands; and altogether I fancy they rank, as to the number of hands, with the
honourable trade. I think the system gets worse and worse. Mr. ——, one of
the best builders on London, is now obliged to give way to competition, and
get up a more scamping sort of work, instead of the fine and beautiful work
that that he used to supply.''

The next point to be noticed is the system of letting and subletting the
work. From an experienced carpenter and his son, also an experienced man
in his trade, I had the following account:—

"I may say," said the father, "I have been seventy-five years in the carpentering trade, for that's my age, and I was born in the business. I worked
nearly fifty years in Somersetshire, chiefly as a journeyman. Forty years ago
the wages were 3s. a day in Taunton — that was the highest wages for the best
men. When I left, five years since, it was a good man who got 2s. 6d.; many
got 2s. a day. The decrease took place about thirty or thirty-five years back,
when the competition and cheap estimates for contract work began. I
remember the time, because a man came from Wellington and undertook
some work which no tradesman in Taunton would undertake — the building
of a market-house, which was put up to competition by the trustees.
Immediately after that wages fell, for cheap contract work spread all over
the neighbourhood . The man from Wellington cut down the wages
directly; many worked for him at 2s. a day. Trade was dull then. It went on
continually on the low system, and continues on that system still. The men
that the market-house contractor employed were mostly inferior labourers,
and he got them cheap. Of course it's the cheaper and worse labourers that
first force the superior workmen to come down. Contracts have reduced
good men as regards wages to the level of bad men, and good men must
scamp it, for scamping is the rule now. I came to London five years ago to
join my family, who were settled here. My family were then at work on a
contract for a lawyer.'' "I knew nothing of the lawyer," said the son of my
first informant, "but I saw a notice up that the carcases of six houses were to
be finished, and made fit for inhabitants, and tenders were to be sent in; the
lowest bidder of course to be accepted. The solicitor, that my brother and I
had the contract from, was the agent of the ground landlord, who was
anxious to have buildings erected on his property. The ground landlord had
advertised that the land would be let on building leases, and that advances
would be made, according to the usual dodge — for dodge it is, sir. A builder
was soon found, one with little or no money, for money in such cases is no
matter — that's an every-day affair. He agreed to erect six houses, and £250
was to be advanced for each house, something more than half a much as

would be required to complete each of them. The builder got the carcases up, and then the agent put the stopper on him, and seized the houses for the ground landlord. Each house, in the manner it was left by the builder, when he was stopped, had full £300 expended on it of *somebody's* money, and materials. For this the builder became bankrupt and he was sent to prison. The houses were then advertised for sale and sold, the agent buying them, and just for the amount advanced − £1,500. So that after full £1,800 had been expended on the houses the agent got them for £300 less. The wages paid to the men employed on the building were as low as contract work usually is, and some carpenters there earned only 2s. 6d. a day of twelve hours. The work was let − brick-work, smith's-work, and all − and at a very low rate. Had fair living wages been paid to all employed the value of the six carcases would have been at least £2,400; so that the lawyer you see, gains £900 by this mode of management. These are the parties who thrive by the contract system. The public gains nothing, for the house is not let for a farthing less rent than if built on a fair wages system; but the owner of his people may get 15 or 16 per cent. for their money. There is the same system now being carried on, and to a very great extent, all over the same neighbourhood. Some as good mechanics as ever took a tool in hand work from four in the morning till eight or nine at night, and earn only 4s. a day. Before the contract system it was 5s. a day of ten hours. Now on this contract system men grow rich on the degradation and suffering of the working man, and on the swindling of the timber merchant, the iron merchant, and the other tradesmen out of the materials. Nineteen out of every twenty speculating builders become bankrupts.'' (I may add, that in the bankrupt lists of last year, 51 are returned as builders; the largest number in any trade, except drapers and victuallers.) "So that," continued my informant, "notwithstanding all the money that these speculating builders wring out of the men, they keep failing every day. The agent I've been speaking of stuck boards up over the neighbourhood, stating that the finishing of the carcases, as I've said, was to be let to the lowest bidder, on certain terms; advances were to be made on the surveyor's report, among other conditions. I knew, if a low figure wasn't sent in, it was no use trying for the job, so my brother and I bid for the work at the lowest possible sum. We reckoned on our own labour being serviceable, as we could do so much among ourselves, and save the expense of a foreman and such like. We hoped to make something, too, out of the extras, that is for extra work not included in the specification, for the specification is never correct. Men now bid very low in hopes of making their profit in this way. My father, my brother, and myself, didn't realize more than 4s. a day, working on an average 13 hours. If we'd been employed by a contractor, who took it at the rate we did, our wages couldnt have been moe than 3s. a day, and that was the reason of our bidding for it. The journeymen in that neighbourhood now get 3s. a day, all the work being let and sub-let. A journeyman will undertake work to pay himelf 4s. a day, and will hire men under him at 3s. – or even less – 14 s. or 15s. a week. One man takes the windows, another the skirtings, another the doors, another the dwarf and high cupboards, another the stairs, another the mouldings, another the boxing shutters for the windows, and another the floors. The average price for labour in contract work windows is 6s. an opening for 25 feet, and according to Skyring's prices (which are low) the charge would be 10s. Doors, double moulded, are paid 2s. 6d. on an average, and they ought to be 5s.; of course, they must be scamped. On this work I must make two doors a day, while one properly made is a good long day's job. Some of these doors don't last above ten years. Staircases are done at £3 a six-roomed houe; it ought to be from £5 to £5 10s. For boxing shutters £1 4s. is the price, instead of from £2 10s. to £3. It's a fortnight's work to do it well; it's 40 feet work, a fair price (Skyring's) being 1s. 4½d. a foot. At Notting-hill, twelve years ago, I had £2 10s. for this same work. Floors, on contract, are 2s. 6d. a square, though that's above the average, and they are honestly worth 5s.; Skyring gives 6s 6d. Skirtings, which they take by the house, are 15s., and ought to be £2 10s. Mouldings, which are taken by the hundred feet sticking (working) are 1s. 6d. the hundred, running measure, the regular price being 4s. 2d. The dwarf and high cupboards are a shameful price by contract – 2s. 6d. each, with shelves folding doors, hanging, and everything complete. These prices are what I know of by my own experience; but when there's a further sub-letting by a journeyman contracting under the contract, and so getting hands at the lowest possible rates, they are even less than I have specified. Contracting altogether is a bad system; it's carried on for the benefit of a few at the cost of the working men, and out of their sweat, and at the cost too of respectable tradesmen many a time. Government contracts are carried on just the same way. I myself have worked at the Post-office, and the man next me had only 18s. a week. Since the present contractor has had it, only 12s. is paid; so you can see what it must all lead to. I reckon that there are from 18,000 to 20,000 working men in my trade in London; and I believe that full two-thirds of them at under wages. One half of the two-thirds will get 4s. a day, and the other third 2s. 6d. In London, as you have stated, sir, no doubt there are 6,405 houses built every year; and at least 6,000 of them are built by contract work, and speculating and scamping builders. All in the suburbs are. These would average (reckon the new houses erected to be chiefly in the suburbs) from £30 to £35 a year rent. One carpenter could frame and finish two such houses a year. That would give employment at the cheap built houses to 3,000 men. These houses are raised on the reduction of the working men's wages, and that reduction, as they now get 20s. where they did get 30s., makes the loss to each working man as much as 10s. a week, or £25 a year, and that amounts in all to £75,000 per annum, which somebody or other gets out of the journeymen carpenters alone. That *somebody* is not the public – that's very clear, for rents are as high if not higher, and since the majority of speculating builders become bankrupts, it's clear that the ground landlords, their solicitors and agents, are the only men benefited by the system. The effect of this reduction on the working men is, as I said, very bad indeed. Respectable masters, who would be fair and honest, are so cut down by competition, that they would almost as soon be without trade as with it. The consequence is, half of the men are unemployed, and when employed get not much more than half wages. If people only knew how the 200 miles of streets that have been built in London in the last ten years had been run up – through what sufferings to the working man and his family – they wouldn't think it quite so grand a thing."

Of the effects of the sub-contracting system an old man gave me the following statement:–

"I have known the trade forty years as a general hand, doing both carpenter's and joiner's work. Things are wonderfully altered since I first knew it. Thirty-five or forty years ago there was no cutting under, and no small masters taking work at prices that wouldn't pay them, and getting it out of the men. Lately I have been working at staircasing, and in houses run up by speculating builders. A journeyman like myself has taken my present work at 18s. a storey for staircasing. Each storey for this house will have 13 steps. A fair price would be £2, or £2 2s. The man who undertakes it at 18s., gives me 4s. a day of ten hours, from six to six. He employs old men – too old for first-rate work – and boys, and anybody that he can get cheap, and they 'scamp' the work as much as they possibly can. The work aint fit to be seen, but anything will do for speculating builders, so as they have it done cheap, and plenty of it. He gives a youth of 17 only 6s. a week – 1s. a day. He finds his own tools, and so do I, and so, do we all; and reckon this boy spends 1s. a week on his tools, he has 5s. a week left for his labour, and he's a handy chap, too. My employer has one old man, and he makes four-pannel square doors, 2 feet 6 inches by 8 feet 6 inches, at 1s. 6d. the door. The regular charge by Skyring's prices, at 5d. a foot, and that for 16 feet, would be 6s. 8d. Of such men and boys he usually employs from 6 to 20. He has built 100 houses, I dare say, by this system of engaging the sort of hands I tell you of, and paying them as I've said. He drives these boys and men like niggers; his son acts as foreman, and sees that they cram 18 hours work into 12; if they don't they're discharged. One man 'stuck' (worked) 400 feet of moulding in a day (10 hours), and he got discharged for not doing more. According to the price-book, it would be 16s. 8d. – the charge being a halfpenny a foot, and his pay was 4s. a day for doing 16s. 8d. worth of work. The master expected 500 feet for 4s. I don't work for the same man, but for one who has taken the stairs of him. He has taken twelve houses of the sort. The speculating builder prefers to let all he can. The work's then let and sublet again. He's now got a man planing floor-boards. He don't get them done at the mills and I'll tell you what he give the man. There's 6 'square' to be done; a 'square' is 100 feet, ¾-inch, white deal, edges shot; and through the proper price is 5s. 6d. a square, or 33s. altogether, he gives only 10s. for 6 square, or 20d. a square; that's for planing, shooting, and laying. A young man does it; he's only 30, and he can't earn more than 2s. a day; but what's a man to do when he's had his hands in his pockets out of work for two or three weeks, with a wife and two children? A man's then obligated to do it. These are the sort of men such as my employer always gets hold of. If I was paid fairly for my work it would come to 7s. a day from the quantity. I should get discharged if I didn't do that quantity of work, and at a moment's notice. When one's on by day there's no notice wanted – you must leave that night. The man who's taken the work I'm now upon was out a long time, and he was obligated to take it to get a crust, and so must put on men worse off than he is. If the staircase was sub-let to me, or such a man as me, I might get 12s. in the room of the 18s. Houses run up this way don't let for one farthing cheaper; they look well outside and a gentleman wouldn't know it was all badly done. It's like a rogue with a good suit of clothes on his back, the house is. These houses won't stand long, some are built without mortar; the builders get the lime that tanners have done with in their trade and make that do; all the nature's out of it; it's no more good than mud, only it's white. The cheapest timber is used, American spruce and that's certain to fill the place with bugs; it always does. The men that work in such buildings are never society men, and are generally given to drink, and can't get work any where else. When I was a young man I had 5s. and 5s. 6d. a day. For the last four years I have had only 4s. a day, and often not more than 3s. I'm now 60. I couldn't get work at the regular prices, and I was obliged to go to a speculating builder or starve. They know all about that. The number of men working low like me has increased greatly in these five years. Many hands come from the country, too, 'specially from the west of England, where wages are 15s. to 18s., so that lots of hands can be had at almost any price in London. To-day an Irish carpenter offered to go to work at 4s. a week rather than starve. Some speculating builders take numbers of apprentices. I've worked for one who had three apprentices and one good hand. This cheap sort of work will ruin the trade altogether if a stop's not put to it. Every year it gets worse and worse, and in time there'll be no good workmen left, as everybody will be forced to scamp it. In many places they won't employ a man turned forty, for fear he can't do work enough. They like strong country fellows. When I first knew the trade there were no contracts. They've been the ruin of the trade among men and masters, who've been cutting one against another for twenty years now. No gentleman will set the most respectable builder in London to work now-a-days without a contract, it's come to such a pitch. Before contracts came into use all in the trade was well off — masters and men. Masters did their work honestly and fairly, and men were comfortable in their homes, and had their good meat dinners on a Sunday, and lived well generally. Now three-fourths of the men are starving, if you could know all, and none of them are contented. If bread and meat weren't reasonable, men couldn't live at all. Our wives had no need to work formerly, except doing their house work; they could mind their homes and their families then properly. Now they must strive and strive, and earn only 4d. or 5d. a day at needlework, and often see their children starving for all that. I know whole families who have to work now, when formerly only the father had to work, and the children are barefoot all the week. Many of our wives go out charing or washing, or they're put to making soldiers' coats. We all do four times the work we once did, families and all, and yet we don't get one-fourth the money for it that we once did. I don't make more than 10s. a week, the year through. My daughter, who is a shoebinder, makes 6d. a day."

In my next Letter I purpose describing the different kinds of machinery employed in the building trade — such as the planing, moulding, and morticing machines. I shall likewise give an account of the establishment of Mr. Thomas Cubitt, at Thames-bank, Pimlico, so that the public may have an opportunity of contrasting the present treatment of the operatives by the worse class of masters with that of the better.

LETTER LXII
Thursday, July 25, 1850

In the present letter I shall conclude my inquiry into the condition of the London carpenters and joiners, with a description of the several applications of machinery to the purposes of their trade. These appear to consist of moulding mills, planing mills, mortising mills, and saw benches for cutting grooves, tennons, and rabbets. To estimate the quantity of manual labour superseded by these means is a very difficult calculation, and only admits of a rough approximation. I have, however, endeavoured to obtain the best information on this point, and the statement here given is, I am convinced, rather below than above the actual amount.

I shall begin with the moulding mills.

One of the most delicate applications of steam to wood work, as regards precision, nicety, and celerity, is seen in the preparation of mouldings. At the mill I visited, and over which I was obligingly shown by the manager, mouldings are prepared for the use of the joiner in house buildings, as well as for the upholsterer and the carver and gilder. A moulding steam-mill was first established in Paddington somewhat less than ten years ago. There had been many attempts previously, which failed of attaining full success. The one I allude to is the largest in the world. The premises in which it is carried on are of great extent, and the constant recurrence of timber, as you walk along, upstairs and down, in doors or out – of timber as it is received from lighters in the Thames (on the banks of which the premises are built), and then piled for use, or in its last stage of preparation – gives the visitor a better impression than any other place I have seen of the vastness of the timber trade of London. The establishment is erected for all the purposes of sawing, planing, and cutting wood (except veneers) by steam; but as I have already – in my letter on the Sawyers – given an account of the other processes, I shall here confine myself to the moulding mills. Any kind of wood can be formed into mouldings; but yellow pine is generally used. This pine is kept four or five years drying before it is fit for use. The wood to be "moulded" – a word which is not expressive of the process, for all is done by cutting – is prepared of the width and substance required. It is then rubbed smooth with glass paper – boys being employed at this work. When ready, it is placed into a frame by a lad, and the machinery is set to work.

This consists of a multiplicity of wheels, cutters, &c., working so rapidly, that the motion of some of them is almost imperceptible, while a shower of little chips of wood – the size of peas or beans, but angular, and larger or smaller, according to the pattern worked – is thrown upon the stander-by. The peculiar construction of the machinery, which cuts the timber into a moulding; the modes of changing it so as to cut the wood to any pattern – some patterns being very elaborate as to curves and outlines, and to the depth of 12 inches – cannot be properly described without the aid of engravings. The moulding is completed in one operation. The boy "keeps feeding the machine," by putting the timber to the frame, and with the usual unconscious look of lads employed in labour the nature and importance of which they know and care nothing about. All is quiet, regular, and orderly. By "quiet," I must be understood as speaking of the demeanour of the people at work, for quiet, in the sense of noiselessness, is unknown in such places. The clatter of wheels, the grinding sound of saws, and the chip-chip of the moulding engines render conversation difficult. The persons employed, however, by a peculiar pitch of their voices, aided by gestures, seemed to make each other readily understand any order or communication. The machinery prepares the moulding complete; it is formed to the pattern – whatever curves or elevation that pattern may comprise. The moulding is also "under-cut;" that is, planed smooth – knots in the wood being no obstacle, on the under or flat side of the wood as "moulded" – and all is executed at one process. Whatever be the pattern, the machine will cut, at an average, twelve feet in a minute. A simple form thus prepared would occupy a skilled and quick mechanic one quarter of an hour. Four steam moulding machines are constantly at work at the establishment I saw, and thus they "mould" 48 feet or 16 yards a minute, 960 yards an hour, and 9,600 yards in a day of 10 hours. Ten hours is a low average, for though time is somewhat lost in changing cutters and such like, the mill is sometimes kept going from six in the morning until ten at night. The day's work is thus about 5½ miles, or 33 miles length of moulding in a week; and reckoning 50 weeks to the year, 1,650 miles in the year are "moulded" in one mill. This is the only mill which "undercuts" the mouldings, and does all by one process. The other mills may do altogether little more than half as much, and that gives, in all, 2,475 miles. For the moulding machines 5 men, over-lookers and directors generally, and 15 boys, are employed. The men earn from 36s. to 40s. a week, the boys 7s. to 15s., according to age and trust-worthiness. The mere errand, jobbing boy, has 4s. a week. A new moulding engine, to cut to the depth of 18 inches, is in course of erection. I may mention here also a new system of steam sawing – a simpler system, and the only one now in operation – which I saw at this mill. A steam engine is placed *above* a frame of saws, the frame containing 48 or any lower number of saws, while the piston of the engine works the saws without the intervention of further machinery.

The next kind of mills that demand our attention are those for planing by steam.

Planing mills for general work have been established in London within these twelve years; the first was Mr. Jackson's, of Pimlico. Prior to that, the process was known, and some of the masters had somewhat similar machinery to that now in use, but worked by hand instead of steam. The introduction of steam planing machines, I am informed on the best authority, was suggested by the uses of a machine in operation some thirty-five years ago, for the cutting of wood into scaleboard. It was thus cut smooth into thin planks, and was used for making hat and bonnet boxes, salve boxes, and the like; and until about fourteen years since, this scaleboard paid 21s. per cwt. duty, as it was a substitute for paper or pasteboard. Very wet timber would then frequently entail a dead loss on account of its weighing heavily. The planing machine is now worked by a steam-engine in the usual way. A shaft from the main shaft works one drum, and that one drum works alike the "endless chain," two saws for edging boards, two spindles for ploughing and tonguing, and two adzes for "thicknessing" the board, or reducing it to one perfect uniformity as regards thickness. The planing irons, two being generally used, are fixtures. The deal to be planed is placed on an iron frame thoroughly smooth and level; and when the board is thus placed upon it and fitted firmly, it is drawn rapidly along by the endless chain, which is impelled by the engines, and so the board is passed under the planing irons. The other processes that I have mentioned, viz., the edging, &c., go on when required, simultaneously with the planing, and at the same frame. Two shavings are in this way planed off the surface of the board, one rough and one fine. The wood thus planed must not exceed 11 inches in thickness. The shavings are useless, and sometimes have to be burnt in considerable quantities, that they may be got rid of. The wood so planed is entirely for the purposes of flooring, and I am informed that a joiner could not plane it so truly — if as smoothly — as the mill; for it is not easy to give, merely by the eye and the touch, a precisely uniform thickness of substance to every portion of the deal or plank. The machine effects this uniformity with infallible precision. The one that I saw planes 450 deals or planks, of the usual length of a plank, in a day. To plane them finely and in the best fashion of workmanship, a good hand would not do more than twenty such planks. Long practice might, however, I was told, enable a joiner to plane thirty in a day, if not in the very best style. Take the average at twenty-five, and the planing machine performs the work of eighteen men. There are, I am told, about eight such public planing machines in London; planing among them eight times 450 deals or planks in a day, or performing the work of 116 men in planing. This, of course, is independent of any planing machines which are private or Government property. The planing process is managed by two men, the frame-man and his assistant; the engine, of course, require the usual amount of attention on the part of the engineer, &c. The highest amount paid to the workmen at the mill I visited was 8s. a day. The frame-men have 5s. a day, but they usually make seven days in the week, owing to the mill being frequently worked over-time. The labourers have 21s. a week. The cost of mill planing runs gradually as regards intermediate sizes, from 1s. 6d. and 2s., respectively, for 6-feet deals and planks, to 5s. 1d. and 7s. for 21-feet deals and planks.

I moreover witnessed the working of a rack timber bench for cutting logs of timber, by steam application, into scantlings and joists of all descriptions for building purposes. This machine can cut any log not exceeding two feet in depth and of any length. It accomplishes in five minutes as much labour as would occupy a pair of sawyers two hours. It will cut thirty loads of timber a day. There are five or six such machines in London, but they are not in constant working, the demand for such labour varying greatly.

Besides the machinery for planing and making mouldings, steam machinery is generally used, on the larger builders' premises, for sawing deals and timber both for flooring and roofing in the carpenters' department. In the joiners' branch there are steam machines for cutting tennons for doors, sashes, and whatever is framed together; also for ploughing, rabbeting, and indeed grooving generally. "In our shop," said one of my informants, "a machine makes any sized tennon by a single motion passed over two saws. That, of all machines, does most harm to the efficient joiners; it will do thirty men's work. We have only this machine and the steam saw. I reckon that twenty-five such machines are kept going in London, and so 750 men's labour is done away with. In one house I know of there is a morticing machine by steam, which will do twelve men's work. I know only of one in London."

In the course of my inquiries I paid a visit to the establishment here alluded to, and was not more surprised at the completeness of all its mechanical arrangements than I was delighted at the regard and consideration exhibited for the comfort and well-being of the men. There science was not only taken advantage of for the performance of the most skilful operations in connection with almost every branch of the art of building, but likewise to promote the health of all the men employed on the premises. There were steam-mills for cutting marble and for polishing it – mills for grinding the lime and cement by steam – steam-mills again for sawing the timber, and steam-mills for grooving, rabbeting, mortising, and making tennons – lathes driven by machinery, for turning wood and iron – drilling and punching machines – all worked in the same manner. But I purpose treating more fully upon this subject at a future time, and especially, upon the consideration shown for the well-being of the men, displaying in this most admirable establishment. I was informed by one of the gentlemen at the head of it that the application of machinery to building purposes generally could not but produce a great revolution in the carpenters' trade. Another gentleman thought that they had, by such means, displaced full 25 per cent of manual labour within the last few years.

I shall now proceed to give an account of a veneer-mill.

The manufacture of veneers, now exclusively made by means of steam-machinery, is among the most curious applications of steam power to mechanical contrivances. About 38 years ago, Sir Isambert, then Mr. Brunel, turned his attention to the preparation of a process by which the sawing of wood might be facilitated by means of the steam-engine. The invention of the machinery, and its adaptation to the working of the steam-engine, as now in use, was Mr. Brunel's; and the first steam-mill for the sawing of deals was that of Mr. Smart, as I have already stated in my account of the sawyers. Mr. Brunel patented his discovery, and sold licenses to those who chose to invest their money in the establishment of the steam-mills. In the course of his experiments to improve the process for the sawing of logs of timber, he thought of applying it to the production of veneers, which, before his discovery, were sawn in the usual manner in the pits, but were rudely, as well as expensively, produced; the failures of the sawyers in the production of a perfect veneer being frequent. For two years, Mr. Brunel, at considerable cost, carried on his experiments, but only with approximations to success. The saws he first used were straight, and were formed of "a solid plate" of one piece of steel. They were very fine; and from the heat produced by the friction of the timber, they soon became useless; for in working they "lengthened" and "buckled," and so lost their accuracy of performance. ("Buckling" is a technical term expressive of the blistering or puckering of the steel.) "It buckled sometimes," said my informant, who was at the time I speak of with Mr. Brunel, "like the frill of a shirt." On one occasion, when watching the working of his saws, Mr. Brunel took a file, and as if struck by a sudden thought, "nicked" the saws in the parts where they "buckled." The machinery was then set a-going, and the saws worked truly, without hitching or irregularity. It then occurred to Mr. Brunel (who was himself surprised, my intelligent informant assured me, at the effect of his simple remedy for the buckling) that saws formed of distinct pieces of steel would be better than those formed of solid plates, and this – when he had given more attention to the subject – led him to apply segment saws, of a circular form, to effect his purpose. These saws were then formed, as they are at present, of different segments of steel, by which any "bucking" or deviation from the nicest accuracy is thoroughly obviated. The first application of the segment and circular saw convinced Mr. Brunel that his discovery was perfected – a conviction which has been justified by a long tried result, for up to the present day no improvement, and indeed no alteration, has been introduced into his process, as regards the use of these saws. The first steam-mill established for the sawing of veneers was at Battersea, thirty-four or thirty-five years ago, and was the property of Mr. Brunel and his partners. This mill is still in full operation.

The veneer saw mill that I visited is the largest in the world, and in its beautiful and scientific arrangements presents a most striking example of the perfection by which the hardest as well as the softest timber can be made available for veneering purposes; a nicety and a perfection utterly unattainable by manual labour or skill. The ground occupied by the buildings covers about six acres, and is situated on the bank of a canal, up which the timber is usually conveyed. Dark and dirty looking logs, some of them of vast size, lie scattered or piled about; but among these, only distinguished by a practised eye, are the most costly and rare of all the foreign woods used in the manufacture of our richest furniture, none but the choicest timber being collected for the formation of veneers. The stateliest trees that some months back graced the forests of St. Domingo, Brazil, or Honduras, lie there until their trunks can be sawn into multiplied divisions, some of them as thin as paper. The principal woods used for veneering are the mahoganies – Spanish, Honduras, or African. The Honduras mahogany is in the most extensive use. Here, too, may be seen satin wood, Amboyna, the many varieties of rose-wood, zebra-wood, ebony, tulip-wood, coromandel, bird's-eye maple, cedar, sandal-wood, and king-wood; besides our native oaks, yews, elms, ashes, birches, walnuts, and sycamores – these woods having of late come into much more frequent use as veneers.

Nor is it the costlier woods alone that are prepared in this great establishment. Deals are consumed in great quantities, and for perhaps the cheapest of all commodities which science has given to general use – the formation of lucifer-matches. The matches, however, are made by a different process from that used to prepare veneers, as I shall presently show.

The wood to be sawn into veneers is first carried into the "adzing-room," where men chip the surface with axes, or level it with planes, so as to remove any grit or dirt which might impede the action of the saw. The logs so adzed are then fixed by an application of Scotch glue to a wooden frame with transverse battens, so as to be held fixedly when subjected to the action of the saw. Scotch glue is used in preference to all others. It may not be so strong as marine glue, but marine glue is not affected by water, and for the business purposes of this mill the glue must be capable of being removed by washing, as the part to which it has been applied must be cleansed.

The timber to be sawn is then taken to the saw-room, a large well-lighted apartment, 120 feet long, 90 wide, and of proportionate height. In this room are eight circular saws, from 7 to 17 feet in diameter. There are 11 such saws in use altogether in the mill; the teeth of the 17 feet saw are five to the inch, and the rest in proportion. In the saw-room, on the occasion of my visit, there was a very agreeable odour, reminding one strongly of the perfume of a library, where the books are bound in Russia leather. Some of the woods give out a strong aroma when sawn. Among these, the rose-woods and ebony are the most pungent and titilating, the dust causing strangers to sneeze, even if the inured to snuff-taking. The sandal and tulip woods also emit a pleasant fragrane, while the cedar, contrary to the popular notion, is not especially agreeable to the sense when being sawn – indeed, a veneer sawyer told me, that once on sawing some wet, and not very sound cedar, the smell given out was so strong and unpleasant, from the liberation of the volatile oils, that the men had to run out and "drink spirits to fortify themselves against its effects."

The timber, affixed to its frame, is placed on an iron beam, and adjusted to the exact approximation to the saw. The saw is then set rapidly revolving, and a sawyer, assisted by a boy, follows the timber as the machinery carries it along, subject to the fine and dividing edge of the saw; he keeps the teeth of the saw clear from the dust, as far as he can, and closely watches, and in some sort directs, the precise adjustment of the timber to the saw, until the veneer is completed. On my visit a large rosewood tree was being sawn, and the veneers looked like huge, dull "watered" ribbons. The strong glowing colours are afterwards brought out by varnish.

The object of my present letter does not entail upon me the necessity of describing the minutiae of the beautiful machinery, so exquisitely adjusted in this mill. I may mention, however, that a person unused to such sights will find the "saw-room" an imposing spectacle when the saws are all going. The clatter of the steam-engine below – the rapid running of broad belts of leather connecting the various parts of the machinery – the peculiar sound of the saw-wheel as it whirls round rapidly, and as rapidly severs the timber – and the close attention and almost unbroken silence of the men at work, with the peculiar atmosphere caused by the work, present certainly a combination only known to great cities and to modern times.

To the courtesy of the proprietor, who was obliging enough to give instructions that every possible information and facility of inquiry should be afforded me, I am indebted for the following account of the extent of his business in the week preceding my visit (as regards the production of veneers). Nine saws were thus employed. The numbers 1, 2, &c., indicate the saws; the second series of figures the logs, trunks of trees, or planks sawn; and the third range of figures the number of feet sawn for veneering:

No. 1	30	4,813
2	24	3,936
3	13	2,332
4	17	7,640
5	12	4,898
6	53	8,269
7	16	8,216
8	12	10,043
9	6	938
	183	51,085

This number, however, is below the average, which may be fairly taken at 200 logs, &c., a week, forming 60,000 feet long of veneers, averaging 10 inches wide. The mill cannot be said to work more than 50 weeks in the year, and that gives a length of 3,000,000 feet or 1,000,000 yards, which is upwards of 568 miles. For this purpose between 3,000 and 4,000 trees are yearly used. The segments of the worn out saws in this mill – now piled up in heaps – would measure in a row 13 miles. I may add that more than once a log of mahogany of the value of £500 has been cut at this mill.

The machinery *can* cut 15 veneers in the inch, though 11 and 12 to the inch is the usual demand. The sawyers can saw but little more than 6 on the average to the inch. The charge at the mill is 1d. a foot for sawing veneers; thirty years ago it was 6d. Each veneer is now canvassed at each end to prevent its splitting; and throughout the establishment are large rooms, heated by steam, for the drying of the veneers or of the timber to be sawn. The extent to which veneering is carried on in London may be estimated by computing 28 saws at work, doing the same, or nearly the same, amount of work as those I have spoken of.

Among the other performances of this mill, I have spoken of the preparation of timber for lucifer matches. For the making of these matches the best America yellow pine is used. It is first sawn into blocks as wide as the tree, or rather plank, will allow, averaging perhaps 12 inches. These blocks are 3 inches thick and 5 and 5¼ in. wide. Five of such blocks are placed on a "feeding bench," and, when the machinery is put into operation, they are subject to the incision of from 45 to 60 cutters, lancet-shaped, which cut into the timber; it is the "slit" to the thickness of a match by the operation of a knife fitted into the machine; but so rapidly is the process carried on, that to the eye the slitting and cutting seem simultaneous. The five blocks are divided into match-wood in 116 strokes of the machine, and the machine performs 122 strokes in a minute or less; so that 16,000 double, or 32,000 single, matches are thus made in that time. Two other machines perform the same quantity of work as the great one I have described. The matches, when cut, slide from the machine into another room underneath, where girls are employed in tying them up into bundles, first fitting them into parcels, which hold six dozen boxes, each box containing 50 splints. In one day 30 hogsheads of matches were sent from the mill to one man in Bristol, each hogshead containing 500 bundles, or 54,000,000 matches in all. In this mill the average of matches thus made is 156,000 gross of boxes a year, each box containing 50 splints – altogether 60 millions of matches. For the manufacture of this quantity 400 cubic feet of timber are used in a week, averaging eight trees, or 400 large trees a year for lucifer matches, only in one mill. My informant thinks that three times the number is so made throughout the country.

In this mill are also rooms for the bending of timber for coach-builders' purposes, for the chopping of dye-woods, logwood, fustic, Campeachy, Nicaraguay, &c., into small particles, for the formation of ship blocks, and for the splitting of wood for lucifer-match boxes.

The veneer-mill sawyers are paid 5s. 6d., and 7s. a-day; but for that payment the saw is "taxed" to perform 5,000 feet in a week, and for all beyond that the veneer mill-sawyer receives 7s. per 1,000 feet – his average the year through is £2 15s. a week. There is no society among these men, and their number in London – where there are eight mills with twenty-eight saws – does not exceed 40. The labourers at the veneer mills are paid 3s. and 3s. 6d. a day, and the men who pile the timber, known in the trade as "gangers," earn 6s., 7s., and 8s. a day. These gangers, however, are a very small body, only four being employed at the great mill in question. In packing and tying the matches twenty girls are usually employed.

To this it is but fair that I should append the statement of one of the most intelligent of the operative carpenters, concerning the influence of machinery upon his trade. I wish it, however, to be distinctly understood that the opinions expressed below are those of the working men, and they are given merely in order that the public should be made acquainted with them: –

"The opinion of the journeymen generally is, that machinery cannot but make the trade worse and worse every year. The public, I know, generally believe it to be the greatest of blessings to have work done as cheap as possible, and as machinery does work cheaper than human beings, of course it is looked upon as a great benefit to society. The reason why the work can be done cheaper by machinery is, because a steam-engine only wants coals, and we require victuals – besides, masters can keep their steam-engines working night and day, and human beings *must* rest. The longer a master can keep his machinery going, the oftener, of course, he turns his capital over. You see directly they get a large quantity of machinery together, so as to keep it going continually, they will work at any price. I'm certain if they was tied to time as we are, we could beat them in our trade, for there's only particular parts that they can do effectually, and the great portion of these is the most laborious. To produce work as cheap as possible is certainly a great benefit to all those who have money to buy with; but to the working classes – that is to those who have no money but what they earn by their labour – machinery cannot but be a curse, since the object of it is to displace the very labour by which they live. Of course the capitalist gets ultimately a greater amount of profit by machinery, because he does more work with it, and so increases the returns on his capital, even though he sells at a less rate; it's by small profits and quick returns that all the fortunes are made in trade. But, only let us have machinery carried out to its full extent and then we shall soon know whether it is really a blessing or a curse to society as at present constituted. No working man that ever I heard but did not admit that machinery might be a benefit in another state of things, but that at present it must do an inconceivable amount of harm. If carried out to its full extent, of course it would displace human labour *altogether* (except the few children that would be required to tend upon it, and the few makers of it) − and when *all* labour is displaced, what is to become of the working men? But there is another point connected with machinery that also requires to be attended to. Suppose, I say, that *all* human labour is done away by it, and the working men are turned into paupers and criminals, then what I want to know is, who are to be the customers of the capitalists? The capitalists themselves, we should remember spend little or none (comparatively speaking) of the money *they* get; for, of course, it is the object of every capitalist to save all he can, and so increase the bulk of money out of which he makes his profits. The working men, however, spend *all* they receive − it's true a small amount is put into the savings bank, but that's a mere drop in the ocean; and so the working classes constitute the great proportion of the customers of the country. The lower their wages are reduced of course the less they have to spend, and when they are entirely superseded by machinery, of course they'll have nothing at all to spend, and then, I ask again, who are to be the capitalists' customers?"

Such then are the opinions of the journeymen generally as to the effects of machinery upon them. That the difficulty of obtaining work has increased among the carpenters considerably of late years, all whom I have seen, both masters and men, agree. This is attributed by many to the increase of machinery, and by many to the introduction of the "strapping' system described in my last letter, by which each man is now compelled to do four times the work that he was once expected to execute; and that this must necessarily tend greatly to overstock the trade with hands there cannot be the least doubt. However, be the cause what it may, the following statement is given as an instance of the difficulty the men find in obtaining employment: −

"I am a jobbing carpenter, and in very great distress. All my tools are gone − sold or pawned. I have no means of living but by parish relief, and picking up what I can in little odd jobs along the waterside. Sometimes I get at a job at painting, glazing, or whitewashing, now that I have lost my own work; sometimes I get a day's work at the London or St. Katherine Docks − anywhere I can get anything to do. And when I can't find any other employment I go to the workhouse yard and get a job there at wheeling the barrows and breaking stones. Sometimes I go to the yard four days in the week, sometimes only one day, and sometimes the whole of the week, according as I can get work. At the workhouse yard I get 1s. 6d. when I'm paid by the day; and when I'm at work on the stones I get 2d. a bushel for all I break, and the most I can do is six bushel in a day. Some men does 9 and 10 bushel, but then they're stronger men than me. I have got a wife and three children to keep out of my earnings, such as they are. My wife does nothing. She has a young child six months old to take care on, so it all lays on my hands. My eldest is a boy of 13 years. He got a place at a glass polisher's, and gets 5s. a week. He lives with his uncle. I've only the two others to look to. On Saturday my wife has a loaf and a shilling given to her from the parish, and that, with the shilling I earn at the yard, is all we has to keep and pay rent for the four of us, from Saturday till Monday. We can't go to work at the yard till Tuesday morning, for on Mondays we has the day to look after a job at some other place. Taking one week with another, I reckon I get, with parish allowance and all, from 5s. to 6s., and out of that I pays 1s. 6d. a week rent for one room – a first floor back, in an alley. It's my own things that's in it, and I'm obliged to scrape up 2d. and 3d. at a time to raise the rent, and give it 'em at the end of the week. I reckon we has generally from 4s. to 4s. 6d. a week at the outside to live upon – all the four. Sometimes it arn't that, for I go down to the docks to look after some work, and lose my day. We live upon bread and butter and coffee or tea, and maybe we manage sometimes to have a herring or two; and if we do have a taste of meat, why it's a bit of bacon – twopennyworth – which I buys instead of butter. Perhaps, if I've been very lucky in the week, I picks up a pound of bits at 4d. on the Saturday night, and we makes a hash on it, with a few taturs, for Sunday. My wife does the washing at home, and the things is dried in the room we live and sleep in. In the winter we all of us goes into the house (the union), because we can't afford to pay for firing outside. I leaves my things, such as they are, with my brother-in-law. To people like myself the cheapening of food has been the greatest of good. I don't know who brought it about, but I'm sure whoever it was, he has blessings for it. It was said that the bread was to be brought down to 4d. a loaf, but it's never been less than 5d. round about us. It's mostly bread that keeps us alive. Sometimes we has a pennyworth of taturs, but that's not our usual food. Half-a-quartern loaf will last us to the next day, and when I goes to work I puts a bit of bread in my hat, and that's my dinner, and all I have until night, when I go home and get a cup of tea. We have a halfpenny candle of an evening and a quarter of a pound of soap on a Saturday. My wife buys 14lbs. of coals for 2d. about twice a week, and that serves for boiling our kettle and such like. That's how we live. This is the way I reckon that our money goes every week:

	s.	d.	
Rent	1	6	per week
Half-quartern loaf a day	1	3	,,
Half a quartern of butter a day	0	8¾	,,
Pennyworth of coffee or tea a day	0	7	,,
One quartern of fourpenny sugar a day.............................	0	7	,,
One halfpenny candle a night	0	3½	,,
Half-pound of soap a week	0	2	,,
Fourteen pounds of coals twice a week	0	4	,,
Four halfpenny bundles of wood a week	0	2	,,
	5	7¼	

Yes, that's just about what it costs me, and if I manages to get a few pence more, why we buys a Dutch plaice (if they're in), and fries it for dinner, or else two or three fresh herrings, or may be, as a great treat, a pound of bits for the Sunday. I dare say there's hundreds in London lives like us, but I'm sure there's no one lives harder. There isn't much room for extravagance in five and sixpence a week among three and an infant – is there? The reason of my being in the state that I am is because I never belonged to no society, nor no clubs nor nothing. I never could have belonged to our regular trade society, because I never was brought up regular to the business. My father was a carpenter, and I used to work for him. He never apprenticed me, nor gave me no education, nor didn't teach me how to do the better kind of joiner's work. I can do the rough work, but sashes and frames is beyond me. When father was alive I had plenty of employment. He was a journeyman. I can't exactly call him a small master. He used mostly to take contracts on his own hands, to finish small houses and shop fronts, and then him and me used to do them together. Sometimes, may be, we'd have another hand on with us, that is, if the job was in a hurry. Father was a Yorkshireman, and I was born in Yorkshire too. He came to London with me and mother and settled here when I was six years old. I did very well till father's death. He used to keep me and give me 10s. a week. He's been dead now 12 years or better. I was 36 when he died. After his death I did pretty tidy for a short time. I got married about twelve months after that. I used to get a good bit of jobbing then from my father's connection. I took contracts, too, but some-how I used to lose a good deal by them. I was obligated to take so cheap. I seldom got above £1 and often only 15s. a week for my labour. After that I went to work for the speculating builders about the suburbs, and then I used to pick up £1 a week as long as it lasted. There is no society nor benefit club for the men as work for the cheap builders; so if they are sick, or out of employment, why the parish must keep them, and that's the way with all the cheap masters as I know on. They screws the men down to the lowest, and leaves them when ill to go to the house for relief. Then there's no allowance for the unemployed who don't belong to society, as there is when they do, so that when a man who works for the cheap builders can't get no employment – and there's hundreds that way in winter every London – why there're obligated to starve, and make away with their tools. When that's done, its all up with a man – he can't never get to work again. I might have had several jobs if I'd had my tools, but they're gone, and so I'm obligated to break stones. It's a twelvemonth since I lost 'em all. I was seized with the cholera in the hot weather last year. In course as I didn't belong to any benefit club why I couldn't get no allowance, so I parted with my things one by one, and last of all with my tools, and when I got well I couldn't find nothing for me to do. I went about and about till I pretty well wore the shoes off my feet, looking for work and trying to keep out of the workhouse as long as I could, but when the winter came, I was forced to get an order to go in − I couldn't hold out no longer. We had made away with everything − blankets off the bed, shirts and petticoats off our backs, and, last of all, the brokers was put in for eight or nine weeks' rent that I owed, and so we made the best of our way to 'the house,' and stopped in it about five months. I've striven every way to work for my living, but all to no good. Since my tools have gone, I haven't tried only one thing, but many. I've worked at the docks. I've made up stools, and tables, and clothes horses, at a shopmate's of mine, who used to let me go and work at his place, and I've hawked 'em about at the brokers, but they wanted 'em so cheap that there was no living at all to be made cut of them. I think the main cause of my being as I am is, because the cheap masters gives men such low wages as they can't afford to subscribe to any benefit club out of them, and so they're left to come upon the parish directly they're took ill, or thrown out of work; and another of the reasons is, because all the hands is now obligated to do double as much work as they formerly used; the consequence is, that one-half of the workmen can't get nothing to do. The men is obligated to work fourteen days to the week at the strapping shops, so where's the use of such as me hoping to get any employment. Then just look here, sir, it's not only me and my wife that's made paupers on, but my two children as well. In course, they'll be brought up in the house as paupers, and the last, you may say, as been regularly born and bred to it. I don't think I shall ever get out of the house again when I goes into it next winter, as I know I must. I'm a broken down man, sir. Work is so uncertain that I'm tired of looking for it. Work for the cheap masters as hard as a man will, he's sure to come to the workhouse at last.''

It now only remains for me to exhibit the relative criminality of the carpenters, as compared with that of other trades. For this purpose the metropolitan police returns have been examined with considerable care, and, in order that as general a result as possible might be come to on this point, an average has been struck for a series of ten years, and the annual number of offenders thus obtained divided into the estimated number of individuals belonging to the craft. The same plan has been adopted with all the other trades cited below, while a similar calculation has been made as to the criminality of the entire population of London. By this means we shall be enabled to discover not only the proportion of the population to one offender belonging to any particular occupation, but also to contrast this with the relative amount of crime in other avocations, and moreover to compare the whole with the average criminality of the entire population of the metropolis. A few of the principal results thus obtained are given in the subjoined table, where those trades that have already been investigated, and some others, are placed in juxtaposition, so that the reader may perceive the tendency of each class to commit any of the crimes there specified:

TABLE SHOWING THE NUMBER OF EACH CLASS (MALES OF ALL AGES) TO ONE OFFENDER, OF THE UNDERMENTIONED TRADES TAKEN INTO CUSTODY BY THE METROPOLITAN POLICE, BEING AN AVERAGE FOR TEN YEARS, FROM 1840—49

	Sawyers	Carpenters	*Turners, &c.	Tailors	Shoemakers	Carvers and Gilders	Coachmakers	Weavers	Sailors	Labourers	All Classes
Murder	1 in 15,020	1 in 22,846	1 in 38,630	1 in 99,495	1 in 61,152		1 in 43,980	1 in 3,781	1 in 6,242	1 in 11,930	1 in 39,818
Manslaughter	,, 15,020	,, 60,923	,, 77,260	,, 39,798	,, 40,768		,, 14,660	,, 7,422	,, 10,701	,, 5,042	,, 20,878
Rape	,, 15,020	,, 7,029	,, 77,260	,, 33,165	,, 27,178		,, 43,980		,, 12,485	,, 5,090	,, 18,337
Assaults (common)	,, 133	,, 127	,, 868	,, 154	,, 205	1 in 80	,, 181	,, 82	,, 59	,, 45	,, 125
Larceny (simple)	,, 182	,, 130	,, 757	,, 181	,, 169	,, 198	,, 448	,, 81	,, 60	,, 32	,, 130
Wilful damage	,, 625	,, 356	,, 3,219	,, 527	,, 655	,, 383	,, 934	,, 340	,, 138	,, 56	,, 286
Coin (counterfeit) uttering, &c.	,, 1,365	,, 862	,, 8,584	,, 861	,, 944	,, 1,568	,, 1,999	,, 562	,, 1,040	,, 347	,, 974
Drunkenness	,, 63	,, 59	,, 580	,, 63	,, 91	,, 89	,, 106	,, 75	,, 13	,, 31	,, 81
Vagrants	,, 143	,, 250	,, 1,030	,, 338	,, 498	,, 297	,, 862	,, 55	,, 71	,, 44	,, 163
Offences against the person	,, 80	,, 70	,, 518	,, 91	,, 119	,, 60	,, 127	,, 58	,, 37	,, 23	,, 76
Offences against property with violence	,, 2,002	,, 1,646	,, 9,657	,, 2,518	,, 2,184	,, 2,875	,, 5,497	,, 773	,, 1,208	,, 588	,, 2,308
Offences against property without violence	,, 100	,, 66	,, 380	,, 84	,, 84	,, 61	,, 227	,, 39	,, 34	,, 14	,, 56
Malicious offences against property	,, 600	,, 354	,, 3,219	,, 525	,, 648	,, 375	,, 934	,, 337	,, 137	,, 55	,, 282
Forgery and offences against the currency	,, 1,201	,, 794	,, 7,726	,, 771	,, 864	,, 1,326	,, 1,832	,, 545	,, 823	,, 330	,, 896
Offences not included in the above classes	,, 25	,, 24	,, 167	,, 25	,, 33	,, 26	,, 55	,, 17	,, 6	,, 7	,, 23
Total	,, 15	,, 13	,, 90	,, 15	,, 18	,, 14	,, 31	,, 9	,, 4	,, 3	,, 12

*This class includes cabinet-makers and upholsterers.

The following conclusions may be drawn from the foregoing table. Of all the trades or occupations above cited the weavers are the most addicted to murder, for they appear to have 1 murderer in every 3,711 of their body. Those who seem to be the least given to this crime − as far as my investigation has already gone − are the tailors, who have only one murderer in 99,495 of their craft. The average of all classes for murder is 1 in every 39,818 individuals. The carpenters stand a little above the ordinary rate in this respect, there being 1 murderer in every 22,846 of their body. With regard to manslaughter, the labourers stand first on the list, and the turners, &c., last. The carpenters are considerably below the average on this point, there being only 1 homicide among them in every 60,793 of the class, whilst the average for *all* classes is 1 criminal in 30,878. As to rape, we find the labourers, again, the most criminal, and the turners, &c., again the least so. In this respect, however, the carpenters are greatly above the average, the number of criminals among them being 1 in 7,029; whilst the average is 1 in 18,337. In assaults, too; the labourers are at the top of the list, whilst turners, &c., still show the least of all. For assaults the carpenters are a trifle below the average, the ratio of all classes being 1 in 125; whilst the carpenters show 1 in 127. These are the principal of the offences against the person; concerning this class of offences generally the greatest amount of crime exists amongst the labourers, and the least amongst the turners, &c. The average stands thus: one criminal in every 76 individuals, while the carpenters number one in every 70 of their craft. For the crime of simple larceny we find the labourers still at the top of the tree, and the turners, &c., again the least criminal of all classes. The carpenters in this case are neither above nor below the average. The other offences against property without violence show the labourers to be still the most criminal, and the turners, &c., the least. The average is 1 in 56, and the carpenters 1 in 66, which is a trifle below it. We next come to wilful damage, and still find the labourers in the most criminal position, whilst the turners are again the least criminal in this respect. The average stands at 1 in 286; and the carpenters appear in this instance to be less criminal than the ordinary run of the people, they being 1 in 356. For the whole of the malicious offences against property the labourers still keep their position, and the turners, &c., theirs. The carpenters rank below the average in this respect, showing 1 criminal in every 354 of their craft, the ordinary rates being 1 in 282. For uttering counterfeit coin we find the labourers still the most criminal, and the turners, &c., the least. The carpenters in this case are somewhat above the average in crime. With regard to forgery and the whole of the offences against the currency, the labourers still hold the same rank; whilst the turners, &c., again show the least criminality. Next comes the vice of drunkenness, in which the sailors take the lead, showing 1 in every 13 of their number. The least drunkenness exists amongst the turners, &c., there being only 1 drunkard in 580 of their body. The carpenters in this case are considerably above the average, viz., 1 in 59; whilst the average stands at 1 in 81. The labourers are still prominent in vagrancy; whilst the turners appear the least vagrant of all classes. For all other crimes not included in the foregoing, the sailors stand the highest, being one in six, and the turners, &c., the lowest, being 1 in 167. The carpenters are a trifle below the average. Upon the whole the labourers appear to produce more criminals than any other classes, there being amongst them 1 offender in every 3 individuals, and the turners, &c., the least criminal, they having only one offender in every 90 of their class. The carpenters are slightly below the average, showing 1 in 13; whilst the average gives for all classes of crimes 1 offender in every 12 individuals. A general summary of the foregoing may be thus concisely expressed. The carpenters rank above the average of all other classes in the following offences:— Murder, rape, coining, and drunkenness; whilst as regards manslaughter, larceny, wilful damage, and vagrancy, they are more or less below the ordinary ratio of the entire population of London. The labourers appear to be the most criminal of all classes, and the turners the least so; whilst the sailors have the greatest tendency to drunkenness, and the weavers to murder.

LETTER LXIII
Thursday, August 1, 1850

Having now set forth the earnngs and condition of the Wood-workers who are engaged in the construction of our houses, I shall treat of those who are engaged in the furnishing of them.

Cabinet-making is the one generic term applied to the manufacture of every description of furniture. Upholstery is, however, a distinct art or handicraft, dealing with different materials. The cabinet-maker is a pure wood-worker; and that, perhaps, of the very highest order. Being generally engaged upon the most expensive woods, his work is required to be of the most finished and tasty description. The art is constantly calling forth a very high exercise of skill, ingenuity, and invention. It is a trade which perhaps, more intimately than any other, is mixed up with the fine arts. Marqueterie is mosaic work in wood; as wood-carving, in its higher branches, is sculpture in wood. The upholsterers, who confine themselves to their own proper branch, are the fitters-up of curtains and their hangings, either for beds or windows; they are also the stuffers of the chair and sofa cushions, and the makers of carpets and of beds; that is to say, they are the tradesmen who, in the language of the craft, "do the soft work" − or in other words, all connected with the cabinet-maker's art in which woven materials are the staple.

The cabinet-maker's trade of the best class, where society-men are employed, is now divided into the *General* and *Fancy* Cabinet-makers. There are also the *Chair-makers* and the *Bedstead-makers*. The General Cabinet hand makes every description of furniture apart from chairs or bedsteads. "A general hand," I was told by an intelligent workman, "must be able to make everything, from the smallest comb-tray to the largest bookcase. If he can't do whatever he's put to, he must go." He is usually kept, however, to the manufacture of the larger articles of furniture − as tables, drawers, chiffoniers, sideboards, wardrobes, and the like.

The Fancy Cabinet-maker, on the other hand, manufactures all the lighter or more portable articles of the trade, and such as scarcely come under the head of furniture. In the language of the craft he is a "small worker," and makes ladies work-boxes and tables, tea-caddies, portable desks, dressing cases, card, glove, gun, and pistol cases, cribbage-boards, and such like.

The Chairmaker constructs every description of chairs and sofas, but only the framework: the finishing, when stuffed backs or cushions, or stuffing of any kind, is required, is the department of the upholsterer.

The Bedstead-maker is employed in the making of bedsteads; but his work is considered less skilled than that of the other branches, as the woodcarver or the turner's art is that called upon for the formation of the handsome pillars of a bedstead of the best order.

To estimate the numerical strength of the cabinet-makers as a distinct body is impossible, for unfortunately the census of 1841 lumps them with the upholsterers (who are a totally different class of workmen, operating upon different materials) because their arts happen to be *locally* associated. The two *trades* are certainly conjoined in commerce, but the two *arts* are essentially distinct; that is to say, the employers are master upholsterers as well as cabinet-makers, but the operatives themselves seldom or never follow both occupations. The circumstances which govern the classification of trades are totally different from those regulating the division of work. In trade the convenience of the purchaser is mainly studied, the sale or manufacture of such articles being associated as are usually required together. Hence the master coachmaker is frequently a harness manufacturer as well, for the purchaser of the one generally stands in need of the other. The painter and house decorator not only follows the trade of the glazier, but of the plumber, too, because these arts are one and all connected with the "doing up" of houses. For the same reason the builder combines the business of the plasterer with that of the bricklayer, and not unfrequently that of the carpenter and joiner in addition. In all of these businesses, however, a distinct set of workmen are required, according as the materials operated upon are different; for, as I before showed, it is the nature of the materials that regulates the character of the work.

The cabinet-makers *and* upholsterers then, at the time of taking the last census, numbered altogether in Great Britain as many as 30,712; of these, 25,000 and odd were resident in England, 4,000 in Scotland, 650 in Wales, and 350 in the British Isles. Besides these, there were the chair-makers, who amounted throughout Great Britain to 5,123; of whom upwards of 4,800 belonged to England, and 218 to Scotland. The bedstead-makers in Great Britain were 396, and they were wholly located in England; so that, adding together these three classes, we arrive at the conclusion that there were in 1841 as many as 36,231 cabinet-makers, upholsterers, chair-makers, and bedstead-makers dispersed throughout Great Britain, and that upwards of 30,000, or five-sixths, of these resided in England.

The number of cabinet-makers and upholsterers located in the metropolis at the time of taking the last census was 6,956. The London chair-makers were 1,325, and the bedstead-makers 296: making altogether as many as 8,577 belonging to the different branches of the London trade.

According to the "Post-office Directory" no less that, 1,008 of these were masters in business for themselves, so that it may be said that in 1841 the London operative cabinet-makers amounted to 7,500 and odd. Such are the Government returns of 1841; and on comparing them with those of 1831, we arrive at the following curious results as to the increase or decrease of the trade in the different countries during that time. –

The greatest increase of cabinet makers from 1831-41 occurred in the county of Sutherland, where in amounted to as much as 272 per cent. above the increase of the population. In Inverness, and in Orkney and Shetland, the increase was 130 per cent.; in Roxburgh, 110 per cent; in Huntingdon-shire, 70 per cent.; in Bedfordshire, 62 pere cent.; in Flintshire, 55 per cent.; in Banff, 54 per cent.; in York city and county, 35 per cent.; and in Buckinghamshire, 32 per cent. above the increase of the population. The greatest decrease, on the other hand, took place in Anglesey, where the number of the cabinet-makers, in comparison with the population, declined no less than 98 per cent. in the ten years. In Renfrew the decrease was 95 per cent.; in Linlithgow, 86 per cent.; in Derbyshire, 73 per cent.; in Cheshire and Cumberland, each 68 per cent.; in Merioneth, 67 per cent.; in Caithness, 66 per cent.; in the West Riding of Yorkshire, 62 per cent.; in Durham, 61 per cent.; and in Bute, 60 per cent. below that of the population. In England generally the cabinet-makers and upholsterers, twenty years of age and upwards, in comparison with the population of that age, decreased from 1831-41 as much as 22 per cent. In Wales there was also a decrease of 11 per cent., while in Scotland there was a still greater decrease – the number of cabinet-makers and upholsterers located there having diminished as much as 33 per cent. in the same space of time. The total for Great Britain shows a decrease in the cabinet makers and upholsterers, of 20 years and upwards, of 4 per cent.; and an increase in the population of the same age of 20 per cent., thus making, in comparison with the increase of the population, a total decrease of as much as 24 per cent. In the metropolis, with which we are here more particularly concerned, the decrease was 1 per cent. – whilst the population, above twenty years, increased as much as 32 per cent., making a decline in the numbers of this class (in comparison with the rest of the population) to the amount of 33 per cent.

The next question that naturally presents itself is, how has this reduction of the number of hands throughout the country affected the trade? According to the law of supply and demand, the decrease of workmen should have given rise to a proportionate increase in the wages, provided there was no corresponding diminution in the quantity of work to be done. As to the effect produced by the decrease of the hands upon the weekly income of the workmen in the provinces, I have no means of arriving at an accurate conclusions. Concerning the metropolis, however, I am differently situated, and to the kindness and consideration of the West-end branch of the General Cabinet-Makers' Society, I stand indebted for much important information. Of course the diminution in the number of workmen between 1831 and 1841 is a fact from which few or no deductions can be drawn, unless we can likewise arrive at some equally authentic facts concerning the increase or decrease of work during the same period. With a view, therefore, of obtaining the best information on this point, I applied to the Cabinet-makers' Society for an account of the number of their unemployed members for a series of years, as well as the number of days they had been out of employment, and the sum the society had paid them during that time. The committee immediately gave directions that I should be furnished with all the information I needed, and the secretary devoted himself for several days to the compilation of a tabular statement, in which the wished-for facts were given for every quarter of a year since 1834. This table, however, being much too long to print here, I have taken the average of the four quarters of each year, and the following is the result: –

	Number of Members.	Number of Unemployed.	Days Unemployed	Paid to Unemployed.
1831	342	—	—	—
1832	290	—	—	—
1833	318	—	—	—
1834	371	40	632	£60 18 8½
1835	435	41	748	67 7 8¾
1836	506	40	566	53 10 1¾
1837	527	90	1,675	156 6 10½
1838	513	82	2,025	185 13 3
1839	518	61	1,321	120 13 11½
1840	504	77	1,873	170 15 7
Average from 1834-40	482	62	1,368	£125 14 7

	Number of Members.	Number of Unemployed.	Days Unemployed.	Paid to Unemployed.
1841	516	102	2,958	£278 3 7¾
1842	464	110	3,482	367 10 10¾
1843	412	85	2,006	216 19 11¼
1844	419	43	934	84 17 5½
1845	460	26	383	35 12 9½
1846	546	47	878	86 18 6¼
1847	506	98	2,901	256 14 8
1848	413	125	4,201	387 13 4½
1849	340	98	2,204	204 13 5½
Average from 1840-49	452	81	1,158	£213 4 11½

A superficial glance at this account will not enable us to come to any conclusion with regard to the state of the trade of the cabinet-makers in the different years above mentioned. In order to do this, we must find out the ratio of the employment to the non-employment of the members of the society; for the number of the unemployed is of no value *pcr sc*. Nor is the number of members out of work alone sufficient for this purpose, for, unless we know the number of days that they were collectively unoccupied in each quarter, the true ratio of the employment to the non-employment cannot be obtained. Again, the sum paid to the unemployed members during any particular quarter is no criterion, unless we ascertain the amount that the employed members would collectively earn in the same time. It is the ratio between these several facts that will alone enable us to arrive at any definite result with regard to the state of the trade. To show the reader at a glance, therefore, the proportion that these facts bear to each other, I have in the first column of the following table given the per centage of the ratio of the days unemployed to those employed. This has been arrived at by finding first the number of days that the whole of the members in the society would have worked in the quarter, provided they had had full employment, and then calculating the proportion between that amount and the aggregate number of days unemployed. In the second column of the same table, I have likewise shown the ratio of the loss to the society by the non-employment of some of its members in comparison with its gains by the employment of the others. This I have ascertained by estimating the value of the unemployed days at the regular wages of the trade, and adding this sum to the amount paid to the members out of work, and then finding the proportion that this sum bears to the amount that the whole of the members would have earned had they been fully employed.

	Ratio of days unemployed employed to those employed.		Ratio of loss by non-employment to gains by employment.	
1834 ...	2.1 per cent.	...	2.9 per cent.	
1835 ...	2.2	,,	...	2.9	,,
1836 ...	1.4	,,	...	1.9	,,
1837 ...	4.0	,,	...	5.5	,,
1838 ...	5.0	,,	...	6.8	,,
1839 ...	3.2	,,	...	4.3	,,
1840 ...	4.7	,,	...	6.3	,,
1841 ...	7.1	,,	...	9.9	,,
1842 ...	9.4	,,	...	13.2	,,
1843 ...	6.4	,,	...	8.9	,,
1844 ...	2.8	,,	...	3.8	,,
1845 ...	1.0	,,	...	1.4	,,
1846 ...	2.0	,,	...	2.8	,,
1847 ...	7.3	,,	...	9.7	,,
1848 ...	13.4	,,	...	17.5	,,
1849 ...	8.3	,,	...	11.2	,,

A glance at the above table will show us that the ratio of loss by non-employment rises and falls in the same manner, though not precisely to the same manner, though not precisely to the same extent as the ratio of days unemployed.

We are now in a position to ascertain in what proportion the wages of a trade rise and fall, according as the hands and the work decrease or increase. It may however be said, that since the society-men of a trade never work for less than an established rate of pay, the earnings of its members cannot be influenced by any such means. This, however, we shall find, is far from the fact; for though it may be true individually, still collectively it is untrue. Even a moment's reflection is sufficient to ensure us that if a body of men contribute a certain sum in the quarter to the support of their unemployed members, it is the same as if their wages had been reduced precisely that sum. If their collective earnings amounted in the year to £40,000, and out of that they gave £250 per quarter to the maintenance of those members who might be out of work, of course their gross income must be reduced one-fortieth. Whether they receive the £40,000 in full and pay the thousand pounds out of it afterwards, or whether they receive collectively £1,000 less for their labour, the result is the same – their aggregate earnings or wages have fallen from £40,000 to £39,000 – the burden is only removed from one shoulder to the other; the pressure, it is true, may not be felt so severely by shifting it, but still there it is, not one atom the lighter, though more easily borne. We can, then, by comparing the ratio of the loss to the society by non-employment to its gains by employment, at one period with that existing at another, obtain an accurate account of the increase or decrease in the earnings of the trade at any given time. By doing the same with the ratio of the unemployed days to those employed, we can likewise ascertain the increase or decrease of work for the same period – while a comparison of the number of workmen belonging to the society in different years will further give us the increase or decrease of the workmen. We have thus a means of demonstrating whether the wages of a trade really depend on the quantity of work to be done and the number of hands to do it.

	Increase or decrease of hands.	Increase or decrease of work.	Increase or decrease of wages.
1835	+ 17.2 per cent	− 0.1 per cent	0.0 per cent
1836	+ 16.3 ,,	+ 0.8 ,,	− 1.0 ,,
1837	+ 4.1 ,,	− 2.6 ,,	− 3.6 ,,
1838	− 2.6 ,,	− 1.0 ,,	− 1.3 ,,
1839	+ .9 ,,	+ 1.8 ,,	+ 2.5 ,,
1840	− 2.7 ,,	− 1.5 ,,	− 2.0 ,,
1841	− 2.3 ,,	− 2.4 ,,	− 3.6 ,,
1842	− 10.0 ,,	− 2.3 ,,	− 3.3 ,,
1843	− 11.2 ,,	+ 3.0 ,,	+ 4.3 ,,
1844	− 1.7 ,,	+ 3.6 ,,	+ 5.1 ,,
1845	+ 9.7 ,,	+ 1.8 ,,	+ 2.4 ,,
1846	+ 18.6 ,,	− 1.0 ,,	+ 1.4 ,,
1847	− 7.3 ,,	− 5.3 ,,	− 6.9 ,,
1848	− 18.3 ,,	− 6.1 ,,	− 7.8 ,,
1849	− 17.6 ,,	+ 5.1 ,,	+ 6.3 ,,

By the above table we perceive that in the year 1835 there were 17 per cent. more hands, and one-tenth per cent. less work than in 1834, and yet the earnings remained the same in that year as in the previous one. In 1836 the hands increased 16 per cent., and the work only 8-10ths per cent., but still the gains rose 1 per cent. In 1842 the hands decreased 10.0 per cent., and the work only 2 per cent., and yet the earnings fell 3 per cent. In 1849, however, the number of workmen declined no less than 17½ per cent., while the quantity of work rose 5 per cent.; the consequence was, that the gains of the members were upwards of 6 per cent. more than they were in the year before. Such facts as these show us that the principle of supply and demand, though undeniably true in general, still is not sufficient to account for all the fluctuations of wages. This will be even more evident when I come to treat of the Slop Cabinet Trade, for then I shall show that notwithstanding the number of cabinet-makers in the metropolis, compared with the rest of the population, decreased no less than 32 *per cent.!* between 1831 and 1841, still the wages of the non-society men (whose earnings are regulated solely by competition) have fallen as much as 400 per cent. – and this while the amount of work done has increased rather than decreased. The cause of this extraordinary decline will be found to be due chiefly to the rapid spread of what are called "Garret Masters" – a class of petty "trade-working-masters," who are precisely equivalent to the Chamber Masters among the boot and shoe makers, and to whom we found the decline of the wages in that trade were mainly attributable. This, indeed, appears to be the great evil likewise of the turner's trade, where, while hands have decreased, and work increased, wages have also fallen almost to the same extent as in the cabinet trade, and that from precisely the same reason, viz. – the increase of the "Small Masters," who are continually underselling each other.

In the present Letter, however, I purpose confining myself to the "honourable" part of the general cabinet-makers' trade. I shall first give a description of the work executed by the cabinet-makers, and then state the regulations of the trade. After which I propose speaking of the social condition of the men generally employed in it, and concluding with the statements of some of the best informed members of the craft.

The general Cabinet hands make the following articles, on which they are principally employed: – *Pembroke Tables*, which are square-cornered, with a wide "bed" (surface) and two small flaps. They are generally of solid mahogany. *Loo Tables*, which are generally round, though a few are oblong. The making of the highest branches of the cabinet-maker's art. The carving alone of one of the most beautiful ever made, for the Army and Navy Club, cost, I am assured, £40. Loo tables are generally veneered; rosewood, maple, and mahogany being the most frequent materials. The *Dining Table* has a narrow bed, with two long "flaps." The "extensible" dining table has telescope slides. Dining tables are all solid. The *Card Table* turns on a frame, and folds over into half the space. There are also "library," "sofa," "occasional," and other tables, which I need not describe. For the furniture of drawing rooms oak is now a fashionable wood: the small tables in recesses, or for the display of any bust or ornament, are now often made of this material. Fine English oak for such a purpose is far costlier than mahogany. *Chairs* are the most changeable in their fashion of all the furniture formed by the cabinet-maker. The Louis Quatorze style, has now come again into fashion – a style which I am informed is always alternating, for, after some very opposite mode in style and form has been established for a limited period, "it works round again to the Louis Quatorze." Nearly all chairs are "worked solid," except that the "splat," or top of the back, is sometimes veneered. Of dining-room chairs I need not speak. Drawing-room chairs are of rosewood, maple, or walnut, and are, in the present fashion (of which alone I speak), covered with rich silk tabaret, or elaborate needlework. The bedroom chairs are of polished or stained birch; sometimes they are japanned, with cane-work or osier bottoms. The chairmaker is, moreover, the artisan employed in the making of sofas. These are known as cabriole, couch, and tête-à-tête is the form of the letter S, and is adapted for two persons only, who occupy the respective bends. *Sideboards* are most frequently made of mahogany, solid or veneered, but in most cases solid. Oak, however, is now the fashionable material for a sideboard, and is elaborately carved. *Cabinets* also are now made, as in the old times, of oak and walnut. For a lady's apartment rosewood is often the material used for a cabinet. *Cheffoniers* are of rosewood or mahogany, solid or veneered. *Drawers* and *Wardrobes* are of the wood which is considered most *en suite* with the other furniture, and with the general decoration of the chamber. *Book-case* making of the best quality is accounted a highly skilled portion of the cabinet-maker's productions. One at the Carlton Club, for its beauty of proportion, and strength as well as delicacy of workmanship, is pronounced by the trade, I heard in several quarters, a perfect masterpiece. It extends 90 feet. The surface is mahogany, veneered; the inferior is the finest deal.

In most large establishments the work is begun and completed on the premises; general cabinet-makers, bedstead-makers, upholsterers, wood carvers, French polishers, and sawyers, all being employed there.

The mode of workmanship pursued by cabinet-makers is very remarkable, as showing a dependance on the skill of the individual workman unknown, perhaps, in any other trade. The best workman among the tailors in a large establishment has but to exert his skill to put together the materials which have been cut to the nicest proportions before they are placed in his hands. So it is with the boot-maker. With the cabinet-maker, however, it is different. The foreman gives him a sketch of the article he has to make, and points out the material in the yard or the ware-room which is to be used in its construction. The journeyman then measures, saws, and cuts the wood to the shape required, and is expected to do so with the greatest economy of stuff, and so to cut it that the best portion of the wood shall occupy the most prominent part of the furniture, and any defective part be placed where it is least visible, or, in the language of the trade, "he must put the best side to London." The journeyman cuts out every portion; not only the front of the article, but every shelf required for the interior, and the minutest partitions or drawers. He then takes the material to his bench in the workshop, and puts it together without any subdivision of labour. The journeymen will assist one another in any elaborate article which is being made by piece-work, but this is an arrangement merely among themselves. The master requires every workman to be able to complete whatever article he is told to make. In a large establishment, at a very busy time (and in some establishments at all times), a foreman, called a chalk foreman, is employed to mark or cut out, in order to facilitate the business; but the method I have described is that usually observed.

The cabinet-makers find all their own tools, a complete set of which is worth from £30 to £40. They all work on the master's premises, which, in establishments where many men are employed, are, with a few exceptions, spacious and well-ventilated rooms, open to the skylighted roof. Valuable timber is generally placed along the joists of the workshop, and there it remains a due time for "seasoning." When the men are at work there is seldom much conversation, as each man's attention is given to his own especial task, while the noise of the saw, the plane, or the hammer, is another impediment to conversation. Politics, beyond the mere news of the day, are, I am assured by experienced parties, little discussed in these workshops. I am told, also, that the cabinet-makers, as a body, care little about such matters.

The operative cabinet-makers of the best class are, to speak generally, men possessed of a very high degree of intelligence. I must be understood to be here speaking of the best paid. Of the poor artisans of the East-end I have a different tale to tell. I was told by a cabinet-maker – and, judging by my own observations, with perfect correctness – that of all classes of mechanics the cabinet-makers have the most comfortable abodes. The same thing may be said also, if in a less degree, of the joiners and carpenters; and the reason is obvious – a steady workman occupies his leisure in making articles for his own use. Perhaps there are not many stronger contrasts than one I have remarked in the course of my present inquiry – that between the abode of the workman in a good West-end establishment, and the garret or cellar of the toiler for a "slaughter-house" at the East-end. In the one you have the warm, red glow of polished mahogany furniture; a clean carpet covers the floor; a few engravings in neat frames hang against the papered wall; and book-shelves or a bookcase have their appropriate furniture. Very white and bright-coloured pot ornaments, with sometimes a few roses in a small vase, are reflected in the mirror over the mantelshelf. The East-end cabinet-maker's room has *one* piece of furniture, which is generally the principal – the workman's bench. The walls are bare, and sometimes the half-black plaster is crumbling from them; all is dark and dingy, and of furniture there is very little, and that, it must be borne in mind, when the occupant is a furniture-maker. A drawer-maker whom I saw in Bethnal-green had never been able to afford a chest of drawers for his own use; "besides," he added, "what do I want with drawers? I've nothing to put in them." What is meant by a "slaughter-house" will be seen in my account of the non-society cabinet-makers in Spitalfields and the adjacent districts. The same establishments in the West-end are generally described as "linendrapers;" they are indeed the drapers who sell every description of furniture and upholstery, but the workmen from whom they receive their goods are the "East-enders." These "linendrapers," and indeed all masters who employ non-society men, are known in the trade as "black" masters. "He's nothing but a black," is a sentence expressive of supreme contempt in a cabinet-maker's mouth.

"Within my recollection," said an intelligent cabinet-maker, "there was much drinking, very much drinking, among cabinet-makers. This was fifteen years back. Now I'm satisfied that at least seven-eighths of all who are in society are sober and temperate men. Indeed, good masters won't have tipplers now-a-days." According to the Metropolitan Police returns, the cabinet-makers and the turners are two of the least criminal of all the artizans; I speak not of any one year, but from an average taken for the last ten.

The great majority of the cabinet-makers are married men, and were described to me by the best informed parties as generally domestic men, living, whenever it was possible, near their workshops, and going home to every meal. They are not much of play-goers, a Christmas pantomime or any holiday spectacle being exceptions, especially where there is a family. "I don't know a card-player," said a man who had every means of knowing, "amongst us. I think you'll find more cabinet-makers than any other trade members of mechanics' institutes and literary institutions, and attenders at lectures." Some journeymen cabinet-makers have saved money, and I found them all speak highly of the advantages they, as well as their masters, derive from their trade society." The majority of the cabinet-makers in London are countrymen. There are some very good workmen from Scotland. One who has been an apprentice to a good London master is, however, considered to rank with the very highest as a skilled workman.

In the honourable trade bonuses to foremen, and "improvers," and "contracts," and "sub-letting," among the journeymen, are at present unknown. "I don't know," it was said to me, "that we have any great grievances to complain of except one — and that's the East-end." I find, however, that the "strapping system," known in this trade as the "cut and run" work is becoming very general among the trade working masters — while any of the more respectable shops are beginning to give out their work by the "lump," instead of the "piece." To the non-existence of contracts, however, there is one exception — in the cabinet work of a great pianoforte and musical instrument maker. There the letting and sub-letting is carried on through the several grades, to the complete or comparative impoverishment of a great majority of the workmen, and the enriching of a few contractors.

The cabinet-maker's trade is generally learned by apprenticeship, and the apprentices to superior masters are often the sons of tradesmen, and are well-educated lads. There is no limit to the number a master may take, but the great firms in the honourable trade take very few, while the masters not in the honourable trade will, I am informed, take very many (one has eleven), and even put run-away apprentices to work. "They go for one thing, sir," a cabinet-maker said to me, "to get things done for half-price; it's little matter how." A journeyman can have his own son apprenticed to him, but only one at a time.

The payment of the journeyman cabinet-maker is, both by the piece and by the week, 32s. a week, being the minimum allowed by the rules of the society as the remuneration for a week's labour, or six days of ten hours each. The prices by piece are regulated by a book, which is really a remarkable production. It is a thick quarto volume, containing some 600 pages. Under the respective heads the piece-work price of every article of furniture is specified; and immediately after what is called the "start" price, or the price for the plain article, follows an elaborate enumeration of extras, according as the article may be ordered to be ornamented in any particular manner. There are also engravings of all the principal articles in the trade, which further facilitate the clear understanding of all the regulations contained in the work. The date of this book of prices is 1811, and the wages of the society men have been unchanged since then. The preparation of this ample and minute statement of prices occupied a committee of masters and of journeymen between two and three years. The committee were paid for their loss of time from the masters' and the journeymen's funds respectively; and what with these payments, what with the expense of attending the meetings and consultations, the making and remaking of models, the cost of printing and engravings, the cabinet-makers' book of prices was not compiled, I am assured, at a less cost than from £4,000 to £5,000.

The trade societies in connection with this branch of art, are those of the cabinet, chair, and bedstead makers. They are divided into three districts, viz., West-end, Middle, and East-end. These districts contain five societies — one at the West-end, another in the centre of the metropolis, and the others at the East-end. Three of these societies are in connection with the cabinet makers' trade; the remaining two belong to the bedstead makers and the chair-makers. The following table shows the number of men in connection with each society, together with the non-society men appertaining to each branch:

	Society Men	Non-Society Men	Total of Society and non-Society
West-end General Cabinet-makers	300	1,400	1,700
East-end ditto	140	1,000	1,140
Fancy Cabinet-makers	47	500	547
Chair-makers	130	1,428	1,558
Bedstead-makers	25	238	263
	642	4,566	5,208

Thus we perceive that the society men constitute not quite one-seventh part of the trade, from which it should be remembered that the upholsterers are here excluded.

These several societies, as is usually the case, have for their object the upholding of the standard rate of wages, and providing such assistance to their members as has been found to best suit the peculiar circumstances in which the workman is placed. They are mostly offered by a secretary, president, and committee, who are differently paid, according to the importance of the body and the nature of the duties required, while the payments of the members partake of the same variable character. The West-end cabinet-makers meet weekly, and pay 6d. per week as their regular trade contribution, and the members who are unemployed obtain for a given time 10s. per week from the funds, and when on strike 16s. There is also a payment for the insurance of tools, for which 1s. 6d. is paid every quarter. The West-end General Cabinet-Makers' Society have paid no less than £11,000 to the unemployed members within the last sixteen years, which is at the rate of very nearly £700 a year. They have also expended in the insurance of tools, since 1836, £1,758, and have received during that time £708 for loss of them by fire.

The members of the East-end body differ from those at the West-end in their rate of pay. They receive 30s. instead of 32s. per week, and when on piece-work they are paid by the job, or in the "lump;" that is to say, a given labour-value is put upon the entire article, whereas the West-end workman receives an additional price for everything which can be considered as coming under the denomination of an "extra." In the East-end, the members likewise meet weekly, but pay the less contribution of 4d. The unemployed members get 8s. per week, and when on strike 15s. The tools of the members are also insured by the society, but at a less rate than in the West-end.

The contributions of the fancy cabinet-makers are lower than in either of the foregoing instances, being but 3d. per week. They in like manner meet weekly. The assistance received by the unemployed, however, is mainly dependent on the state of the society's funds, 2s. per week being the lowest amount to be granted and 6s. the highest. They also have a legitimate weekly wage of 30s.; but this at present is very rarely to be obtained. The generality of this class work in their own homes, and take out the work in the "lump," the custom of paying for extras in the fancy cabinet trade being virtually extinct.

The chair-maker's weekly contribution is 6d., the same as that of the West-end cabinet maker; he gets, also, 10s. a week when unemployed; while, in cases of strike, the pay is as high as £1 per week for four weeks, and 16s. for another four weeks. Their standard wages are 32s. per week, while their piece work is regulated by their book of prices, with every description of extra or additional work carefully specified. Like the general cabinet makers, they prefer this mode of employment to being paid by the week. An insurance is also taken out by this society for the tools of the members.

The bedstead-makers only meet once a month, and pay their contributions by the month, which is 1s. 4d. When employed by the week they get 32s.; but they receive 3s. 6d. per day when sent out to a gentleman's house, to do such repairing (including cleaning) as may be required in their line of trade. This society also insures the tools of members, at the optional values of £12, £18, or £25, the latter sum being the highest. No payments have been made by this body either to the unemployed, or to parties on strike, for so long a time now that the custom in these cases has fallen into total disuse.

As a general rule the members of all the above societies are opposed to strikes, preferring the system of arbitration.

There is no superannuation or sick fund in connection with any of these societies. When the societies of cabinet-makers first commenced, the houses of call were established upon the same principle as the tailors' − that is to say, as the labour market of the trade; but now it is oftener the case that a man calls upon the master or his foreman, instead of receiving a call from the society house. Sometimes a man gets recommended to a master or foreman by a brother workman, and so obtains employment. The non-society men call upon the masters and ask for work.

Tramps are not encouraged, as these societies have no correspondence with the country societies. If, perchance, a tramp should call at a shop, he may get a few halfpence, but that is all. The brisk season continues during the spring and summer, and the autumn and winter months are the slack period of the trade. The following table shows the average ratio of non-employment at different seasons from 1834 to 1849. It will here be seen that the periods of greatest slackness are the first and last quarters, and the period of the greatest briskness the second quarter of the year:

TABLE SHOWING THE AVERAGE RATIO OF DAYS UNEMPLOYED TO
THOSE EMPLOYED IN EACH QUARTER OF THE UNDERMENTIONED
YEARS

	August, 1st Quarter	August, 2d Quarter	August, 3d Quarter	August, 4th Quarter
1834−40..................	4.5 per cent	3.0 per cent	3.9 per cent	3.8 per cent
1840−49..................	8.3 ,,	4.6 ,,	6.0 ,,	6.2 ,,
1834−49..................	6.9 ,,	3.9 ,,	5.1 ,,	5.1 ,,

A good-looking man, who spoke with a hardly perceptible Scotch accent, gave me the following account of his experience as a *general cabinet-maker* of the best class. His room was one of the sort I have described in my preliminary remarks:

"I am a native of ——, in Scotland," he said, "and have been in London a dozen years or so. My mother was left a widow when I was very young, and supported herself and me as a laundress. She got me the very best schooling she could, and a cabinet-maker without some education is a very poor creature. I got to be apprenticed to Mr. ——, who took me because he knew my father. I got on very well with him, and lived at home with my mother. When I had been five years or so at the business I went with my master to Lord ——'s a few miles off, to do some work, and among other things we had to unpack some furniture that had come from London, and to see that it wasn't injured. My lord came in when he had unpacked a beautiful rosewood loo table, and said to my master, 'you can't make a table like that.' 'I think I can, my lord,' said my master, and he got an order for one, and set me to make it as I had seen the London table, but he overlooked me, and it gave great satisfaction, and that first made me think of coming to London, as it gave me confidence in my work. I had only occasional employment from my master when I was out of my time, and as my mother was then dead I started off for London before I got through my bit of money. I walked to Carlisle and was getting very tired of the road, and very footsore. What a lot of thoughts pass through a countryman's mind when he's first walking up to London! At Carlisle I had about a month's work, or better, as an order had just come in to Mr. —— from a gentleman who was going to be married, and the furniture was wanted in a hurry. I gave satisfaction there and that encouraged me. I walked to London all the way, coming by Leeds and Sheffield, and Leicester, and the great towns, where I thought there was the best chance for a job. I didn't get one, though. In my opinion, sir, there ought to be a sort of lodging-house for mechanics and poor people travelling on their honest business. You must either go to a little public-house to sleep, and it's very seldom you can get a bed there under 6d., and many places ask 9d. and 1s. − or you may go to a common lodging-house for travellers, as they call it, and it would sicken a dog. Then, in a public-house, you can't sit by the fire on a wet or cold night without drinking something, whether you require or can afford it or not. I knew nobody in London except two or three seafaring people, and them I couldn't find. I went from place to place for three weeks, asking for work. I wasn't a society man then. At last I called at Mr. ——'s, and met with the master himself. He asked me where I'd worked last, and I said at Mr. ——'s, of ——, and Mr. ——'s, of Carlisle. 'Very respectable men,' said he, 'I haven't a doubt of it, but I never heard their names before. And he then asked me some questions, and called his foreman and said, 'R——, we want hands; I think you might put on this young man; just try him.' So I was put on, and was there four or five years. I had many little things to learn in London ways, to enable a man to get on a little faster with his work, and I will say that I've asked many a good London hand for his opinion, and have had it given to me as a man should give it. I do the same myself now. A good workman needn't be afraid: he won't be hurt. I work by the piece. I have been very fortunate, never having been out of work more than a month or six weeks at a time – but that's great good fortune. These are my earnings for the last eight weeks. I've only lately begun to keep accounts, all at piece-work, and a busy time: 32s. 2d., 41s. 3d., 40s. 1d., 36s., 29s. 6d., 28s., 35s. 10d., 35s. 9d. An average of near 35s. is it? Well, no doubt I make that all the year round. I can keep a wife and child comfortably. I wouldn't hear of my wife working for a slop tailor. I'd rather live on bread and water myself than see it. Slop means slavery. In my opinion, if the black master, or the slaughtermen, as they call them at the other end, didn't keep men always going, or didn't force them to keep them always going, they'd be troubled to get hands. But when men are always struggling for a living, they have no time to think or talk, and so they submit, and, indeed, their wives and families make them submit.''

A young man, well spoken, and well dressed, gave me the following account as to the earnings of a chair-maker of the better class:

''I was brought up as a general hand in the country, in Yorkshire, and in country towns a cabinet-maker makes everything in his own line, and some-times does a little joiner's work. I came right away to London, between eight and nine years ago, as soon as I was out of my time. My master had seven apprentices, and didn't employ any journeymen. His was a 'cutting' shop, but he made very capital furniture, when he had a fair price. I have heard the old men in the trade say that when they were young, 40 or 50 years back, a cabinet-maker wanting work used to try York, or Leeds, or Sheffield, or Manchester, or Liverpool, before he thought of London; but now we all make for London. If a man asks for work at a country master's now, the first question generally is, 'Have you worked in London?' I was two months out of work in London, and then got on for a very good man who fitted up offices in the best style; such as for banks and insurance offices – that's cabinet-maker's work; but it's often done by joiners. We consider that they encroach on our department there. I was at this work about a year, making better than 30s. of a week, and then was out of work seven weeks. I knew a man who worked for a 'linendraper' just started in the tally system, in Westminster; and I went to make a few chairs along with him, just not to be idle. I worked a week alongside of him, and he hawked my chairs on the Saturday with his. For that week's hard work I got 7s. 3d. clear, and my chairs were abused by the tallyman as if they weren't good enough for his rubbishing place. But after he'd growled out his fault-finding, he said 'You may bring the same next week, if you like, at 1s. the half dozen less.' I made a resolution just then and there that I'd starve before I'd touch a piece of slaughter-house stuff again; and I haven't − but then I was a single man, and am still. If I'd had a family, I suppose I must have 'slaughter-housed' on. They couldn't have waited. By pawning my watch I raised 25s., and that kept me going for three weeks, until I got work at a good shop. I had joined the society before, and have been pretty lucky in keeping work ever since. I haven't kept any particular account, but I know I make about 34s. every week. I make nothing but chairs and sofa frames; chiefly drawing-room chairs. I can do best at them, and have been a chairman these four or five years. I'm afraid the linendrapers will pull down the good masters, and down with them must go the good men."

Bedstead making is, as I have stated, a distinct branch of the cabinet-maker's business. It is, however, generally carried on in the same premises as the other branches, but in some establishments bedsteads are the principal manufacture. The bedstead-maker has not to cut out his material in the same way as the cabinet-maker, as the posts are fashioned by the turner or the wood-carver ready for his purpose, and the other portions of his work are prepared by the sawyers in the sizes he requires. He is the putter together of the article, in every part, except the insertion of the sacking bottom, which is the work of the porter.

From a well-informed man, a member of "society," I had the following statement, which embodies information (which I found fully corroborated) of the social condition of the men, and the fashions of the trade. I am informed that in the society of bedstead-makers there is not one unmarried man.

"When I first knew the business, 40 years ago, I could earn at bedstead-making, by hard work, 50s. or 60s. I have heard men brag in a public-house that they could make more than 60s. and masters got to hear of it, and there was great dis-satisfaction. We always work by piece and did so when I was an apprentice in London. The prices paid to society men are, on the whole, the same as in 1811. We all find our own tools, and a good kit is worth £30. I consider the bedstead-makers an intelligent, sober class. I'm speaking of society men − gentlemen I may call them. I don't know much of the others. The majority of us are members of literary institutions, and some of us have saved money. There is great improvement since I first knew bedstead-makers, in point of temperance. There used to be hard drinking and less working. In 1810, when we met for society purposes, our allowance of fourpence a night per man that had to attend was drunk in an hour; now its not consumed in the course of the meeting. Several of us are house-keepers, and can support our wives and families comfortably. I don't think one of the wives of the members of our society work in any way but for the family. I have brought up seven children well, and now five are working at other trades, and two girls at home. Very few good hands now earn less than 30s. a week, and some 8s. or 9s. more I do that, and I've been very rarely out of work. There is no importation of French bedsteads now; there used to be, but they didn't stand. When I first made bedsteads, tents, four-posters, and half-testers were the run; now half testers and tents are never asked for. Then came the Waterloo bed, which turns up with a curtain over it. The French bedstead next came in, with and without canopies. The Arabian bed is the present fashion. It resembles a half-tester. The iron-work has interfered greatly with my trade. I remember when there were no iron bed-steads at all; now —— sends out 60 or 70 in some weeks. The iron bedsteads came into more general use about ten years ago. People fancy they're free of vermin, but I have had to take some to pieces, and have found them full of bugs in the lath and sacking parts. We've no grievances – not a bit of them. I think workmen themselves might remedy some of their grievances. They should be united, and they shouldn't encourage low-priced shops of any kind by buying things there. I pay 12s. a pair for my shoes, and one of my sons tells me it's foolish to do so, but the shoemaker has as good a right to a good week's earnings as I have, and to encourage slop work is to help on our own trouble.''

I shall now concluded with the following statement, which I received from an elderly man, the second member, in point of seniority, of the present Cabinet-makers' Society of the eastern district of London. My informant is a freeman of the Ancient Joiners' Company of the City: –

''I went apprentice to a cabinet-maker,'' he said, ''my friends paying £50 premium with me, a sum which very few can pay now. That was in 1812. Trade was then in full swing. There was a general war in Europe and men and subsidies were required to keep up the armies. When peace came, in 1815, and large armies came to be disbanded, the men naturally sought employment at the trades they were taken from. Then trade came to a stand still. To meet one declining markets, employers began to reduce wages; the corn-laws were passed, so that no great reduction in the price of provision took place. Workmen found they could not get so remunerative a price for their labour, and a great many commenced masters on their own account. Trade not improving caused further competition, so that by the time my term of apprenticeship expired, in 1819, I found the price of work reduced from 20 to 30 per cent. From that period to the present, fashion and style have been continually altering; while those alteration have generally thrown more work into *jobs*, with no proper remunerating pay for the same. Understand at the East-end there is no regular or fixed price to work for – the jobs are invariably what is called "lump" – little day-work employ, with few exceptions. From the above circumstances men have been induced, and especially those who do not belong to the society, to confine themselves to one line of work – taking apprentices and employing youngsters from the country, who are not proficient workmen. Timber-yards now carry on a profitable business by retailing small lots, so that a man can purchase stuff for a job in the same way one can for a pair of shoes – say, for a chest of drawers, the top ends, fronts, sides, &c., &c. So with a table, and other furniture. These articles are hawked from Bethnal-green, Curtain-road, and along Holborn, Fleet-street, taking the west route to Hammersmith and its vicinity, of a Saturday, the wood having been in the timber-yard the Saturday previous." (Here my informant gave an account of the system of hawking to the "slaughter" houses similiar to what I have given, and to the injury they inflicted upon the masters in the honourable trade, as well as upon the men. He continued.) "As for me, I have before now been driven, in a slack time, to purchase material to make up a job; and in some instances I have not been able to realise the price of a day's work, say 5s., above the cost of materials, though upwards of a week has been consumed in manufacturing the article – the consequences being short fare, scanty clothing, a selling and pledging of all the necessary articles of home, neglect of children's education, and, should a longer continuance of want of employment have ensued, every vestige of home must have been swept away. The question seems to me, what are the remedies to be applied to this state of things? An attempt to regulate the price of labour, to legislate for supply and demand, would be to disturb an hornets' nest. Still the general impression of the working classes is, that if a properly constituted Labour Board was established by the Legislature, empowering employers and men to agree to a fair remunerating price of labour in their respective trades, great good would arise. The working classes, it is true, are not themselves free from blame, for they have yet a great power to ensure many advantages, if they would but unite for the best purposes."

In my next Letter I shall give an account of the better-paid fancy cabinet-makers, the carvers, the buhl-cutters, the marqueterie-workers, &c., and I shall then pass on to describe the slop-trade in connection with these different branches of art.

Letter LXIV
Thursday, August 8, 1850

The "art and mystery" of cabinet-making consists of two main branches – "general," and "fancy" cabinet work. The general cabinet-makers, as I have before stated, are employed upon all the large work, such as the manufacture of tables, cheffioniers, bookcases, wardrobes, sideboards, chairs, sofas, couches, and bedsteads. The fancy cabinet-makers, on the other hand, are the "small workers" of the trade, manufacturing the lighter articles, such as desks, dressing-cases, work-tables and boxes, cribbage and chess boards, tea-caddies and tea-chests, &c. In my last Letter I gave a description of the condition and earnings of the "general cabinet-makers," working at the best shops for the best prices. In the present Letter I purpose treating of the other branch of the art – namely, the "fancy" part of it, or rather that portion of the fancy cabinet- workers who belong to the "honourable" trade; reserving till my next communication all account of the cheap or slop work, in connection with this and the "general" branch of cabinet-making.

In almost all trades there are two broadly distinguished classes of workmen, known as "society" and "non-society" men; that is to say, a certain portion (usually about one-tenth of the whole) of the operatives belong to a "society" for upholding the standard rate of wages, as well as supporting their unemployed members. These society-men constitute what may be termed the aristocracy of the trade. They are not only for the most part the more intelligent and respectable of the craft, but by far the more skilful workmen. They are staunch upholders of their order, and the sturdiest of sticklers for what they believe to be their rights. To give them their due, however, if they will not allow their employers to wring any of their body, they also will not permit any of their body to wrong their employers. In the general cabinet-makers' trade, for instance, if a society man overdraws his account with his master, the members make a point of seeing the extra money refunded; so, in the tailors' societies, the members are answerable for the due execution of the work by any of their association. The wages, moreover, which they are bound to uphold, have generally been agreed upon by a committee composed of an equal number of operatives and employers, and in some cases the price-book in which the rate of pay for the making of the different articles belonging to the trade is fixed, has been got up at an expense of several thousand pounds. Further, the sums which they contribute to the support of their members out of work amount to many hundreds in the course of the year.

The wages of "society men," are regulated by *custom;* those of the non-society men, however, are determined solely by *competition*. It is the competitive men who are invariably the cheap workers, and the prey of the slopsellers of every trade. Of the latter class belonging to the cabinet-making trade I shall speak in my next communication. For the present I purpose confining my remarks to the condition and earnings of the society-men employed at the fancy branch of the business.

Let me, however, first give a description of the several kinds of work pertaining to the craft. Of fancy cabinet-makers there are two classes, viz., those engaged in the manufacture of the cases or exteriors, and those employed upon the fitting up or interiors of the different articles produced in the trade. Those employed upon the exteriors are makers of dressing-cases, writing desks, work-boxes and tables, jewel, glove, card, gun, and pistol-cases, chess, and backgammon-boards; tea-caddies and tea-chests (the difference being that the "chest" contains a glass for sugar, while the "caddy" does not). Those employed upon the interiors of the above articles are the "pine-worker," who makes the partitions of work-boxes, &c.; the fitter up, who arranges the compartment of dressing-cases; and the liner, who covers the several parts of the interiors with coloured paper, silk or satin, as the case may be. Contrary to what I have remarked of the "general" trade, the employers of the fancy cabinet-makers require the operatives to confine themselves as much as possible to one especial branch; that is to say, the deskmaker is expected to make only desks – the dressing-case only dressing-cases – and so through all the divisions. I was told that the "scamping," or low-priced, masters encouraged this close division of labour, as they thought it made the men more dependent. A man employed on low terms at desk-making was, for instance, unwilling to leave that for dressing-case making, at which, perhaps, his hand "was out;" and so, to avoid a change, he would submit to reduction upon reduction in his wages. All concurred in asserting that fancy cabinet work is becoming more and more "scampish" every year – the exception of "honourable" employers in it being one in forty. Thus we have another instance of the privations and degradations which working men are called upon to endure, not for the production of the necessaries of life, the articles which the poor and even the pauper must eat and wear, but for the manufacture of *cheap luxuries* – of wares demanded not by necessity, but as a matter of taste, of mere convenience, or mere parade. "If we are fairly paid," said a fancy cabinet-maker to me, "we work all the better, but now quantity is the object with the greater part of us instead of quality. Twenty years ago I had 6d. an inch for the making of a 20-inch desk of solid mahogany – that's 10s. for the entire article; now I've 2s. 3d. for the same thing. Smaller desks, with four brass caps and four brass corners to them, *did* average to us – large and small – 6s. each for wages; now they average to us 1s. large and small, and 1s. extra if inlaid with brass. But prices – that is, masters' prices – have not at all lowered in proportion to the lessening of our wages. Let ladies be told that we've had for making 12-inch workboxes, with plate and 'scutcheon, 3s. 6d. and 4s. a-piece twenty years ago – beautiful wood, rosewood or any fancy thing, and beautiful work, such as a man might feel pride in when he thought it would go into a good lady's hands – and now for such workboxes 5s. a dozen is paid, 5d. a piece, but they're given out in dozens; 7d. a piece, or 7s. a dozen, for better work. Many are half starving in making workboxes and desks for ladies, and can't help themselves." This man spoke with bitter indignation as to the state of his trade.

Desk makers and the other branches of the fancy cabinet trade are further divided into "solids" and "veneers," and the handicraftsman working at the one is unable to work so quickly or well at the other, though he does it when required. The "solid" work is the nicer art. The payment for such work has, however, fallen in a more rapid ration than almost in any other trade. "I don't understand about per cents." was said to me," but this I do know, the prices I get have, within these 20 years, fallen from 4s. to 5d., I might say 4½d., take it at the outside 5d." Another man calculated that twenty-six years ago the wages were from 300 to 400 per cent. better than they are at present. Where they formerly got 15s. they now receive but 5s., or even 4s. Among this class, as among others, I found unanimity in one complaint – that while wages were so much reduced, while all kinds of provisions were much lower in price, the rent of their rooms had increased rather than diminished. I speak of men in "society," be it remembered; the state of the non-society men is still worse. I find, moreover, that masters pretty generally have raised the wages of their men 3d. a dozen within these two months. The other divisions of the craft are those of the "pine-worker" and the "fitter-up." The pine-worker is the man who makes the interior of ladies' workboxes, the divisions for thread, &c. He is, for inferior work, one of the worst paid of all. For the mere labour which, 15 years ago in some cases, and 20 or 25 years ago in all, brought him 2s. 6d., he now receives 6d., and he must, moreover, find the material, which (with glue and glass paper) reduces his 6d. to 4d., and sometimes even to 3d. His tools, new and for repairs, may cost him 6d. a week more. Among these men 12s. is considered a good and full week's work, and frequently they are unemployed. Many pine-workers are, however, continually at work on their own account, without having any definite order, and the work so accumulated is sold to the hawkers to complete the boxes, or is ready incase of a hurried demand. The pine-worker's family sometimes cover the interiors with paper or silk –

and sometimes the masters employ their own workwomen or girls to do so.

The "fitter-up" makes the interior of the dressing-case, as the pine-worker does that of the workbox. The fitter-up usually does nothing else. For the interior of a dressing-case, which, as an average "regulation" in a 12-inch case, must contain partitions for four razors – a pair of boot hooks – two, and sometimes three, places for shaving powders or soaps – a shaving brush – a hair brush – a clothes brush – one, two, or three scent bottles (and gentlemen's dressing-cases now-a-days have generally as many divisions for scent bottles as ladies'), and "a looking glass for the head" – for this work the fitter-up, even of the better class – a "society man" – receives 6d.; but that 6d. is subject to the same deductions as I have recorded in the case of the pine-worker. The "casemaker," as the artisan who makes the exterior case case is called, receives 10s. a dozen, and despite the "fitters-up" being less skilled labourers, they do not unfrequently earn more than the casemakers.

Women are employed in fancy cabinet work as "liners." They affix the paper, or other linings, to work-boxes, but are invariably employed in that department of labour. They do the same usually with dressing-cases, but far less frequently with jewel-cases; "for," said a workman, " jewel-cases generally require greater care and nicety in the lining, and so men do them." The wives and daughters of the workmen are usually the parties thus employed, and concurrent testimony proves the young women thus employed to be virtuous and prudent, with very few exceptions. Of all the branches of the fancy cabinet maker's work, wages for the making of jewel cases have fallen the least. This work requires a very nice admeasurement, an accurate eye, and great tastefulness in the workman, especially when the case is made in "angles;" that is, not to present a flat, but a projecting and receding exterior. The fall within fifteen years has been from twenty to thirty per cent.; but some masters have reduced the wages 200 per cent. for inferior work, and on that the operative and his family may starve while making jewel-cases.

A great quantity of French fancy cabinet-work is imported into London. Of this, however, the better class of workmen made no complaint, as the French work is undersold, sometimes as much as thirty and even fifty per cent., by the London slop work. I found, among the men, moreover, a universal opinion, that French fancy cabinet-work, if more tasteful, or rather – for that was the word used – more "showy" than English work, was less solid, and altogether not so well made; it not very unfrequently dropped asunder, I was told, so that ladies were getting tired of it.

The fancy cabinet-makers are, I am informed, far less political than they used to be. The working singly, and in their own rooms, as is nearly universal with them now, has rendered them more unsocial than they were, and less disposed for the interchange of good offices with their fellow-workmen, as well as less regardful of their position and their rights as skilled labourers. "Politics, sir," said one man, in answer to my inquiry, "what's politics to me, compared to getting my dinner – and what's getting my dinner, compared to getting food for my children?"

The amusements of the cabinet-makers, I was told by one of the older workmen, used to be principally the play. Some were very fond of going to the Polytechnic Institution. "Now, however," he said, "few comparatively can afford the 1s., or 6d. that's wanted, and they go to penny concerts, and get to think that 'Sam Hall' or some nigger case I've seen Liston play *Paul Pry,* and Farren play the *Colonel,* and Mrs. Glover the *Housekeeper.* I think that was the cast at the start, but I'm not quite sure. I went to see it, sir, at least eight times at my own expense. Latterly I've been to the play only once these three years, and then I had an order." Card-playing, dominoes, and games that are carried on without bodily exertion, seem now to be the chief recreations of the fancy cabinet-makers. The fancy cabinet trade has of late years almost entirely sunk into low prices and inferior workmanship. There are still five or six West-end masters who give good wages – six times as much as I have detailed – but none of the masters employ more than two or three hands, and for these hands there is not, at the fancy cabinet trade, half employment, so they become general workmen.

A complete set of fancy cabinetmaker's tools, which they find themelves, is worth £10. The tools of the pine-workers and fitters-up are worth from 40s. to 50s.

Before proceeding to give the subjoined statement of a desk-maker, I premise that "solid" desks are made out of a plank of mahogany, as it comes from the sawyer, or of whatever wood is the material required. This plank the deskmaster has to plane and to cut to his purpose. He has generally the material for twelve desks given to him at once. If the manufacture be "veneers" the same rule is observed, and the journeyman then receives a quantity of deal commensurate to the veneer. The journeyman executes the ink range, or the portion devoted to holding ink bottles, pens, pencils, wafers, &c., and indeed every portion of the work in a desk, excepting the "lining" or covering of the "flaps," or sloping portion prepared for writing. This "lining" is done by females, and their average payment is 15d. a dozen. Desks now are getting "lap-dovetailed;" that is, the side edges of the wood are made to lap over the adjoining portion of the desk.

The person from whom I received the following narrative was an elderly man, and a workman of great intelligence. He resided in a poor and crowded intelligence. He resided in a poor and crowded neighbourhood. His wife was a laundress, and there was a comfortable air of cleanliness in their rooms. I give this man's statement fully, as it contains much that has been repeated to me by others in different branches:

"I've known the London fancy cabinet trade," he said, "for forty-five years, as that's the time when I was apprenticed in London. My father was a button-maker in Birmingham, and gave a premium of fifty guineas with me. But he failed, and came to London, and was for some time a clerk with Rundell and Bridge, the great jewellers. My master was a tyrannical master; but he certainly made a workman of me and of all his apprentices. I don't recollect how many he had. I think that now even a little master treats his apprentices middling well; for if he don't they turn sulky, and he can hardly afford their being sulky, as he depends on them for work and profit, such as it is. I got work in a good shop immediately after I was out of my time. No good hand need, then, be a week out of work. Masters clamoured for a good man. I have made £3 3s. a week, and one week I made £3 15s. For twenty years after that I didn't know what it was to want a job. I once during that time had three letters altogether in my pocket from Mr. Middleton, the great fancy cabinet-maker – you may have heard of Middleton's pencils, for he was the first in that line too – pressing an engagement upon me. Then I prided myself (and so did my mates) that I was a fancy cabinet-maker. I felt myself a gentleman, and we all held our heads like gentlemen. I was very fond at that time of reading all that Charles Lamb wrote, and all that Leigh Hunt wrote. As to reading now, why, if we have a quarter of cheese or butter, I get hold of the paper it's brought in, and read it every word. I can't afford a taste for reading if it's to be paid for. I got married twenty-five years ago, and could live very comfortably then without my wife having to work to help me. We had two houses towards the West-end, and let them out furnished. But twenty years ago, or less, I resisted reductions in our wages, and fought against them. I fought against them for 3¾ years, and things went wrong – uncommon wrong – and I had to sacrifice everything to meet arrears of rent and taxes, and I was seized at last; for it wanted a weekly lift through a man's earnings to keep all prosperous. I've done all sorts of work in my time, but I'm now making desks – 'ladies' school,' or 'writing' – of mahogany, rosewood, and satin-wood. Those are the principal; though every now and then another fancy wood is used. Walnut sawn solid makes a beautiful desk or box. I think walnut's coming into fashion again for that work. Twenty years ago I made 35s. at the least a week the year through. My family then, and for five, six, or seven, or more years after that time, had the treat of smelling a real good tasty Sunday dinner of beef, or pork, or mutton, as it came hot from the baker's, steaming over the potatoes. And after smelling it we had the treat of eating it, with a drop of beer to wash it down. On week days, too, we had the same pretty regular. I've had six children. Now we have still the smell and the taste of a Sunday meat dinner, but there it stops. We have no such dinners for week days. I'm forced now-a-days to work on Sundays too, and almost every Sunday. People may talk as they like about Sunday labour; I know all about it; but an empty cupboard is stronger than everything. If I have the chance I may make 15s. a week at present prices. I work, as we mainly do, at my own bench, in my own place, and find my own tools, glue, glass-paper, candles, and et ceteras; so that my 15s. a week sometimes falls down to 12s. clear. I work for masters, but not always, that find their own materials; but a great many of us have to find material and all. When our work's taken in, if the key breaks, the foreman – and the foreman is often the master's very convenient tool – fines a man 2d., or he may take back the work, and make it good, if he's found the material – that's called 'stopping.' Locks for the low-priced works are paltry, infamous things. Good locks used to be put to good work; they cost 10d. and 1s. for inferior, and averaged 2s. for better, and from 5s. to 7s. for desks and boxes, where security was wanted. Now locks costs 2d. and 2½d. – slop things, that's no safeguard. What was reckoned, and indeed was, inferior box-locks, was 6d., and is now 1½d. Work's huddled together any how. How it'll all end with me is a poser. I suppose in the work-house. I almost always worked at piece-work, and don't object to it when wages are fair; indeed, piece-work is better for a good hand, and he's more independent. If a man was on by day he would be expected to do so much work a week, and that would come to about the same thing. In 1825 or 1826 I had 4s. for making a lady's workbox if it was ordered to be first-rate, as the customer was very particular; 3s. 6d. was the regular wages, and I could make ten or eleven, or, in long days, twelve, in a week. Candlelight isn't well adapted for our trade; and when a man works in his own room, as I've mostly done, and as has been and is the custom in our trade, he don't think of gas. Cheap provisions is a great blessing. No one knows what we suffered in '47, when bread was 11d. to 1s.; and when it was at the highest our wages were reduced. When I was first a journeyman I had 10s. for making a 20 inch desk, and it fell to 8s., and 7s., and 6s., and by little and littles down to what it is now, 4s.; and it's pretty well two days' work to make it properly, but it aint made properly nineteen times out of twenty. It can't be done at the money. Perhaps a scamping hand might make five such things in a week, or six if he worked on Sundays, and if we was kept regularly at it, but he never is, or very seldom. In my young days an inferior hand couldn't get work in London; now he has a better chance. I think that machinery has been a benefit to us: it increases the material for our work. If there wasn't so much veneering there wouldn't be so much fancy cabinet-work. To show how wages have fallen, I'll mention this. A month back I walked through the Lowther-arcade, and saw fancy boxes, made of different kinds of wood, marked 2s. 6d., and I've had twenty years ago – aye, and fifteen years ago, but not so often – 3s. for the more making of them, and found nothing at all. The material couldn't cost less than 1s. or from that to 1s. 6d. altogether. Such boxes are plastered together by boys – or most likely by girls, if a man has sharpish girls in his family, and works at his own bench. Hawkers have sold such boxes so that they didn't get 1½d. a piece for making them. The French goods, in my opinion, don't harm us now; they did at one time. I fancy that little masters sprung up twenty years ago, and have gone on increasing. How many of them there are I don't know; Lord knows there's too many. I'm satisfied that a scamping hand will do his work in one quarter of the time that a good hand will. I can't scamp. A man must be brought up to it to do it.''

Work-boxes, whether solid or veneered, are made after the same plan as desks; the "pine-worker's" portion of the labour being always done independently of the case-making. The lining, as I said before, is the work of women and girls.

The work-box maker whom I saw gave me a statement not dissimilar to that of the desk-maker. Like him, he was an old man, had been regularly apprenticed to the trade, and had passed his youth in comfort and respectability. He got married when he was between forty and fifty, and after that the expense of a family, together with the falling off in the wages of his business, exhausted whatever he had accumulated, and he was reduced to poverty. He told me he thought of trying the country, the neighbourhood of Bath, for employment, as there he had friends. He is still known as a first-rate workman. He is slow, I was told, but firm and solid. He would rather trundle a barrow, he said, at Covent Gardens – if he could get one to trundle – than do what he was doing. For every 35s. that he earned in a week twenty years ago – and he had on rare occasions, and working night and day, earned 63s. – he now earned from 9s. to 12s. and had a wife and five children to support. He couldn't adapt himself to the demands of the scamping masters, and so, as he must work slow and well, he wasn't for their turn.

Dressing-cases are made after the same mode as work-boxes. The material is given out by the employer and prepared by the workmen. Nine out of every ten dressing-cases made at present are veneered. Three-fourths of the veneers are now rosewood; mahogany being less and less used. Some dressing-caes are made of deal and covered with ornamental leather, but these belong to the department of "the pine-worker." The interior is made by "the fitter-up," and the furniture, the bottles, brushes, &c., are added by "the shopkeeper," as the cutler, toyman, perfumer, silversmith, or whatever tradesman supplies the case to the customer, is called. From one of the most respectable workmen in the trade (as I was assured) I had the following statement. I found him at work in what is generally the under-ground kitchen of a small house, but which, with him, was altogether devoted to the purposes of a workshop:

"I have been ten years in the trade, and am a 'society man.' I think if our society were more numerous it would be far better both for masters and men. These cases here are twelve inches. They have twelve brass corner-hoops and four brass caps. I get 3s. a piece for making them. No doubt, at a first-rate. West-end shop, I should have 9s., or 10s. a piece for the work, but in those shops it's odd jobs only that way, and under employers such as mine we have a quantity in at one time, and so can keep at work regularly. I was not apprenticed, but served five years to the trade under an agreement, which is the same thing. Sometimes the master or foreman affixes the fitter's-up work himself – indeed generally so; sometimes it's sent to us to have that done. By working long hours I can make eight of these boxes a week. For average hours, say ten hours a day, I can make 20s. a week at my work, but against that there's the wear and tear of tools, which I find myself; there's the expense of glue and glass-paper, and so the 20s. is about 18s. clear. I make also common dressing-cases, which have no brass corners or caps. They are 1s. a piece. A good hand is expected to be able to make two dozen of them in a week, but he won't make more money at them than at the better ones. There's all the more glue, &c., used. We send our work home unvarnished. A French polisher does the varnishing.''

The making of tea-chests and tea-caddies does not differ from the making of dressing-cases; but the whole work is done by one man. The earnings are in the same ratio. There is no subordinate branch of fitters-up. The 20-inch chests are 5s. in a middling, and 7s. in a good shop for wages, and as low as 3s. 6d. among the worst-paid workmen, and out of this, too, deductions for glue, &c., have to be made.

A young man gave me the following account. As with other branches, the pine-worker saws, planes, and in all respects prepares the material as it is given out by him by the master:

"I served seven years apprenticeship as a fitter-up of dressing-cases, and most in my line do the same. We most of us serve apprenticeships. I served with a little master, for he was so then, but he is now a large master. I was an in-door apprentice, and had no fault to find with my usage. I now do journey-work, and have done so for six or seven years. The material is given to us by our employers; it is always clean pine, and we have it in "leaf stuff," that is the whole or half the length of the tree from which it is cut. It is cut at the veneer mills, 4 or 5-cut we call it; that is, 4 or 5 cuts to the inch in thickness. We are paid by the dozen. The largest size I have made in dressing-cases is 20 inches in length, and in that may be a dozen partitions. By hard work and long hours, a man may earn 20s. a week at fitting-up – that's of the best description of work. Trade's uncertain. I'm not to call busy above six months in the year – the spring and summer parts. After that I have only about half or three-quarters work in the week, and sometimes none at all. 14s. a dozen is the price for fitting-up a dozen 20 inch desks, and other sizes in proportion. I've nothing at all to complain of. I'm not a married man, and have only myself to care for.''

A pine-worker for a better-class shop gave me information almost identical as to prices and employment.

The "liners," a class of which I have previously spoken, are, with the exception of those employed in the "getting up" of jewel cases, invariably women. To execute the work tastefully and skilfully, and with an economy of material, no little tuition and no little skill is necessary. From a respectable young woman, residing in a good house, with a large garden in front, who, I was informed, was the best in the trade, I had the following information:

"I was brought up to the business, and I think every person, to do the work well, ought to be. I now live here with my sister. My friends were in the line. The work of the better class is usually given out to the liners at their own houses, at it is now generally to me. It is my business to cut it so as to fit it precisely to the parts of the work required to be lined. I have in this way every kind of coloured paper given to me for lining, as well as all colours and qualities in silks, satins, and velvets. I use both paste and gum, but each must be of the best and most delicate kind. I do not work by any regular scale of prices, so I cannot give prices. I only do the best work, and for houses where I am known. I take or send the work in when completed, and receive what the master thinks proper. But my own labour I can make from 15s. to 20s. every week. I have sometimes to employ an assistant. I had rather not state anything more; indeed I don't know anything more that I have to state. I have understood that many women in my line are wretchedly paid and wretchedly off, but of their earnings or their characters I know nothing personally."

Such is an account of the earnings of those working at the better-paid branches of the Fancy Cabinet-trade. There are, however, several descriptions of work, belonging both to the general and fancy trade, that still remain to be described. These are the Marqueterie-workers, the Buhl-cutters, and the Wood-carvers – each of these having, like the other branches, its skilled and slop-labourers. I shall for the present merely give an account of the more skilful and better-paid workmen belonging to these arts.

The beautiful art of *Marqueterie,* which had fallen somewhat into disuse in this country, experienced a revival ten or twelve years ago. Marqueterie is the inlaying of coloured woods, so as to present a group of flowers, or any object, in their proper forms and appropriate hues. It is generally used for the adornment of furniture, such as ladies' work-tables and loo tables, but it is sometimes – though very rarely in this country – applied to the internal decoration of a house. There is an inlaid floor in Buckingham Palace, executed by order of George IV.; but the workmanship, I am informed, is inferior to that of the present day, as, at the time the floor was inlaid, there were not three thoroughly good artificers in marqueterie in England. The woods used in this art are holly, pear-tree, and sycamore, which are all fine-grained, and take the dye readily; for the wood used is all dyed, and always worked from veneers. Four veneers are held firmly together in a frame, and the outer veneer has been marked, after a drawing, to the pattern to be cut. The workman in cutting uses saws made out of the hardest-tempered, thinnest, and narrowest watch-springs; the saw is attached to a slender frame, and forms what may be described as the string of a bow, and this fine saw, which is made by the workman himself, is directed according to the pattern marked until the shape required is cut out. No cavity can be seen where the saw has done its work, so fine and delicate is the process. Thus four portions are cut at one operation. By the old system each veneer was dyed *before* it was sawn, and so there was a uniformity of colour, which made a group of flowers, for instance, look flat, hard, and unnatural.

About four or five years ago, however, Mr. Bayles, who lately received, at the hands of Prince Albert, the prize awarded by the Society of Arts for the finest specimen of marqueterie, introduced a decided improvement. Mr. Bayles dyes the woods *after* they have been cut, and by his peculiar art gives them the great advantage of "shading." For his dyes he resorts both to boiling and scorching the wood. When the respective portions of the pattern are cut out, they are fitted together and fixed to the furniture. The making of the furniture, apart from the marqueterie, is the work of the cabinet-maker, who now uses walnut for the material of the table, or whatever be the furniture, more frequently than any other wood; as the flowing and delicate shades of walnut blend best with the hues of the marqueterie.

Of the English workmen in this art there are now in London upwards of 100, of whom eight or nine are pronounced highly accomplished artists, the others being for the most part those engaged in the mechanical portion of the art. The divisions in the trade are the designer, cutter, dyer, and putter-together. The departments of the designer and dyer require the largest amount of skill. Twenty-five years ago the marqueterie workers could earn 30s. a day, and be employed, if they chose, the year through. Now the best hands earn 7s. and 8s. a-day, the employment being all by the day, and the work, is more uncertain – nine months in the year, or somewhat less than nine, being the average of employment. The marqueterie workers find their own tools, which are chiefly their saws. They have no society, but are steady men, and pretty well informed. I was told that they might, as a body, advantageously interest themselves more in the progress of the fine arts, were it but to the same extent as the wood carvers. The mode of acquiring a knowledge of the trade is by apprenticeship, it being at least twelve months before a boy can be of any use with his saw. The great decline in the wages of the men has been in the last two years, when their wages fell in some cases about one half, having gradually fallen from the 30s. a day of 25 years ago. The decline was owing to the great influx of foreigners practising this art who hurried over from France and Germany on the breaking out of the revolutions, and who continue to arrive still. The prices of marqueterie work fell at once about 100 per cent from the competition, and the English masters were compelled to reduce wages. The foreigners now employed in marqueterie in London are about double the number of the English. They are about double the number of the English. They are not considered superior, and rarely equal, workmen to the English, as they do not excel in "effect." As to whether the work of the Englishman or the foreigner may be the more durable, there is hardly a means of judging; for, as was observed to me, "no man can expect to outlive a marqueterie table." The impression is, however, that the English work is the best adapted for durability.

The habits of the foreigners, I am told, are sober and penurious. They manifest little care for what an English artisan frequently prides himself upon – "a respectable appearance;" and, indeed, show no great regard for the comforts or decencies of life. "Ten or twelve of them," I was told by a person (an Englishman) familiar with their habits, "master and men, all pig together, sleeping where they work."

A very intelligent man, in a very comfortable abode, gave me the following account:

"I've been a buhl-cutter for fourteen years, and served a seven years' apprenticeship to it, and then became a little master on my own account. There are very few journeymen among us; we are mostly little masters. There are two kinds of buhl cutting, 'plain' and 'French ornament.' The plain is mother of pearl laid on to the veneer; the 'French ornament' is brass and green shell (foreign snail shell) greatly variegated. The brass is cut first and fitted into the wood, and then the brass is cut to admit the green shell, and cut by myself or my fellows in the trade. It is an art demanding the utmost nicety. I work almost entirely by my eye, but the slopworkers make a sad mess of it. The buhl worker then introduces a wire scroll into the pattern, and a few little brass pips (tacks). When finished, I clean it off with a 'toothing iron' and a file. When it's so cleaned off, it's sent to the cabinet-maker, and he must be a first-rate workman for the French ornament work. Then it's sent back to me to engrave. There are not above 20 good buhl-cutters in London, and none anywhere else. Of an interior sort there may be 100. The pearl-worker prepares the material for us, grinding it down to a uniform charge by the job. I could once earn £1 a day, but now I can only earn £2 a week. The slop-fellows get my good patterns, and I form my own patterns and we all do, and they imitate our patterns. I adopt a pattern now and then from any tasteful engraving I see, or anything in my way. My tools are all very small and niggling, and will cost altogether about £5. The chief tool for size is called 'a neddy' with the shops, which is something like a saddler's or boot-closer's claims, but we do not hold it between our legs – we sit astride on the frame, and so go to work with our saws. Another of our principal tools is a frame-saw. I defy anybody to learn our business without great practice. It's a business always changing, and always demanding some new exercise of skill. When my work has been fitted into the dressing-case, or whatever it may be, the cabinet-maker completes the article, and then it is sent back to be 'engraved up,' – generally crests, cyphers, and coats of arms. We have no scale of prices, and no society. Jobbing is generally 9d. an hour, because master must have a profit after mine, but I've little jobbing. The first worker in buhl in this country was a German – I forget his name – between twenty and thirty years ago. He did well, but would not communicate his secret. A man he employed found out his secret, and improved upon it, and so the art grew. The best buhl-cutter after that is now in Birmingham, and very poor. His style is altogether superseded.''

The *carvers of wood,* for cabinet-making and other purposes, are divided into the carvers of hard and white woods. The carving of the hard woods, such as oak, walnut, mahogany, and rosewood, now comprises the most skilled portion of the art. At one period, and indeed up to the time when George IV. (then Regent) renewed many of the ornaments of Windsor Castle, under the direction of Sir J. Wyattville, the carving of the white woods was the most skilled. The white woods carved are chiefly pine and lime tree. The white-wood carver, until within the last fifty years, executed the work for the gilder's purposes, such as picture and mirror frames, but now such labour is entirely superseded by the use of composition ornaments and machine-cut mouldings. There are still some very tasteful and elegant artificers in white-wood carving, and in the Grinling Gibbons' style – game, fruits, and trophies being so carved in lime. The art reached its perfection in the hands of Grinling Gibbons. I am assured, however, on the best authority, that many carvings have been sold as Gibbons's which were far more modern than his era. Mowatt, a Frenchman, exhibited great skill in the flowers he executed at Windsor Castle for George IV., and may be considered to rank next to Gibbons. Mowatt is less bold in style, more conventional, but remarkable for delicacy and finish. (These opinions, it is right I should state, were what I heard expressed by a working man.) Hard-wood carving is now chiefly required for furniture, such as mahogany sideboards, &c., also for church work – oak being then the material on which the artificer's skill is exerted. The styles most popular now for churches are the Norman-Gothic, and the early English. Very little of the mediaeval style is at present, or has been lately, demanded from the wood-carvers. The most recent style introduced is the Italian, "which is becoming," I was told, "the most fashionable for churches, though introduced less than five years ago." Until the revival of this art, which is within these twenty years, the styles followed were the Roman and Louis Quatorze. Then sprung up a demand for the Elizabethan and *renaissance* (Italian) styles, and the demand has progressed, and very superior skill has been elicited. I heard this revival of a taste for the wood-carver's beautiful and enduring art attributed, among other causes, to the establishment of the Schools of Design in Somerset-house. Until then there was, I was told, really no artistic education for the young wood-carver. The opening of Hampton-court, &c., to the public, I was assured by a practical man in the trade, with great powers and means of observation, had tended to create and foster this taste. The Houses of Parliament, too, at one time gave employment to eighty wood carvers, and another impetus was thus given to the progress of the trade, but the eighty are now reduced to twenty. They are paid from 36s. to £2 a week. The grotesque figures of animals in the Gothic church-carvings are accounted the most difficult portion of the art. Figure-carving is also the "high art" of furniture woodwork, and is demanded most for sideboards, but not to any very great extent. The figures so carved are chimerae, fruits, flowers, "strap-work" (interlacing bands), and foliage. The rate of wages in this business ranges from 30s. to £3 a week; 36s. being about the average earnings of the operative when at work. His employment, however, is very uncertain, being greatly dependent on the outlay of the wealthier classes in tasteful furniture and decorative embellishments. Within the knowledge of my informant, the trade suffered greatly after the panic of 1826, and after every subsequent panic. "The passing of the Reform Bill," said a trades-man of the first class to me, "depressed wood-carving to a great degree, as many members of the aristocracy became alarmed, and put a check on their accustomed patronage of art." Even now the trade, I am informed, has hardly recovered from the depressing effects of the panic of '47, many excellent workmen being unemployed. The wood-carvers of the best class number from 250 to 300. Those of an inferior and underpaid description, residing chiefly in Moor-fields, the Curtain-road, and Bethnal-green, are about as numerous. These men are wretchedly paid for so skilled a kind of labour, some not earning 15s. a week. They work in their own rooms, or have a bench and sleep under it. The West-end carvers used to be altogether employed on the cabinet-maker's premises – an arrangement, however, now becoming less prevalent. Machinery has not affected the purely artistic portion of the carver's business, but it has been applied (six such machines are now in use at the new Houses of Parliament) to "rough out" the carving. The men of the best class are paid both by the piece and the day. If by day, a good workman receives 6s. and 7s., and can generally earn about that by piece work. They have a society (to which employers are admissible), but it is only for the obtaining of casts and books required for the artificers' advancement in their calling. There is no benefit society, nor any which at all deals with the regulation of wages. The wood-carvers are now a remarkably well conducted class. Some have saved money, and others have insured their lives. "I don't know," said one of them, "an habitual drunkard in my trade, but I only speak of the West-end workmen, as I'm acquainted with none else; but I fear that, except in the very highest departments of furniture work, they will be driven down by Moorfields competition, and then they may take to drink." About twenty-five years ago nearly all the best workmen (most of them Scotchmen) were hard drinkers. At that time the body was not a third, perhaps not more than a quarter, so numerous as it is now, and the men easily earned £4 a week. The majority, or a very large proportion, of wood-carvers are now countrymen, the best "Gothic" carvers are now countrymen, the best "Gothic" carvers coming from Norwich, Lincoln, and other cathedral towns. There are no foreigners among these operatives. The restoration of York Cathedral did little for the art, as, at the time of Jonathan Martin's incendiarism, a great deal of the carved wood work was sent to be executed in Holland for cheapness. Apprenticeship is the mode by which the young wood-carver is taught his business in London, and generally by apprenticeship to small masters. An average fee is £15 out of doors, and £40 or £50 if in doors. Country apprentices usually, as it is called, "try London," and many of them remain. For two years a boy is almost use less as an assistant in the carving. The wood-carvers find their own tools. They are almost entirely gouges, with which the artificer scoops out the wood to the pattern, drawing, or model spread before him on his bench. A good set of tools is worth £5, and the wear and tear of them will not amount to 1s. a week. There are no recognised subdivisions in this trade; but if an artificer manifests peculiar skill in any one department, he is frequently employed in that department – as in the carving of Gothic figures, for instance. This, done by piece, ensures the highest amount of remuneration. There is no scale of prices; merely an understanding or an arrangement as to the amount between master and man. The regulation, however, as to employment in one particular branch, is dependent on an employer's discretion. The same workmen are employed on side-boards as are employed on fonts and pulpits.

LETTER LXV
Thursday, August 15, 1850

The Cabinet Makers, socially as well as commercially considered, consist, like all other operatives, of two distinct classes; that is to say, of "society" and "non-society men," or, in the language of political economy, of those whose wages are regulated by *custom,* and those whose earnings are determined by *competition.* The former class numbers between six and seven hundred of the trade, and the latter between four and five thousand. As a general rule, I may remark that I find the "society men" of every trade comprise about one-tenth of the whole. Hence it follows, that if the non-society men are neither so skilful nor so well conducted as the others, at least they are quite as important a body, from the fact that they constitute the main portion of the trade. The transition from the one class to the other is, however, in most cases, of a very disheartening character. The difference between the tailor at the West-end, working for the better shops at the better prices, and the poor wretch slaving at "starvation wages" for the sweaters and slop-shops at the East-end, has already been pointed out. The same marked contrast was also shown to exist between the society and non-society boot and shoemakers. The Carpenters and Joiners told the same story. There we found society men renting houses of their own – some paying as much as £70 a year – and the non-society men overworked and underpaid, so that a few weeks' sickness reduced them to absolute pauperism. Nor, I regret to say, can any other tale be told of the Cabinet Makers – except it be that the competitive men in this trade are even in a worse position than in any other. I have already portrayed to the render the difference between the homes of the two classes – the comfort and well-furnished abodes of the one, and the squalor and bare walls of the other. But those who wish to be impressed with the social advantages of a fairly-paid class of mechanics should attend a meeting of the Wood-carvers' Society. On the first floor of a small private house in Tottenham-street, Tottenham-court-road, is, so to speak, the museum of the working men belonging to this branch of the Cabinet Makers. The walls of the back room are hung round with plaster casts of some of the choicest specimens of the arts, and in the front room the table is strewn with volumes of valuable prints and drawings in connection with the craft. Round this table are ranged the members of the society – some forty or fifty were there on the night of my attendance, discussing the affairs of the trade. Among the collection of books may be found "The Architectural Ornaments and Decorations of Cottingham," "The Gothic Ornaments of Pugin," "Tatham's Greek Relics," "Raphael's Pilaster Ornaments of the Vatican," "Le Pautre's Designs," and "Baptiste's Collection of Flowers" (large size) – while among the casts are articles of the same choice description. The objects of this society are, in the words of the preface to the printed catalogue, "To enable wood-carvers to co-operate for the advancement of their art, and by forming a collection of books, prints, and drawings, to afford them facilities for self-improvement, also by the diffusion of information among its members, to assist them in the exercise of their art, as well as to enable them to obtain employment." The society does not interfere in the regulation of wages in any other way than by the diffusion of information on the subject, so that "both employers and employed may, by becoming members, promote their own and each other's interests." The collection is now much enlarged, and, with the additions which have been made to it, offers aid to the members which in many cases is invaluable. As a means of facilitating the use of this collection, the opportunities of borrowing from it have been made as general as possible. The meetings of the society are held at a place where attendance is unaccompanied by expense; and "they are therefore," says the preface, "free from all objection on account of inducements to exceed the time required for business." All this appears to be in the best possible taste, and the attention of the society being still directed to its improvement, assuredly gives the members, as they say, "good reason to hope that it will become one of which the wood-carver may be proud, as affording valuable assistance both in the design and execution of any style of wood-carving." In the whole course of my investigations I have never experienced more gratification than I did on the evening of my visit to this society. The members all gave evidence, both in manner and appearance, of the refining character of their craft; and it was indeed a hearty relief from the scenes of squalor, misery, dirt, vice, ignorance, and discontent with which these inquiries too frequently bring one into connection, to find oneself surrounded with an atmosphere of beauty, refinement, comfort, intelligence, and ease.

The public generally are deplorably misinformed as to the character and purpose of Trade Societies. The common impression is that they are combinations of working men, instituted and maintained solely with the view of exacting an exorbitant rate of wages from their employers, and that they are necessarily connected with "strikes," and with sundry other savage and silly means of attaining this object. It is my duty, however, to make known that the rate of wages which such societies are instituted to uphold has, with but few exceptions, been agreed upon at a conference of both masters and men, and that in almost every case I find the members as strongly opposed to "strikes," as a means of upholding them, as the public themselves. But at all events the maintenance of the standard rate of wages is not the *sole* object of such societies – the majority of them being organised as much for the support of the sick and aged as for the regulation of the price of labour; and even in those societies whose efforts are confined to the latter purpose alone, a considerable sum is subscribed annually for the subsistence of their members when out of work. The General Cabinet Makers, I have already shown, have contributed towards this object as much as £1,000 per annum for many years past. It is not generally known how largely the community is indebted to the Trade and Friendly societies of the working classes dispersed throughout the kingdom, or how much expense the public is saved by such means in the matter of poor-rates alone.

According to the last Government Returns, there are at present in England, Scotland, and Ireland, upwards of 33,000 such societies, 14,000 of which are enrolled, and 8,000 unenrolled – the remaining 11,000 being secret associations, such as the Odd-Fellows, Foresters, Druids, Old Friends, and Rechabites. The number of members belonging to those 33,000 societies is more than three millions; the gross annual income of the entire associations is £4,980,000; and their accumulated capital – £11,360,000. The working people of this country, and, I believe, of this country alone, contribute therefore to the support of their own poor nearly five millions of money every year, which is some thousands of pounds more than was dispensed in parochial relief throughout England and Wales in 1848. Hence it may be truly said that the benefits conferred by the Trade and Friendly societies of the working classes are not limited to the individuals receiving them, but are participated by every ratepayer in the kingdom; for, were there no such institutions, the poor-rates must necessarily be doubled.

I have been thus explicit on the subject of Trade Societies in general, because I know there exists in the public mind a strong prejudice against such institutions, and because it is the fact of belonging to some such society which invariably distinguishes the better class of workmen from the worse. The competitive men, or cheap workers, seldom or never are members of any association, either "enrolled" or "unenrolled;" the consequence is, that, when out of work, or disabled from sickness or old age, they are left to the parish to support. It is the slop-workers of the different trades – the cheap men, or non-society hands – who constitute the great mass of paupers in this country. And here lies the main social distinction between the workmen who belong to society, and those who do not – the one maintain their own poor, the others are left to the mercy of the parish. The wages of the competitive men are cut down to a bare subsistence, so that, being unable to save anything from their earnings, a few days' incapacity from labour drives them to the workhouse for relief. In the matter of machinery, not only is the cost of working the engine but the wear and tear of the machine considered as a necessary part of the expense of production. With the human machine, however, it is different − slop wages being sufficient to defray only the cost of keeping it at work, but not to compensate for the wear and tear of it. Under the allowance system of the old poor-law, wages, it is well known, were reduced far below subsistence point, and the workmen were left to seek parish relief for the remainder; and so, in the slop part of every trade, the under-paid workmen, when sick or aged, are handed over to the State to support.

As an instance of the truth of the above remarks, I subjoin the following statement which has been furnished to me by the Chairmakers' Society concerning their outgoings:

Average number of members, 110

Paid to unemployed members from 1841−1850	£1,256	10	0
Ditto for insurance of tools	211	10	0
Ditto loss of time by fire	19	2	8
Ditto funerals of members	120	15	0
Ditto collections for sick	60	4	0

"The objects which the London chairmakers have in view by associating in a Trade Society," says the written statement from which the above account is extracted, "is to insure, as near as possible, one uniform price for the work they execute, so that the employer shall have a guarantee in making his calculations that he will not be charged more or less than his neighbours, who employ the same class of men; to assist their members in obtaining employment, and a just remuneration for the work they perform; to insure their tools against fire; to provide for their funerals in the event of death; and to relieve their members when unemployed or in sickness; − the latter being effected by paying persons to collect voluntary subscriptions for invalid members (such subscriptions producing on an average £5 in each case). The members have, moreover, other modes of assisting each other when in difficulties."

I may as well here subjoin the statement I have received from this society, concerning the circumstances affecting their business:

"Our trade," say they, in a written communication to me, "has suffered very materially from a change which took place about thirty years ago in the system of work. We were at that time chiefly employed by what we term 'Trade-working masters,' who supplied the upholsterers with the frames of chairs and sofas; but since then we have obtained our work directly from the sellers. At first the change was rather beneficial than otherwise. The employer and his salesman, however, have now, in the greater number of instances, no knowledge of the manufacturing part of the business, and this is very detrimental to our interest, owing to their being unacquainted with the value of the labour part of the articles we make. Moreover the salesman sends all the orders he can out of doors to be made by the middleman, though the customer is led to believe that the work is executed on the premises; whereas only a portion of it is made at home, and that chiefly the odd and out of the way work, because the sending of such work out of doors would not answer the end of cheapness. The middleman, who executes the work away from the premises, subdivides the labour to such an extent that he is enabled to get the articles made much cheaper, as well as to employ both unskilful workmen and apprentices. Placed in the position where the employer gets the credit of paying us the legitimate price for our labour, it would appear that we have no cause of complaint; but owing to the system of things before stated, as well as to the number of linendrapers, carpet-makers, and others who have recently entered the trade, without having any practical knowledge of the business, together with the casualty of our employment, our social position has become scarcely any better, or so good, as that of the unskilful or the dissipated workmen; while from the many demands of our fellow-operatives upon us in the shape of pecuniary assistance, we have a severe struggle to maintain anything like a respectable footing in the community. The principal source of regret with us is, that the public have no knowledge of the quality of the articles they buy. The sellers, too, from their want of practical acquaintance with the manufacturing part of the business, have likewise an injurious effect upon our interests, instead of seconding our efforts to keep up a creditable position in society.

"The subjoined is the amount of the capital of our society at the present time:

Property in the Funds £300
Out at use 175
Other available property in the shape of Price-books, &c.* 200
                                                                    ____
                                                                    £675"

* "The Price-books are our exclusive right as well as copyright, we selling them to masters, journeymen, and the trade, and deriving a profit therefrom."

Such, then, is the state of the society men belonging to the Cabinet Makers' trade. These, as I before said, constitute that portion of the work-men whose wages are regulated by custom, and it now only remains for me to set forth the state of those whose earnings are determined by competition. Here we shall find that the wages a few years since were from three to four hundred per cent better than they are at present — 20s. having formerly been the price paid for making that for which the operatives now receive only 5s., and this notwithstanding that the number of hands in the London trade from 1831 to 1841 declined 33 per cent relatively to the rest of the popula-tion. Nor can it be said that this extraordinary depreciation in the value of the cabinet-maker's labour has arisen from any proportionate decreases in the quantity of work to be done. The number of houses built in the metropolis has of late been considerably on the increase. Since 1839 there have been 200 miles of new streets formed in London — no less than 6,405 new dwellings having been erected annually since that time; and as it is but fair to assume that the majority of these new houses must have required new furniture, it is clear that it is impossible to account for the decline in the wages of the trade in question upon the assumption of an equal decline in the quantity of work. How, then, are we to explain the fact, that while the hands have decreased 33 per cent and work increased at a considerable rate, wages a few years ago were 300 per cent better than they are at present?

The solution of the problem will be found in the extraordinary increase that has taken place within the last twenty years of what are called "garret masters" in the cabinet trade. These garret masters are a class of small "trade-working masters," supplying both capital and labour. They are in manufacture what "the peasant proprietors" are in agriculture – their own employers and their own workmen. There is, however, this one marked distinction between the two classes – the garret master cannot, like the peasant proprietor, *eat* what he produces; the consequence is that he is obliged to convert each article into food immediately he manufactures it, no matter what the state of the market may be. The capital of the garret master being generally sufficient to find him in materials for the manufacture of only one article at a time, and his savings being but barely enough for his subsistence while he is engaged in putting those materials together, he is compelled, the moment the work is completed, to part with it for whatever he can get. He cannot afford to keep it even a day, for to do so is generally to remain a day unfed. Hence, if the market be at all slack, he has to force a sale by offering his goods at the lowest possible price. What wonder, then, that the necessities of such a class of individuals should have created a special race of employers, known by the significant name of "slaughter-house men" – or that these, being aware of the inability of the "garret masters" to hold out against any offer, no matter how slight a remuneration it affords for their labour, should continually lower and lower their prices until the entire body of the competitive portion of the cabinet trade is sunk in utter destitution and misery. Moreover, it is well known how strong is the stimulus among peasant proprietors, or, indeed, any class working for themselves, to extra production. So it is, indeed, with the garret masters; their industry is almost incessant, and hence a greater quantity of work is turned out by them, and continually forced into the market, than there would otherwise be. What though there be a brisk and a slack season in the cabinet-maker's trade as in the majority of others – slack or brisk, the garret masters must produce the same excessive quantity of goods. In the hope of extricating himself from his overwhelming poverty he toils on, producing more and more – and yet the more he produces the more hopeless does his position become; for the greater the stock that he thrusts into the market, the lower does the price of his labour fall, until at last he and his whole family work for less than half what he himself could earn a few years back by his own unaided labour.

Another cause of the necessity of the garret master to part with his goods as soon as made, is the large size of the articles he manufactures, and the consequent cost of conveying them from slaughterhouse to slaughterhouse till a purchaser be found. For this purpose a van is frequently hired; and the consequence is that he cannot hold out against the "slaughterer's" offer, even for an hour, without increasing the expense of carriage, and so virtually reducing his gains. This is so well known at the slaughter-houses, that if a man, after seeking in vain for a fair remuneration for his work, is goaded by his necessities to call at a shop a second time to accept a price that he had previously refused, he seldom obtains what was first offered him. Sometimes, when he has been ground down to the lowest possible sum, he is paid late on a Saturday night with a cheque, and forced to give "the firm" a liberal discount for cashing it.

For a more detailed account, however, of the iniquities practised upon this class of operatives, I refer the reader to the statements given below. It will be there seen that all the modes by which work can be produced cheap are in full operation. The labour of apprentices and children is the prevailing means of production. I heard of one small trade working master, who had as many as eleven apprentices at work for him; and wherever the operative is blessed with a family, they all work, even from six years old; for it is generally in the worst paid trades that the labour of children is valuable, and hence a premium is given for the over population of a business that is already too fully stocked with hands. The employment of any undue number of apprentices – a system which I find is invariably adopted in those trades where the remuneration has fallen below the standard of men's labour – also tends to increase the very excess of hands from which the trade is suffering; and thus it is that the lower wages become, the lower still they are reduced. There are very few – some told me there were none, but there are a few – who work as journeymen for "little masters"; but these men become little masters in their turn, or they must starve in idleness, for their employment is precarious. There is among the East-end cabinet makers no society, no benefit or sick fund, and very little communion between the different classes. The chair-maker knows nothing of the table maker next door, and cannot tell whether others in his calling thrive better or worse than he does. These men have no time for social intercommunication. The stuggle to live absorbs all their energies, and confines all their aspirations to that one endeavour. Their labour is devoted, with the rarest exceptions, to the "slaughter-houses," "linen-drapers," "polsterers," or "warehouses." By all these names I heard the shopkeepers who deal in furniture of all kinds, as well as drapery-goods, designated. These shopkeepers pay the lowest possible prices, and in order to insure a bare livelihood under them, the cabinet-makers must work very rapidly. This necessity has led the men to labour only at one branch, at which an artisan becomes expert; but he can do little or nothing else, and that again makes him more dependent on the warehouses. The loo table maker only makes loo tables; the cheffonier maker, only cheffoniers. The men find their own material, and hawk the article when completed to the different warehouses. Even a wet Saturday is a disadvantage to the poor artizan, for his goods become either damaged, or lose their freshness of appearance if they get wet, and the man is unwilling to subject them to a further wetting by exposing them still further to the weather, so that often enough, rather than take his goods back or hawk them to another warehouse, the poor fellow accepts the first warehouse-man's paltry offer. "One Saturday afternoon, sir," said a respectable artizan to me, "I happened to hear a slaughter-house keeper say, 'I hope to God it'll rain hard to-night, that'll put £20 into my pocket.' " The necessity of raising money on a Saturday night, to buy materials on Monday morning for the next week's toil, is often an irresistible motive for accepting the very worst offer, if it be but barely the price of the material.

These men work in their own rooms in Spital-fields and Bethnal-green, and sometimes two or three men if different branches occupy one apart-ment and work together there. They are a sober class of men, but seem so perfectly subdued by circumstances that they cannot, or do not, struggle against the system, which several of them told me they knew was undoing them.

This remarkable monopoly and subdivision of labour was brought about gradually. The warehouses I have described began to flourish about twenty years since, and fifteen years ago they increased, and have increased rapidly since. The proprietors of these places purchased ready-made furniture of any one, and in large or small quantities; and men out of work eagerly seized the opportunity to employ their time in making goods for them, and so the system grew gradually to what it is now. "There's another thing, sir," said a man to me; "many a man didn't like the restraint of a shop, and didn't like the master or the foreman, and to work on his own account was the very thing that pleased him, so such a one would try his hand for the slaughter-houses. They've found it out since, that they have."

The subdivisions of this trade I need not give: they are as numerous as the articles of the cabinet-maker's calling.

I have mentioned that the "black" houses, or "linendrapers," at the West-end of London were principally supplied from the East-end. In the neighbourhood of Tottenham-court-road and Oxford-street, for instance, most of my readers will have had their attention attracted by the dust-covered appearance of some poor worker in wood carrying along his skeleton of an easy chair, or a sofa, or a couch, or his two or three office or parlour chairs, to dispose of in some shop; while, occasionally, two persons may be seen staggering and sweating beneath the heavier load of a large chest of drawers, or even a wardrobe. Often, too, a carter has to be employed for the same purpose – the man getting sixpence an hour for this service, while the charge for the horse is 1s.; so that for every hour this sale-seeking has to be continued the cost is 1s. 6d., and thus even but two hours will exhaust the very fullest value of a long day's labour to this class of workmen, and four or six hours the earnings of two or three days. From a furniture carter of this description I received some most shocking details of the miseries of having to "busk" it, as this taking about goods for sale is called by those in the trade.

From a pale feeble-looking man whom I met on a Saturday evening at the West-end, carrying a mahogany cheffonier, I had the following statement:

"I have dragged this cheffonier with me," he said, "from Spitalfields, and have been told to call again in two hours (it was then half-past seven). I am too tired to drag it to another linendraper's, and, indeed, I shouldn't have so good a chance there, for if we go late the manager considers we've been at other places; and he'll say, 'you needn't bring me what others has refused.' I was brought up as a general hand at ——; but was never in society, which is a great disadvantage. I feel that now. I used to make my 25s. to 28s. a week six or seven years back; but then I fell out of employ, and worked at chair-making for a slaughter house, and so got into the system, and now I can't get out of it, at least I don't know how to set about it. I have no time to look about me, as, if I'm idle, I can't get bread for my family. I have a wife and two children; they're too young to do anything, but I can't afford to send them to school, except every now and then, 1d. or 2d. a week, and so they may learn to read perhaps. The anxiety I suffer is not to be told. I've nothing left to pawn now, and if I don't sell this cheffonier I must take it back, and go back to a house bare of everything, except perhaps 3s. or 2s. 6d. my wife may have earned by ruining her health for a tailor's sweater, and 1s. 6d. of that must go for rent. I ought to have £2 for this cheffonier, for it's superior mahogany to the run of such things, but I ask only 35s., and perhaps may be bid 28s. and get 30s., and it may be sold perhaps by the linendraper for £3 3s. or £3 10s. Of course we're obliged to work in the slightest manner possible, but good or bad, there's the same fault found with the article. I have already lost 3½ hours, and there's my wife anxiously looking for my return to buy bread and a bit of beast's head for to-morrow – it's hard to go without a bit of meat on Sundays – and indeed I must sell, at whatever price, it don't matter, and that the linendraper depends upon."

An elderly man whom I found at work with his four sons, all grown up, or nearly so, in a good sized room, gave me the following account:

"I've been 45 years a cabinet-maker, and indeed was born one, as my father before me was one, but I was put to learn my trade with my uncle. I've worked all those years in London, except nine that I was abroad. I was away in his Majesty's service. You see I had a taste for a roving life, so when I'd been two years more at the trade I ran away, and got service on board the

Redwing, sloop of war. That was easy enough done in them days. I didn't much like the service. There was lots of flogging. I got my liberty at nine years' end, and I was pretty well sobered by that time. I went back to work at my own business, and as I'd been more used to table making than anything else I stuck to that, and got employment chiefly in making Pembroke tables, doing other work now and then, but I had relations in the trade, and so did better than I could otherways. At that time I had 9s. a piece for 'Pembrokes,' and found nothing but tools. All the material was given me, and 3d. was allowed for glue. I could make by working hard six a week − I make them at my own place. 20 years ago things continued good; there was no slaughter-houses then that I know'd of. I worked only for regular cabinet-makers, or cabinet-brokers. The 'polsterers (Upholsterers) too, then did little or nothing beyond fitting up bed hangings and curtains, and such like. Now they go for everything. Perhaps it's 15 years ago when things began to decline. I still work at Pembrokes and must work from six to eight and later to get 18s. for my labour, where I did get 54s. in a week − that's just a third. I could in the old times give my children good schooling and good meals, and all right every way. Now children has to be put to work very young. I have four sons working for me. I never had any 'prentices; I never had any journeymen either; indeed you can't get any but some inferior hands not worth 10s. a week. I pay my eldest son 15s. or 16s. a week, because he's married and lives away from me. The others I don't pay anything regular to, but I keep them and find them all they want. Altogether we do pretty well, but I couldn't do so well if I hadn't my family at work. They've never made anything but Pembrokes. I know it's a bad plan. I know it's bringing them up to knock under to the slaughterhouses, but I can't help it. They couldn't live on anything else when I'm gone. I was very badly off till one and a half or on to two years back, when I came into possession of a little money, and that kept me from sinking, as I could buy materials better, and, bless you, the slaughterers soon found that out, and didn't try it on with me so much when I wasn't so depending on 'em. Oh, they're a bad crew. Now, I may take six Pembroke tables of solid mahogany − all mahogany − to a slaughterer's in ——, and ask 18s. a-piece for them, and at that price I couldn't make more than 18s. a week at them, and work long hours every day, without losing time in hawking. Well, the slaughterer will offer 12s. − that's his standing price. He knows they're not bread and water to a man at that, but what does *he* care? He depends upon a man's being hard up. Why, before I got my bit of a rise, I've waited at his door two or three hours, and then had a blackguard price offered me, and was sometimes forced to take it. We can't pawn our goods now; they won't take them. He keeps men waiting just to get things at his own price; they keep open late on purpose to catch us. Now look you here, sir, as to a Pembroke for 12s. I find all the material, everything, myself, same as others − in course solid mahogany.

The material costs 9s. or 10s., and a man working hard may make three a week. Now, how's he to live honestly if he must sell at 12s. a table?"

Such is the statement of what may be called "the family worker" of the garret-masters. I now subjoin a statement of another garret-master – a maker of loo tables – who was endeavouring to make a living by means of a number of apprentices:

"I'm now 41," he said, "and for the last ten or twelve years have been working for a linen-draper, who keeps a slaughterhouse. Before that I was in a good shop, Mr. D——'s, and was a general hand, as we are in the fair trade. I have often made my 50s. a week on good work of any kind – tables, drawers, or cheffoniers. Now, with three apprentices to help me, I may make 25s. Work grew slack, and rather than do nothing, as I'd saved a little money, I made loo-tables, and sold them to a linen-draper, a dozen years back or so; and so somehow I got into the trade. For tables that eighteen years ago I had in a good shop 30s. for making, now 5s. is paid, but that's only in a slaughterer's own factory when he has one. Of course it's every way inferior, shockingly scamped, rubbish. I've been told oft enough by a linen-draper, 'Make an inferior article, so as it's cheap. If it comes to pieces in a month, what's that to you or me?' Now, a 4-foot 'loo' is an average, and if for profit and labour, and it's near two days' work, I put on 7s., I'm bid 5s. less. I've been bid less than the stuff, and have on occasions been forced to take it. That was four years ago, and I then found I couldn't possibly live by my own work, and I had a wife and four children to keep. So I got some apprentices. I have now three, and two of them are stiff fellows of 18, and can do a deal of work. I pay them 5s., 7s., and 9s. a-piece a week, and they live at their homes. I'm obliged to do that to live myself, but it's not what I call a fair system – certainly not, but then I was so drove down. For a 4-foot 'loo' I have only £1, though the materials cost from 11s. to 13s., and it's about two days' work. There's not a doubt of it that the linen-drapers have brought bad work into the market, and have swamped the good. They were just gamblers in the trade when they began, but now they go on by system. For in their own shops a very inferior quality, both in stuff, substance, and workmanship is used to what was used eight or ten years back. For work that ten or twelve years ago I had £3 5s. to £3 10s. from them I have now 30s. Of course it's inferior in quality in proportion, but it doesn't pay me half as well. I know that men like me are cutting one another's throats by competition. Fourteen years ago we ought to have made a stand against this system; but then we must live."

A *drawer maker,* a young man working in the same room as a furniture tassel turner, gave me the following information:

"I served my time to a drawer maker, a small master (he had nine apprentices), and I then started as a small master myself. I make only drawers or wardrobes, or anything in the drawer line, but I can take a turn at tables, but it don't suit out of one's own line. I make drawers, and hawk them to the slaughterhouses. I can make 12s. a week with luck, and by cutting away hard. I've been six years this way, and can't get a penny ahead. This drawers that I'm at work on now is a 3ft. 6in. It's a cheap deal for japanning. I must first go and buy my stuff at the timber-yard, and it'll cost me 10s. 6d., and it'll take me two days to make it, and I'll ask 16s. 6d. for it at a slaughterhouse, and can hardly get it if I lose half a day over it. I'm always bid less than I ask at a slaughterer's, and I have been offered less than the price of the stuff, and that the slaughterers know well enough, and I have been forced to take it. I've wanted many a meal's victuals. When I've had to sell for less than the stuff cost, I had to begin next week on a smaller article, say a wash-hand stand, or any little thing with drawers, and, as I may, raise money to get drawer stuff again. For journeywork at drawer making for a little master a man may get 5s. or 5s. 6d. for a 3ft. 6in., or two day's labour. But it's so seldom a journeyman's wanted by a little master, that a journeyman, if he can work at all, must be a little master himself, like me, and hawk like me. A veneered mahogany chest of drawers, 3ft. 6in., sides and top and all veneered, will cost me 20s. for material, or 18s. for inferior stuff, and it's good 2½ days' work, and I can only get 30s. for it at a slaughterer's, and sometimes only 25s. If it rains while I'm on the busk (hawking) I can't get so much by 5s., for wet spoils the appearance of the article. I've known slaughterhouse men beg and pray for a wet Saturday. I'm married, but as yet have no family. My wife works for a slop tailor, and may make 3s. 6d. a week.''

A pale young man, working in a room with two others, but in different branches, gave me the following account:

"I have been two years making looking-glass frames. Before that I was in the general cabinet line, but took to this when I was out of work. I make frames only. The slaughter-houses put in the glasses themselves. If I had other work I couldn't afford to lose time by going from one to another that I wasn't so quick at. I make all sizes of frames, from nine-sevens to twenty-four-eighteens (9 inches by 7, and 24 inches by 18). Nine-sevens is most in demand, and the slaughter-houses give 10s. 6d. a dozen for them; two years back they gave 15s. All sizes has fallen 3s. to 4s. a dozen. I find all the material; it's mahogany veneered over deal. There's only five or six slaughter-houses in my way; but I serve the Italians or Jews, and they serve the slaughter-houses. There's no foreigners employed as I'm employed; it's not foreign competition as harms us, it's home. I always ask more than I mean to take, for I'm always bid less than a fair price, and so we haggle on to a bargain. The best weeks I have had I cleared 25s.; but in slack times, when I can hardly sell at all, only 12s. Carrying the goods for sale is such a loss of time. Things are very bad now, but I must go on making, and get a customer when trade's brisker, if I can. Glass has rose 1s. a foot, and that's made a slack in the trade, for my trade depends greatly on the glass trade. Things get worse and worse. I know of no women employed in my trade, and no apprentices. We are all little masters.''

A hale-looking elderly man, with a good open countenance, who was working in a decent garret in Hoxton, gave me information concerning his trade as a *Wood-carver:*

"I've known the trade as a worker at it," he said, "for 49 years – I'm now turned 60. I served my time with my father, and gave him £2 a week to be my own master the last year of my apprenticeship, but he was to keep and clothe me. That year I made almost every week £2 5s. When I was my own master I made from 40s. to 50s. a week, at not very hard work, the year through – 7s. a day was then a regular thing, and more for better hands. Twenty years back things got worse. I have worked both at Gothic and other things, but 15 years or so back I could not work as I once could for the West-end; so I came here, and am now chiefly on chair carving, and earn from 12s. to 18s. a week – just as there's a call for my work. They can't work at the East-end as they can at the West. It's like a blackguard trying to be a gentleman. So here I'm a topper. We have no scale of prices – men grasp at anything they can get – and no society. When I'm past work I've only the parish to look to. I did belong to a benefit club, but it failed. I now get one meat dinner where I did get six. I can't make out how it's all come to pass. I'm no politician, and I never was. If I could be a gatekeeper or anything that way, at 15s. a week, wouldn't I give up my tools?''

I shall now proceed to the other branch of the trade. The remarks I have made concerning the wretched social condition and earnings of the fancy cabinet makers who are "in society," apply even more strongly to the *non-society men.* The society men are to be found chiefly in Clerkenwell – the non-society men in Spitalfields and Bethnal-green. With these unfortunate workmen there is yet a lower deep. The under-paid men of Clerkenwell work generally "to order," if the payment be never so inadequate. But the still more underpaid men of Spitalfields work almost universally on speculation. They supply the "slaughter-houses," as they designate the large warehouses at the East-end, where every kind of fancy cabinet work is sold, alike for the supply of the retail dealers in town, and in all parts of the United Kingdom (many of these warehousemen sending out travellers), and for exportation. The proprietors of these establishments very rarely give an order, and if they do (as is shown in a narrative I have given), it is hardly an advantage to the makers. The Spitalfields Cabinet-maker finds his own material, which he usually purchases of the great cabinet-makers or the pianoforte-makers, being the veneers which are the refuse of their work. The deal required can be "picked-up," as it was worded to me, "at any shop." The poor fellow thus loses time in finding out the cheapest marts; and, if the wood be deficient in quality, the article is pretty certain of rejection at a warehouse. The supply of the East-end warehousemen is derived from "little masters" – men who work at their own abodes, and have the assistance of their wives and children. It is very rarely that they, or their equally underpaid fellows in the general cabinet trade, employ an active journeyman. Almost every man in the trade works on his own account, finds his own material, and goes "on the busk to the slaughter-houses" – that is, hawks his goods to the warehouses for the chance of a customer. There are, however, a few journeymen to be engaged, but as they are generally masters as well as journeymen, they know that their services are required only upon an emergency, and they demand a payment which is considered equivalent to their employer's earnings. When at the busiest they demand 15s. a week. The old and the sickly, however, are glad to be employed as journeymen at the barest remuneration – at piece-work labour which may leave them 5s. or 6s. a week. "This is how it is," said a tea-caddy maker to me; "I don't like to put on a hextr hand ven the varehouses is brisk, because they may turn on me any time and say, 'Not vanted, not at all,' just as I've taken in my goods and expects sale and pay. If I don't sell, I can't pay my journeymen, and that the slaughter 'ouses knows, and so they pulls up stiff and von't buy if there's a notion it's a try on in a brisk time."

I found these fancy cabinet-makers certainly an uninformed class, but patient, temperate, and resigned. Some few could neither read nor write, and their families were growing up as uninformed as the parents. The hawking from door to door of workboxes made by some of the men them-selves, their wives assisting them with hawking, was far commoner than it is now, but it is still practised to a small extent.

An elderly man, with a heavy careworn look, whom I found at work with his wife and family, gave me the following information concerning his occupation as *a little master*. He was then engaged in making tea-caddies, his wife and daughter being engaged in "lining" work-boxes for the husband's next employment. They resided inn a large room, a few steps underground, in a poor part of Spitalfields. It was very light, from large windows both back and front, and was very clean. A large bed stood in the centre, and what few tables and chairs there were were old and mean, while the highly-polished rosewood tea-caddies, which were placed on a bare deal table, showed in startling contrast with all the worn furniture around. The wife was well-spoken and well-looking; and the daughter, who was also well-looking, had that almost painful look of precocity which characterises those whose childhood is one of toil:

"I have been upwards of 40 years a fancy cabinet-maker," the man said, "making tea-caddies and everything in the line. When I first worked on my own account I could earn £3 a week. I worked for the trade then, for men in the toy, or small furniture, or cabinet line only. There was no slaughter-shops in those days. And good times continued till about 21 years ago, or not so much. I can't tell exactly, but it was when the slaughter-houses came up. Before that, on a Saturday night, I could bring home, after getting my money, a new dress for my wife, for I was just married then, and something new for the children when they came, and a good joint for Sunday. Such a thing as a mechanic's wife doing needlework for any but her own family wasn't heard of then, as far as I know. There was no slop needlewomen in the wives of my trade. It's different now. They must work some way or other. Me and my father before me, for he brought me up to the business, used to supply honourable tradesmen at a fair price, finding our own material; all the family of us is in the trade, but there was good times then. This part didn't then swarm with slaughter-houses, as it does now. I think there's fifty at this end of the town. I have to work harder than ever. Sometimes I don't know how to lie down of a night to rest best, from tiredness. The slaughtermen give less and less. My wife and family help me, or I couldn't live. I have only one daughter now at home, and she and my wife line the work-boxes as you see. I have to carry out my goods now, and have for 15 years or more hawked to the slaughter-houses. I carried them out on a sort of certainty, or to order, before that. I carry them out complete, or I needn't carry them out at all. I've now been on tea-caddies, 12-inch, with raised tops. The materials − rosewood veneers, deal, locks, hinges, glue, and polish − cost me £1 for a dozen. I must work hard and very long hours, 13 or more a day, to make two dozen a week, and for them I only get at the warehouse 28s. a dozen, if I can sell them there. That's 16s. a week for labour. Sometimes I'm forced to take 25s. − that's 10s. a week for labour. Sometimes I bring them back unsold. Workboxes is not better pay, though my wife and daughter line them. If I get an order − and that's very seldom, not once a year − for a number of tea-caddies, I must take them in at a certain time, because they're mostly for shipping, and so I must have some help. But I can't get a journeyman to help me unless I can show him he'll make 15s. a week, because he knows I just want him for a turn, and can't do without him, and so the profit goes off. Old men can't work quick enough. They may be employed when there's no particular hurry. If I'm not to time with a shipping order, it's thrown on my hands. The slaughter-house men will often say to my asking 28s. for a dozen caddies, "Oh, we don't want them; and we can get better at 25s.; but we don't mind giving you that." Many a time, when trade's been very slack, I've had 20s. offered, or 19s., which is less than the stuff cost. They knew that, but say they must make their harvest. And they know well enough that we have no society, and no benefit fund, and nothing to look to but the workhouse. I have to buy my materials at the great cabinet-makers and at the pianoforte-makers, such as is over in their work − the odds and ends. If any of the veneer's flawed the slaughterer won't have it − it's flung on my hands, as many an article is, for pretended faults. No man on my earnings, which is 15s. some weeks, and 10s. others, and less sometimes, can bring up a family as a family ought to be brought up. Many a time I've had to pawn goods that I couldn't sell on a Saturday night to rise a Sunday's dinner." "Yes, indeed," interposed the wife, "look you here, sir; here's forty or fifty duplicates (producing them) of goods in pawn. If ever we shall get them out, Lord above knows." "Yes, sir," said the man, taking up a ticket, "and look at this. Here you see the pawnbroker has lent me 2s. 6d. on this box. It's such as is sold in cheap shops at 5s. 6d. Well, after walking my feet off, I couldn't get more than 24s. a dozen offered at a slaughter-house. That's 2s. a piece, and I got 2s. 6d. at a pawn-shop. And here's another; it was the largest size, and the pawnbroker lent 5s. 6d. on it; more than I could get offered at a slaughter-house; though in Lowther Arcade, such an one will be marked 22s. 6d., just with the addition of a glass basin, which costs only 1s. wholesale. I haven't any apprentices; it wouldn't suit me, because I haven't any sure sale for my goods. The men that has apprentices is either slaughterers, or people they keep going."

This man sent his daughter to show me a house I had next to call at, but had not been able to ascertain the number. She was quick, but told me she could neither read nor write. She couldn't spare time to learn if she could be taught for nothing. She was eleven, and worked at the lining, and could work, she thought, as well as her mother. She had been thus working since she was six years old.

I called on an old couple to whom I was referred as to one of the few parties employed in working for the men who supplied the warehouses. The man's appearance was gaunt and wretched. He had been long unshorn, and his light blue eyes had that dull half-glazed look which is common to the old when spirit-broken and ill-fed. His room – a small garret in Spitalfields, for which he paid 1s. 3d. a week – was bare of furniture, except his workbench and two chairs, which were occupied by his wife, who was at work lining the boxes her husband was making. A blanket rolled up was the poor couple's bed. The wife was ten years younger than her husband. She was very poorly clad, in an old rusty black gown, tattered here and there, but she did not look very feeble.

"I am 63," the man said – and he looked 80 – "and was apprenticed in my youth to the fancy cabinet trade. I could make £4 4s. a week at it, by working long hours, when I was out of my time, forty-two years back. I have worked chiefly on workboxes. I didn't save money – I was foolish, but it was a hard living, and hard drinking time. I'm sorry for it now. Thirty years ago thing weren't quite so good, but still very good, and so they was twenty years back. But since the slaughter-houses came in men like me has been starving – starving as we makes good work for rich people. Why here, sir, for a rosewood workbox, like this, which I shall get 6d. for making, I used to give a brother of mine 6s. 6d. for making twenty years ago. I've been paid 22s. 6d. twenty years ago for what I now get 2s. 6d. for. The man who employs me now works for a slaughter-house, and he must grind me down, or he couldn't serve a slaughter-house cheap enough. He finds materials, and I find tools and glue, and I have 6s. a dozen for making these boxes, and I can only make a dozen a week, and the glue and others odds and ends for them costs me 6d. a dozen. That, with 9d. or 10d. a week, or 1s., that my wife may make, as she helps me in lining, is all we have to live on. We live entirely on tea and bread and butter, when we can get butter. Never any change − tea, and nothing else, all day; never a bit of meat on a Sunday. As for beer, I haven't spent 4s. on it these last four years. When I'm not at work for a little master I get stuff of one, and make a few boxes on my own account, and carry them out to be sold. I have often to go three or four miles with them; for there's a house near Tottenham-court-road that will take a few from me generally out of charity. When I'm past work, or can't meet with any, there's nothing but the workhouse for me.''

LETTER LXVI
Thursday, August 22, 1850

The decline which has taken place within the last 20 years in the wages of the operative Cabinet-makers of London is so enormous, and, moreover, it seems so opposed to the principles of political economy, that it becomes of the highest importance, in an inquiry like the present, to trace out the circumstances to which this special depreciation is to be attributed. It has been before shown that the number of hands belonging to the London cabinet trade decreased, between 1831 and 1841, 33 per cent in comparison with the rest of the metropolitan population; and that, notwithstanding this falling off, the workmen's wages in 1831 were at least four hundred per cent better than they are at present − 20s. having formerly been paid for the making of articles for which now only 5s. is given. To impress this fact, however, the more strongly upon the reader's mind, I will here cit a few of the many instances of depreciation that have come to my knowledge. "Twenty years ago," said a workman in the fancy cabinet line, "I had 6d. an inch for the making of 20-inch desks of solid mahogany − that's 10s. for the entire article; now I get 2s. 3d. for the same thing. Smaller desks used to average to us 6s. each for wages − now they don't bring us more than 1s. Ladies' 12-inch workboxes twenty years ago were 3s. 6d. and 4s. a piece making, now they are 5d. for the commoner sort, and 7d. for those with better work." "I don't understand per cents," said another workman, "but this I *do* know, the prices that I get have within these 20 years fallen from 4s. to 5d., and in some cases to 4½d."

Here, then, we find that wages in the competitive portion of the cabinet trade − that is, among the "*non-society* hands" (the wages of the "*society*" men, I have before explained, are regulated, or rather *fixed*, by custom), were twenty years ago 400 per cent. better in some cases, and in others no less than 900 per cent. higher, than they are at present; and this while the number of workmen has decreased as much as one-third relatively to the rest of the population. How, then, is this extraordinary diminuation in the price of labour to be accounted for? Certainly not on the natural assumption that the quantity of work has declined in a still greater proportion that the number of hands to do it; for it has also been proved that the number of new houses built annually in the metropolis, and therefore the quantity of new furniture required, has of late years increased very considerably.

In the Cabinet Trade, then, we find a collation of circumstances at variance with that law of supply and demand by which many suppose that the rate of wages is invariably determined. "Wages," it is said, "depend upon the demand and supply of labour," and it is commonly assumed that they cannot be affected by anything else. That they *are*, however, subject to other influences, the history of the cabinet trade for the last twenty years is a most convincing proof; for there we find that, while the quantity of work, or, in other words, the demand for labour has increased, and the supply decreased, wages – instead of rising – have suffered a heavy decline. By what means, then, is this reduction in the price of labour to be explained? What other circumstance is there, affecting the remuneration for work, of which economists have usually omitted to take cognizance? The answer is, that wages depend as much on the distribution of labour as on the demand and supply of it. Assuming a certain quantity of work to be done, the amount of remuneration coming to each of the workmen engaged must, of course, be regulated, not only by the number of hands, but by the proportion of labour done by them respectively; that is to say, if there be work enough to employ the whole of the operatives for sixty hours a week, and if two-thirds of the hands are supplied with sufficient to occupy them for ninety hours in the same space of time, then one-third of the trade must be thrown wholly out of employment; thus proving that there may be surplus labour without any increase of the population. It may therefore be safely asserted that any system of labour which tends to make the members of a craft produce a greater quantity of work than usual, tends at the same time to overpopulate the trade as certainly as an increase of workmen. The law may be summed up briefly in the expression that *overwork makes under-pay*.

Hence the next point in the enquiry is as to the means by which the productiveness of operatives is capable of being extended. There are many modes of effecting this; some of these have been long known to students of political economy, while others have been made public for the first time in these letters. Under the former class are included the division and co-operation of labour, as well as the "large system of production;" and to the latter belongs the "strapping system," by which men are made to get through four times as much work as usual, and which I described in Letter LXI. But the more effectual means of increasing the productiveness of labourers is found to consist, not in any system of supervision, however cogent – nor in any limitation of the operations performed by the work-people to the smallest possible number – nor in the apportionment of the different parts of the work to the different capabilities of the operatives; but in connecting the workman's interest directly with his labour, that is to say, by making the amount of his earnings depend upon the quantity of work done by him. This is ordinarily effected in manufacture by means of what is called piece-work. "Almost all who work by the day, or for a fixed salary, that is to say, those who labour for the gain of others, not for their own, have," it has been well remarked," no interest in doing more than the smallest quantity of work that will pass as a fulfilment of the mere terms of their engagement. Owing to the insufficient interest which day labourers have in the result of their labour, there is a natural tendency in such labour to be extremely inefficient – a tendency only to be overcome by vigilant superintendence (such as is carried on under the strapping system among the joiners) on the part of the persons who *are* interested in the result. The 'master's eye' is notoriously the only security to be relied on. But superintend them as you will, day labourers, are so much inferior to those who work by the piece, that, as was before said, the latter system is practised in all industrial occupations where the work admits of being put out in definite portions, without involving the necessity of too troublesome a surveillance to guard against inferiority (or scamping) in the execution." But if the labourer at piece work is made to produce a greater quantity than at day work, and this solely by connecting his own interest with that of his employer, how much more largely must the productivenes of workmen be increased when labouring wholly on their own account. Accordingly it has been invariably found that whenever the operative unites in himself the double function of capitalist and labourer, making up his own materials or working on his own property, his productiveness, single-handed, is considerably greater than can be attained even under the large system of production where all the arts and appliances of which extensive capital can avail itself are brought into operation.

Of the industry of working masters or trading operatives in manufactures there are as yet no authentic accounts; we have, however, ample records concerning the indefatigability of their agricultural counterparts – the peasant proprietors of Tuscany, Switzerland, Germany, and other countries where the labourers are the owners of the soil they cultivate. "In walking anywhere in the neighbourhood of Zurich," says Inglis, in his work on Switzerland, the south of France, and the Pyrenees, "one is struck with the extraordinary industry of the inhabitants . . . . . . When I used to open my casement between four and five in the morning to look out upon the lake and the distant Alps, I saw the labourer in the fields; and when I returned from an evening walk long after sunset – as late, perhaps, as half-past eight – there was the labourer mowing his grass or tying up his vines." The same state of things exists among the French peasantry, under the same circumstances. "The industry of the small proprietors," says Arthur Young, in his "Travels in France," "was so conspicuous and so meritorious, that no commendation would be too great for it. It was sufficient to prove that property in land is of all others the most active instigator to severe and incessant labour." If then this principle of working for oneself has been found to increase the industry, and consequently the productiveness, of labourers to such an extent in agriculture, it is but natural that it should be attended with the same results in manufactures, and that we should find the "small masters," like the "peasant proprietors," toiling longer and working quicker than labourers serving others rather than themselves. But there is an important distinction to be drawn between the produce of the "peasant proprietor" and that of the "small master." Toil as diligently as the little farmer may, since he cultivates the soil not for profit, but as a means of subsistence, and his produce contributes *directly* to his support, it follows that his comforts must be increased by his extra production, or, in other words, that the more he labours the more food he obtains. The small master, however, producing what he cannot eat, must carry his goods to market and exchange them for articles of consumption; hence, by overtoil, he lowers the market against himself, that is to say, the more *he* labours the *less* food he ultimately obtains; and this is true the more especially of the artificers of those articles the demand for which is limited, and the lowering of the price of which, therefore, by any extra supply, is not necessarily attended with any increased desire for it on the part of the community. Whether there will be a greater permanent supply of a commodity after its production has been cheapened, depends on the question whether or not a greater quantity is wanted at the reduced value. "But there are many articles," says Mr. De Quincey, "for which the market is absolutely and merely limited by a pre-existing system to which those articles are attached as subordinate parts or members." The demand for cabinet work, for example, must invariably be regulated by the quantity of new houses built in the kingdom. It is impossible to find a sale for more tables and chairs, sofas and cheffoniers, than there are rooms to hold them. Hence it is evident that in a trade where the supply cannot be extended beyond a certain limit, any circumstances tending to stimulate the labourer to further production cannot but tend at the same time to deprive others of work, or else so to increase the supply beyond the power of disposing of it, that the harder the workmen slave the less they will get for their labour.

But not only is it true that overwork makes underpay, but the converse of the proposition is equally true, that underpay makes overwork — that is to say, it is true of those trades where the system of piecework or small mastership admits of the operative doing the utmost amount of work that he is able to accomplish; for the workman in such cases seldom or never thinks of reducing his expenditure to his income, but rather of increasing his labour, so as still to bring his income, by extra production, up to his expenditure. This brings us to another important distinction which it is necessary to make between the peasant proprietor and the small master. The little farmer cannot increase his produce by devoting a less amount of labour to each of the articles – that is to say, he cannot scamp his work without diminishing his future stock. There is no cheating nature by palming off inferior workmanship as equal to the most skilful. Agriculture has at least one great advantage over manufacture – it is impossible to have any slop-work in it. A given quantity of labour must be used to obtain a given amount of produce. None of the details can be omitted without a diminution of the result – "scamp" the ploughing, and there will be a smaller crop. It is the same with the employment of bad materials as with slovenly labour: use inferior seed or manure, and the produce is decreased, not only in quality, but in quantity too. In manufactures, however, the result is very different. There, one of the principal means of increasing the productions of a particular trade, and of the cabinet trade especially, is by decreasing the amount of work in each article; indeed, it is one of the necessary consequences of all *interested* labour, such as piecework and small mastership, where the operative's earnings depend upon the quantity of articles made by him rather than the time he has been employed upon them, that it necessarily leads to "scamp work" – that is to say, to the omission of all such details as can be left out without the inferiority of the workmanship being detected. Hence, in such cases all kinds of schemes and impositions are resorted to to make the unskilled labour appear equal to the skilled, and thus the market is glutted with slop productions till the honourable part of the trade, both workmen and employers, are ultimately obliged to resort to the same tricks as the rest. We find that, as the wages of a trade descend, so do the labourers extend their hours of work to the utmost possible limits – they not only toil earlier and later than before, but the Sunday becomes a work-day like the rest (amongst the sweaters of the tailoring trade Sunday labour, as I have shown, is almost universal); and when the hours of work are carried to the extreme of human industry, then more is sought to be done in a given space of time, either by the employment of the members of their own family, or apprentices, upon the inferior portion of the work, or else by "scamping it." "My employer," I was told by a journeyman tailor working for a large West-end show shop, "reduces my wages one-third, and the consequence is, I put in two stitches where I used to give three." "I must work from six to eight and later," said a pembroke table-maker to me, "to get 18s. now for my labour where I used to get 54s. a week – that's just a third. I could in the old times give my children good schooling and good meals. Now children have to be put to work very young. I have four sons working for me at present." Not only, therefore, does any stimulus to extra production make overwork, and overwork make underpay, but underpay, by becoming an additional provocative to increased industry, again gives rise in its turn to overwork – so that, the wages of a trade once reduced, there appears to be no means of predicting to what point they shall ultimately descend.

Let us now seek to apply these principles to the reduction of prices which has lately obtained among the competitive portion of the cabinet trade. In the first place it should be observed that almost every craft suffers from some system of labour peculiar to itself. The wages of a few, for instance, are found to be depressed below subsistence point, because their labour is brought into competition with that of paupers and criminals, whose subsistence is supplied them by the State. Others, again, do not obtain a fair living price for their work because, as in the case of the needleworkers and other domestic manufacturers, their livelihood is supposed to be provided for them by the husband or father, and hence the remuneration is viewed rather as an aid to the family income than as an absolute means of support. The ballast-heavers and lumpers again were found not to be suffering so much from the depression of wages, as from a compulsory system of drinking for the benefit of their employer – the publican. The evil of the tailors' trade, on the other hand, was the sweating or middleman system, by which one operative traded on the toil of another. The carpenters and joiners were labouring under a similar grievance, viz., the letting and sub-letting of work. The sawyers had been deprived of employment by the introduction of machinery. The bane of the dock labourers was the uncertainty of their work – their living being at the mercy of the winds to such an extent that an easterly breeze prevailing for a week was sufficient to deprive thousands of their bread. The street sellers, on the other hand (numbering 20,000), were often reduced to starvation by a few days' continuous rain; and now we find the cabinetmakers, like the boot and shoemakers, depressed by the increase of "small-masters" – that is to say, by a class of workmen possessed of just sufficient capital to buy their own materials, and to support themselves while making them up. I purpose, therefore, inquiring more minutely than I have yet done into the history of this order of operatives – the motives for their passing from the state of *employés* into that of "masters," as well as the facilities for their so doing – their usual time of labour, together with the quantity of work they do, and the quality of it – the nature of the "helps" they employ when they require extra hands – their dependence in sickness and old age – the time lost in finding purchasers for their goods – and lastly, the effect they have had, and are likely still to have, upon the more honourable part of the trade.

First, then, as to the history of "small," or, as they are frequently called, "garret masters" in the cabinet trade.

Little masters, both in the general and fancy cabinet trade, are now, strictly speaking, the men who purchase the material of the articles they manufacture, and who avail themselves of their own labour, that of their families, not unfrequently that of apprentices, and very rarely, that of journeymen. In fact, they unite in their own persons the two functions of employer and employed, as they provide their own materials, set themselves to work, and execute the work by their own exertions, with the occasional aids I have mentioned. They work on speculation, carrying their goods, when made, to the "slaughter-houses" for sale. This mode of business was hardly known until about twenty years ago. Prior to that time a little master was a man of limited means, having a front shop for the display of his goods, and a contiguous workshop for their manufacture. He worked usually "to order," and was an employer; but in most cases he worked himself along with those he employed, and in all cases prepared or "cut out" the stuff which his journeymen made into furniture, on his own premises. He employed from two to five journeymen, having the greater number when trade was brisk. These journeymen were non-society men, but they were paid tolerable wages, and always, as now, by the piece, earning from 20s. to 35s. a week; the wages were generally 15 per cent. lower than those of society men. Inferior work was not then the common practice of the little masters. They sold their goods at from 15 to 25 per cent. lower than the great houses. There are still some of these little masters in the cabinet trade, but since the establishment of the warehouses some fifteen years back they have dwindled away to one-fiftieth of their number. Some of them, when business fell off, "worked journeywork" for the better houses; some of the younger men among them emigrated, and some are now working for the "slaughter-houses."

There were also, twenty years ago, a numerous body of tradesmen, who were employers, though not salesmen to the general public, known as "*Trade Working Masters.*" These men, of whom there are still a few, confined their business solely to "supplying the trade." They supplied the greater establishments, where there were "show rooms," with a cheaper article than the proprietors of those greater establishments might be able to have had manufactured on their own premises. They worked not on speculation, but "to order," and were themselves employers; some employed at a busy time from twenty to forty hands, all working on their premises, which were merely adapted for making, and not for selling of "showing" furniture. There are still such "trade working masters," the extent of their business not being a quarter what it was; neither do they now generally adhere to the practice of having men to work on their premises, but they give out the material, which the journeymen make up at their own abodes.

A trade working master, now carrying on that business in the fancy cabinet line, told me that he was about withdrawing himself from it. He worked to order, and always kept a supply of goods for "stock," from which either town or country tradesmen could select whatever they required. He paid fair wages, and dealt only in good articles. Now, however, he assures me that it is impossible to compete with the warehousemen, who purchase of the garret or little masters, and avail themselves of those poor men's necessities. And so my informant is relinquishing the business, as he says it is "not fit for honest men – it is now only fit for scamps and scamping masters."

"About twenty years ago," said an experienced man to me, "I dare say the small masters formed about a quarter of the trade. The slacker trade becomes, the more the small masters increase; that's because they can't get other work to do, and so, rather than starve, they begin to get a little stuff of their own, and make up things for themselves, and sell them ås best they can. Anything's better than standing idle and starving, you know. The great increase of the small masters was when trade became so dead. When was it that we used to have to go about so with our things? About five years since wasn't it?" said he, appealing to one of his sons, who was at work in the same room with him. "Yes, father," replied the lad; "just after the railway bubble; nobody wanted anything at all then." The old man continued to say, "The greater part of the men that couldn't get employed at the regular shops then turned to making up things on their own account, and now I should say there's at least one-half working for themselves. About twelve years ago masters wanted to cut the men down, and many of the hands, rather than put up with it, took to making up for theirselves. Whenever there's a decrease of wages there's always an increase of small masters; for its not until men can't live comfortable by their labour that they take to making things on their own account."

Such then, is the history of this class of workmen in the Cabinet Trade. Concerning the motives for men to become small masters, I had the following statement from one of the most intelligent workmen belonging to the craft: –

"One of the inducements," he said, "for men to take up making up for themselves is to get a living when thrown out of work until they can hear of something better. If they could get into regular journeywork there ain't one man as wouldn't prefer it – it would pay them a deal better. Another of the reasons for the men turning small masters is the little capital that it requires for them to start themselves. If a man has got his tools he can begin as a master-man with a couple of shillings. If he goes in for making large tables, then from 30s. to 35s. will do him, and it's the small bit of money it takes to start with in our line that brings many into the trade, who wouldn't be there if more tin was wanted to begin upon. Many works for themselves, because nobody else won't employ them, their work is so bad. Many weavers has took to our business of late. That's quite common now – their own's so bad; and some that used to hawk hearthstones about is turned Pembroke table-makers. The slaughterers don't care what kind of work it is, so long as it's cheap. A table's a table, they say, and that's all we want. Another reason for men turning little masters is because employment's more certain like that way; a man can't be turned off easily, you see, when he works for himself.

Again, some men may prefer being small masters because they are more independent like; when they're working for themselves, they can begin working when they please, and knock off whenever they like. But the principal reason is, because there an't enough work at the regular shops to employ them all. The slaughterers have cut down their prices so low that there aint no work to be had at the better houses, so men must go on making up for the 'butchers' (slaughterers) or starve. Those masters as really would assist the men couldn't do it, because they're dead beat out of the field by the slaughter-houses. There was a large house lately as used to employ sixty men at fair living wages was broke up owing to the master going to the Cape of Good Hope, and then the whole of the men was turned adrift. Well, what was to be done? Some was lucky enough to get into a job, but a good part was obligated to buy a bit of stuff for themselves, and to set to working on their own account. Half a loaf you know is better than no bread at all, and nobody knows that so well as the slaughterers.''

I now come to the amount of capital required for an operative Cabinet-maker to begin business on his own account.

To show the readiness with which any youth "out of his time," as it is called, can start in trade as a garret cabinet-master, I have learned the following particulars:— The lad, when not living with his friends, usually occupies a garret, and in this he constructs a rude bench out of old materials, which may cost him 2s. If he be penniless when he ceases to be an apprentice, and can get no work as a journeyman, which is nearly always the case for reasons I have before stated, he assists another garret master to make a bedstead perhaps, and the established garret master carries two bedsteads instead of one to the slaughter house. The lad's share of the proceeds may be about 5s., and out of that, if his needs will permit him, he buys the materials for a small clothes-horse, or any trifling article, and so proceeds by degrees. Many men, to "start themselves," as it is called, have endured, I am informed, something very like starvation most patiently. The tools are generally collected by degrees, and often in the last year of apprenticeship, out of the boy's earnings. They are seldom bought "first-hand," but at the marine store shops, or at the second-hand furniture broker's, in such places as the New Cut. The purchaser grinds and sharpens them up at any friendly workman's, where he can meet with the loan of a grindstone, and puts new handles to them himself, out of pieces of waste wood; 10s., or even 5s., thus invested has started a man with tools; while 20s. has accomplished it in what was considered "good style," Old chisels may be bought from 1d., 1½d., 2d., to 5d.; planing irons from 1d. or 1½d. to 3d.; hammer heads from 1d. to 3d.; saws from 1s. to 2s. 6d., and rules and the other tools equally low. In some cases the friends of the boy, if they are not poverty-stricken, advance him 40s. to 50s. to begin with, and he must then shift for himself. When a bench and tools have been attained, the young master buys such material as his means afford, and sets himself to work. If he has a few shillings to spare, he makes himself a sort of bedstead, and buys a rug and a sheet or a little bedding. If he has not the means to do so, he sleeps on shavings stuffed into an old sack. In some few cases, he hires a bench alongside some other garret-master, but the arrangement of two or three men occupying one room for their labour is more frequent when the garrets where the men sleep are required for their wives' labour in any distinct business, or when the articles the men make are too cumbrous, like wardrobes, to be carried easily down the narrow stairs.

A timber-merchant, part of whose business consists in selling material to little masters, gave me two instances, within his own knowledge, of journeymen "beginning to manufacture on their own account."

A fancy cabinet-maker had 3s. 6d. at his command. With this he purchased material for a desk as follows:—

	s.	d.
3ft. of solid five-eighths mahogany	1	0
2ft. of solid three-eighths cedar, for bottom, &c.		6
Mahogany top		3
Bead cedar, for interior		6
Lining		4
Lock and key (no wards to lock)		2
Hinges		1
Glue and sprigs		1½
Lining		4
	3	3½

The making of the desk occupied four hours, as the man bestowed extra pains upon it, and he sold it to a slaughterer for 3s. 6d. he then broke his fast on bread and water, bought material for a second desk, and went to work again, and so he proceeds now; toiling and half-starving, and struggling to get 20s. a head of the world to buy more wood at one time, and not pause so often in his work. "Perhaps," said my informant, "he'll marry, as the most of the small masters do, some foolish servant of all-work who has saved £3 or £4, and that will be his capital."

Another general cabinet-maker commenced business on 30s., a part of which he thus expended in the material for a 4-foot chest of drawers:—

	s.	d.
Three feet six inches of cedar for ends	4	0
Sets of mahogany veneers for three big and two little drawers	2	4
Drawer sweep (deal to veneer the front upon)	2	6
Veneer for top	1	3
Extras (any cheap wood) for inside of drawers, partitioning, &c	5	0
Five locks	1	8
Eight knobs, 1s., glue, sprigs, &c	1	4
Set of four turned feet, beech stained	1	6
	19	7

For the article when completed, he received 25s., toiling at it for 27 or 28 hours. The tradesman from whom I derived this information, and who was familiar with every branch of the trade, calculated that three-fifths of the working cabinet makers of London make for the warehouses – in other words, that there are three thousand small masters in the trade. The most moderate computation was that the number so employed exceed one-half of the entire body of the five thousand metropolitan journeymen.

The next point in this enquiry is concerning the industry and productiveness of this class or workmen. Of over-work, as regards excessive labour, and of over-production from scamped workmanship, I heard the following accounts, which different operatives, both in the general and fancy cabinet trade, concurred in giving; while some represented the labour as of longer duration by at least an hour, and some by two hours, a day than I have stated.

The labour of the men, who depend entirely on the slaughter-houses for the purchase of the articles, with all the disadvantages that I described in a former letter, is usually seven days a week the year through. That is, seven days – for Sunday work is all but universal – each of 13 hours, or 91 hours in all; while the established hours of labour in the "honourable trade" are six days of the week, each of 10 hours, or 60 hours in all. Thus 50 per cent. is added to the extent of the production of low-priced cabinet work merely from "over hours;" but in some cases I heard of 15 hours for seven days in the week, or 105 hours in all. The exceptions to this continuous toil are from one hour to three hours once or twice in the week, when the workman is engaged in purchasing his material of a timber merchant, who sells it in small quantities, and from six to eight hours when he is employed in conveying his goods to a warehouse, or from warehouse to warehouse, for sale.

Concerning the hours of labour, I had the following minute particulars from a garret-master who was a chairmaker: –

"I work from six every morning to nine at night; some work till ten. My breakfast at eight stops me for ten minutes. I can breakfast in less time, but it's a rest; my dinner takes me say twenty minutes at the outside, and my tea, eight minutes. All the rest of the time, I'm slaving at my bench. How many minutes rest is that, sir? Thirty-eight; well, say three quarters of an hour, and that allows a few sucks at a pipe when I rest; but I can smoke and work too. I have only one room to work and eat in, or I should lose more time. Altogether I labour 14¼ hours every day, and I must work on Sundays – at least forty Sundays in the year. One may as well work as sit fretting. But on Sundays I only work till it's dusk, or till five in summer. When it's dusk I take a walk. I'm not well dressed enough for a Sunday walk when it's light, and I can't wear my apron on that day very well to hide patches. But there's eight hours that I reckon I take up every week, one with another, in dancing about to the slaughterers. I'm satisfied that I work very nearly 100 hours a week the year through; deducting the time taken up by the slaughterers, and buying stuff — say eight hours a week — it gives more than 90 hours a week for my work, and there's hundreds labour as hard as I do, just for a crust."

This excessive toil, however, is but one element of over-production. "Scamping," adds at least 200 per cent. to the productions of the cabinet-maker's trade. I have ascertained several cases of this over-work from scamping, and adduce two. A very quick hand, a little master, working, as he called it, "at a slaughtering pace," for a warehouse, made 60 plain writing-desks in a week of 90 hours, while a first-rate workman, also a quick hand, made 18 in a week of 70 hours. The scamping hand said he must work at the rate he did to make 14s. a week from a slaughter house; and so used to such style of work had he become, that, though a few years back he did West-end work in the best style, he could not now make eighteen desks in a week, if compelled to finish them in the style of excellence displayed in the work of the journeyman employed for the honourable trade. Perhaps he added, he couldn't make them in that style at all. The frequent use of rosewood veneers in the fancy cabinet, and their occasional use in the general cabinet trade gives, I was told, great facilities for scamping. If in his haste the scamping hand injure the veneer, or if it has been originally faulty, he takes a mixture of gum shellac and "colour" (colour being a composition of Venetian red and lamp black), which he has ready by him, rubs it over the damaged part, smooths it with a slightly heated iron, and so blends it with the colour of the rosewood that the warehouseman does not detect the flaw. Indeed, I was told that very few warehousemen are "judges" of the furniture they bought, and they only require it to look well enough for sale to the public, who knew even less than themselves. In the general cabinet trade I found the same ratio of "scamping," compared with the products of skilled labour in the honourable trade. A good workman made a four-foot mahogany chest of drawers in five days, working the regular hours, and receiving at piece-work price 35s. A scamping hand made five of the same size in a week, and had time to carry them for sale to the warehouses, wait for their purchase or refusal, and buy material. But for the necessity of doing this the scamping hand could have made seven in the 91 hours of his week, of course in a very inferior manner. "They would hold together for a time," I was assured, "and that was all; but the slaughterer cared only to have them viewed and cheap." These two cases exceed the average, and I have cited them to show what *can* be done under the scamping system.

I now come to show this "scamp work" is executed — that is to say, by what helps or assistants, when such are employed. As in all trades where lowness of wages is the rule, the apprentice system prevails among the cheap cabinet workers. It prevails, however, among the garret masters, by very many of them having one, two, three, or four apprentices, and so the number of boys thus employed through the whole trade is considerable. This refers principally to the general cabinet trade. In the fancy trade the number is greater, as the boys' labour is more readily available; but in this trade the greatest number of apprentices is employed by such warehouse-men as are manufacturers, as some at the East-end are – or rather by the men that they constantly keep at work. Of these men, one has now eight and another fourteen boys in his service – some apprenticed, some merely "engaged" and dischargeable at pleasure. A sharp boy, thus apprenticed, in six or eight months becomes "handy;" but four out of five of the work-men thus brought up can do nothing well but their own particular branch, and that only well as far as celerity in production is considered.

In some cases the master takes boys without a fee, and the boy then lives with his parents or friends. For the first two years such an apprentice receives nothing; he is merely instructed. After that he receives half what he earns at piece-work prices. It is these boys who are put to make, or as master of the better class distinguished it to me, not to *make* but to put together, ladies' workboxes at 5d. a piece, the boy receiving 2½d. a box. "Such boxes," said another workman, "are nailed together; there's no dove-tailing, nothing of what I call *work* or workmanship, as you say about them, but the deal's nailed together, and the veneer's dabbed on, and if the deal's covered, why the thing passes. The worst of it is that people don't under-stand either good work or good wood. Polish them up and they look well. Besides, and that's another bad thing – for it encourages bad work – there's no stress on a lady's work box, as on a chair or a sofa, and so bad work lasts far too long, though not half as long as good; in solids especially, if not in veneers."

The usual assistants of the small masters are their own children. Upon this subject I received the following extraordinary statement:–
"The most on us has got large families. We put the children to work as soon as we can. My little girl began about six, but about eight or nine is the usual age." "Ah, poor little things," said the wife, "they are obliged to begin the very minute they can use their fingers at all. The most of the cabinet-makers of the East-end have from five to six in family, and they are generally all at work for them. The small masters mostly marry when they are turned of twenty. You see our trade's come to such a pass that unless a man has children to help him he can't live at all. I've worked more than a month together, and the longest night's rest I've had has been an hour and a quarter – aye, and I've been up three nights a week besides. I've had my children lying ill, and been obliged to wait on them into the bargain. You see, we couldn't live if it wasn't for the labour of our children, though it makes 'em. poor little things, old people long afore they're growed up." I leave you to judge how we're to live by our labour," said the man. "Just look here," he continued, producing a rosewood tea caddy. It was French polished, lined

with tinfoil, and with lock and key. "Now, what do you think we get for that, materials, labour, and all? Why, 16d.; and out o f that there's only 4d. for the labour. My wife and daughter polishes and lines them, and I make them, and all we get is fourpence, and we have to walk perhaps miles to sell them for that." "Why I stood at this bench," said the wife," with my child, only 10 years of age, from four o'clock on Friday morning till ten minutes past seven in the evening, without a bit to eat or drink. I never sat down a minute from the time I began till I finished my work, and then I went out to sell what I had done. I walked all the way from here (Shoreditch) down to the Lowther Arcade, to get rid of the articles." Here she burst out in a voilent flood of tears, saying, "Oh, sir, it *is* hard to be obliged to labour from morning till night as we do − all of us, little ones and all − and yet not to be able to live by it either." "Why, there's Mr. ──, the warehouseman, in ─────── " the husband went on, "offered me £6 a gross for the making of these very caddies, as I showed just now, and that would have left me only 1½d. a dozen for my labour. Why, such men won't let poor people remain honest. And you see, the worst of it is this here − children's labour is of such value now in our trade that there's more brought into the business every year, so that it's really for all the world like breeding slaves. Without my children I don't know how we should be able to get along. There's that little thing," said the man, pointing to the girl of ten years of age before alluded to, as she sat at the edge of the bed, "why, she works regularly every day from six in the morning till ten at night. She never goes to school; we can't spare her. There's schools enough about here for a penny a week, but we could not afford to keep her without working. If I'd ten more children I should be obliged to employ them all the same way. And there's hundreds and thousands of children now slaving at the business. There's the M──'s; they've a family of eight, and the youngest to the oldest of them all works at the bench; and the oldest ain't fourteen, I'm sure. Of the two thousand five hundred small masters in the cabinet line, you may safely say that two thousand of them, at the very least, has from five to six in family, and that's upwards of 12,000 children that's been put to the trade since the prices has come down. Twenty years ago I don't think there was a young child at work in our business, and I'm sure there isn't now a small master whose whole family doesn't assist him. But what I want to know is, what's to become of the 12,000 children when they're grow'd up, and come regular into the trade? Here are all my young ones growing up without being taught anything but a business that I know they must starve at."

In answer to my inquiry as to what dependence he had in case of sickness? "Oh, bless you, he said, there's nothing but the parish for us. I did belong to a benefit society about four year ago, but I couldn't keep up my payments any longer. I was in the society above five-and-twenty year, and then was obliged to leave it after all. I don't know of one as belongs to any friendly society, and I don't think there is a man as can afford it in our trade now. They must all go to the workhouse when they're sick or old."

From a man who, with his wife and young child, occupied rather a decent room in Spitalfields, I had the following statement as to his mode of living. He was a fancy cabinetmaker:—

"I get up always at six, summer and winter. I wake natural at that hour, if I'm ever so tired when I go to bed and sleep ever so dead. If it's summer I go to work in the daylight at six; if it's winter by candle-light. My wife gets up an hour afore me. Indeed she can't well sleep in the room I'm working in. (We've only one-room.) She makes the fire and boils the kettle, and gets breakfast ready at eight. It's coffee and bread and butter. I may take ten minutes to it, sometimes only five. She has dinner ready at one, and that's coffee and bread and butter three days at least in the week, and that's finished in ten minutes too. Then, I've tea, not coffee, for a change about five, and I go to bed at ten without any supper — except on Sundays — about sixteen hours' labour, just with a few breaks, as I've told you. Most people in my way, who are as badly off as I am, work on Sundays. All that I know do, but *I* don't. I haven't strength for it after sixteen hours' work for six days, and so I rest on Sunday, and stay in bed till twelve or after. When we haven't coffee for dinner we have a bit of cheap fish — mackerel at 1½d. or 1d. a piece, or soles at 2d. a pair, and a potato with it. Sometimes they're almost as cheap as coffee for dinner. For breakfast for me, my wife, and a child five years old, coffee, half an ounce, costs ½d.; bread and butter, 3½d. — 1d. butter, and 2½d. bread. Dinner the same, but an ounce of coffee instead of half an ounce as at breakfast; so that's 4½d., and about the same if it's fish, or 1d. or 1½d. more, but there isn't as much fish as we could eat. Tea's ½d. more than breakfast. No supper, and to bed at ten. On Sundays we have mostly half a bullock's head, which costs 10d. to 1s. We have it boiled, with an onion and a potato to it; or when we're hard up we have it without either for dinner, and warm it for supper. There's none left for Monday sometimes, and never much. I don't taste beer above once a month, if that. In winter, fire and candlelight cost me 3s. to 4s. a week for some weeks, or 4s. 6d. a week when there's a fog, for my place isn't very light, and I'm forced to burn candles all day long then, and I must have a bit of fire all times for my glue-pot. There *have* been times — but things are cheaper now, though work's not so brisk — when we've had no butter to our bread, and hardly a crumb of sugar to our coffee. My rent is 1s. 10d. a week, and my own sticks. It costs at least 7s. to keep us, and that's 8s 10d. altogether. I don't earn more than 12s. a week the year through, so that the extra fire and candle in the winter takes it every farthing, and more; and then we're forced to go without butter. There's 3s. 2d., say, left in summer time for clothing, and all that; but I haven't bought a new thing that way since I got married seven years back. My wife earns, perhaps, 2s. a week at charing, but her health's bad. I work for a slaughterer; not one in particular, but one is my principal customer. I began as a little master when I'd been a fortnight out of my time. My mother lent me 20s. She's middling off, and in service. I'd picked up tools before. Then my wife had saved on to £5 in service which furnished the room, with what I made myself. I think most of us marry servants that have saved a trifle. A good many have, I know. My little girl's too young to do anything now, but she must work at lining with her mother when she's old enough. Children soon grow to be useful, that's one good thing. She goes to a Sunday school at present, and is learning to read."

To show the time consumed – or, as the men universally call it, "lost" – in the conveyance of the goods to the warehouses, I am able to give the following particulars. There can be no doubt, as I have stated, that more than one-half of the working cabinet-makers in London work for the supply of the warehouses; but that I may not over-estimate the number, I will say one-half. The least duration of time expended by these men in their commerce with the "slaughter-houses" is an average of eight hours weekly per man. But this is not all. At least one-fourth of their number expend 2s. 6d. each in the hire of carts and trucks for the conveyance of the heavier articles to the warehouses. Sometimes, when the bulk of the articles admits of it, trucks or barrows are used, the charge for which is 2d. an hour. But lighter articles of furniture are carried on the shoulder. "Why, sir," said one man to me, "I have sometimes carried as much as threequarters of a hundred weight on my shoulder, and have taken that weight as far as Knightsbridge and Pimlico and back again, and then not sold it. I have then been obliged to take it out again the next day in a different direction, as far as Woolwich, and have took what I could get for it, or else go without victuals. I find about Thursday to be the best day, and the most profitable, as I can generally get more on a Thursday for an article than on a Saturday or Monday, because if you call on Saturday they think you are hard up for Sunday's dinner, and if you take it on Monday they think you are hard up for rent, and so they play upon you, and, besides, they think you couldn't get rid of it on Saturday. The usual rounds we take for the sale of our articles are Moorfields, Tottenham-court-road, Oxford-street, Edgeware-road, Knightsbridge, Pimlico, and other parts of the West-end." Another party informed me that he has had to call no less than seven or eight times for his money after he had "sold his goods to a butcher," and then only got about half of what was coming to him. At these slaughterhouses, I was informed, "the butchers occasionally pay part cash and part by check, due in two months. But when we get outside, their clerks meet us to know if we have any checks to cash, for which they charge 3d. in the pound."

Concerning the employment of a carter I had the following account from one of the body:—

"I am a tradesman – a cornchandler – and having a horse and cart I am in the habit of doing little jobs for persons in this neighbourhood (Hoxton). I never let out to hire. I am often employed by the numerous small cabinet manufacturers in this locality, to take their work out with them, on what is called the 'biz,' *i.e.* (the hawk). The goods I am employed to carry out consist of loo tables, cheffoniers, pembroke tables, oak chairs, and other large articles of cabinet work, and for this I charge on the average 1s. per hour. Whether the goods are sold or not my charge is the same. Sometimes I am paid after the articles are sold, and sometimes I have to trust. There are no particular days in the week for the sale of the articles, but mostly Saturdays. There are dozens employed in the same line as myself. I generally start about nine or ten o'clock in the morning, calling first at several houses in Tottenham-court-road, then to Oxford-street, Wardour-street, Knights-bridge, and often back again with the whole lot to ————'s, where the articles are left and sold for what the slaughterer likes to give. In case of rain I cover the goods. Sometimes the articles are sold directly, and sometimes in five or six hours. The longest time I have known it to take to dispose of the goods is seven hours in one day and five the next. It is no uncommon occurrence for a poor working man to stand an hour, two, or three at a slaughter-house door before the master butcher will condescend to give him an answer." In answer to my inquiry where do they get their meals while out selling, the reply was, "Why they starve till the goods are sold."

I have before alluded to the utter destitution of the cheap workers belonging to the cabinet trade, and I now subjoin the statement of a man whom I found last winter in the Asylum for the Houseless Poor:—

"I have been out of work about a twelvemonth, as near as I can reckon. When I was in work I was sometimes at piece work and sometimes at day work. When I first joined the trade (I never served my time — my brother learnt me) there was plenty of work to do. For this last twelvemonth I have not been able to get anything to do — not at my own trade. I have made up one dozen of mahogany chairs on my own account. The wood and labour of them cost me £1 5s. I had to pay for a man to do the carving and sweeping of them, and I had to give £1 for the wood. I could get it much cheaper now; but then I didn't know anything about the old broken 'ship' wood that is now used for furniture. The chairs I made I had to sell at a sacrifice. I was a week making them, and got only £2 for the dozen when they were done. By right I should have had at least 50s. for them, and that would have left 25s. for my week's work, but as it was I had only 15s. clear money, and I have worked at them much harder than is usual in the trade. There are two large houses in London that are making large fortunes in this manner. About a fortnight after I found out that I couldn't possibly get a living at this work, and as I didn't feel inclined to make the fortunes of the large houses by starving myself, I gave up working at chair making on my own account. I then made a few clothes-horses. I kept at that for about six months. I hawked them in the streets, but I was half-starved by it. Some days I sold them, and some I was without taking a penny. I never on one day got rid of more than half a dozen, and they brought 3s.; out of which there was the wood and the other materials to pay for, and they would be 1s. 6d. at least. If I could get rid of two or three in a day, I thought I did pretty well, and my profit upon these was about 9d. – not more. At last I became so reduced by the work, that I was not able to buy any more wood, and the week after that I was forced to quit my lodging. I owed three weeks' rent, at 1s. 6d. a week, and was turned out in consequence. I had no things for them to seize – they had all gone long before. Then I was thrown upon the streets. I had no friends (my brothers are both out of the country), and no home. I was sleeping about anywhere I could. I used to go and sit at the coffee houses where I knew my mates were in the habit of going, and they would give me a bit of something to eat and make a collection to pay for a bed for me. At last this even began to fail me, my mates could do no more for me. Then I applied to some of the unions, but they refused to admit me into the casual ward on account of my not being a traveller. I was a whole week walking about in the streets without ever lying to rest. I used to got to Billingsgate to get a nap for a few minutes, and then I used to have a doze now and then on a door step and under the railway arches. All this time I had scarcely any food at all – not even bread. At last I was fairly worn out, and being in the neighbourhood I applied at St. Luke's, and told them I was starving. They said they could do nothing for me, and advised me to apply at the Houseless Poor Asylum. I did so, and was admitted directly. I have been four nights in the Asylum already, and I don't now what I shall do when I leave. My tools are all gone – they are sold; and I have no money to buy new ones. There are hundreds in the trade like me, walking about the streets with nothing to do, and no place to put their heads in.''

I shall now conculde this letter with the following statement as to the effects produced by the slop cabinet business upon the honourable part of the trade, I derived my information from Mr. ——, one of the principal masters at the West-end, and who has the highest character for consideration for his men. Since the establishment of slaughter-house – ''and aptly, indeed,'' said my informant, ''from my knowledge of their effects upon the workmen, have they been named – the demand for articles of the best cabinet work, in the manufacture of which the costliest woods and the most skilled labour London can supply are required, has diminished upwards of 25 per cent. The demand, moreover, continues still to diminish gradually. The result is obvious. Only three men are now employed in this trade, in lieu of four, as formerly, and the men displaced may swell the lists of the underpaid, and even of the slop workers. The expense incurred by some of the leading masters in the honourable trade is considerable, and for objects the designs of which inferior masters pirate from us. The designs for new styles of furniture add from five to ten per cent. to the cost of the more elaborate articles that we manufacture. The first time any of these novel designs comes to the hammer by the 'sale of a gentleman's effects,' they are certain of piracy, and so they pattern descends to the slaughter-houses. These great houses are frequently offered prices, and by very wealthy persons, which are an insult to a tradesman anxious to pay a fair price to his workmen. For instance for an 8ft. mahogany book case, after a new design, and made in the very best style of art, the material being the choicest, and everything about in admirable keeping, the price is 50 guineas. 'O, dear,' some rich customer will say, "Fifty guineas? I'll give you twenty, or, indeed, I'll give you twenty-five.!' " (I afterwards heard from a journeyman that this would be the cost of the labour alone.) The gentleman I saw spoke highly of the intelligence and good conduct of the men employed, only society men being at work on his premises. He feared that the slop-trade, if not checked, would more and more swamp the honourable trade.

LETTER LXVII
Thurday, August 29, 1850

In the present Letter I shall speak of the earnings and condition of the London Turners.

The number of turners in Great Britain at the time of taking the last census was 7,159; of these, 5,925 were resident in England; 1,042 in Scotland, 147 in Wales, and 45 in the British Isles. Out of the 7,159, 5,941 were males and 83 females of 20 years of age and upwards; while of those under 20 years, 1,113 were males and 22 females. Whether the female turners belonged to the operative or trading class the Government returns do not afford us any information. I find, however, that females have often been known to work at the trade.

This was the number of hands in the business in 1841. In 1831 the number of male turners of twenty years of age and upwards was 5,905. In England, the hands had decreased no less than 218 during ten years between 1831 and 1841; whereas in Scotland they had increased 197, and in Wales 22. Whether the wages of the turners rose in the English counties where the decrease took place, I have, as I said before, no means of ascertaining. It is clear, however, that according to the mere law of supply and demand, the price paid to the operatives for their labour should have increased precisely in the same ratio as the hands decreased – provided, of course, that the quantity of work to be done, or, in other words, the demand is the turners' labour, remained the same.

As regards the Metropolis, however, I have been at considerable pains in collecting information both as to the amount of work and the prices paid for it between 1831 and 1841; so that the public may have another instance, in addition to that of the cabinet trade, that the wages of a trade may, under particular circumstances, decline, while the supply of hands is decreasing, and the demand for their labour is increasing.

The number of turners of twenty years of age and upwards who were resident in London in 1841 amounted to 1,320; in 1831, however, there had been 150 more hands in the metropolis – that is to say, according to the census of that date, the London turners of the same age amounted to 1,470. Here, then, was a decrease in the number of hands, very nearly equal to 10 per cent.; so that, allowing the quantity of work to have remained stationary during that time, wages ought to have risen 10 per cent. from 1831 to 1841. But, strange to say, the quantity of work actually increased — for it was during that period that it became the fashion to have several articles, such as door-knobs, curtain poles and rings, &c., made of wood which had before then been manufactured of brass — and yet, notwithstanding this augmentation of the ordinary amount of turning work, and the decrease in the quantity of hands in the trade, wages were 400 per cent. better in 1831 than they were in 1841.

The turners themselves, it will be seen, attribute the decline in their wages to the same cause as that in the cabinet trade, — viz., to the competition of the small masters in reducing the prices of the articles they produce. I shall now proceed to describe the different varieties of the operatives, and then to give the statements of the most intelligent individials belonging to each of these varieties.

The trade of a turner has many ramifications. In the first place, as regards the materials used, there are general turners, hard wood and ivory turners (the hard woods being principally lignum vitie, ebony, cocoa tree, saffron and rose-wood.) Then, as regards the articles made, there are tassel and fringe mould turners, cotton bobbin, lace bobbin, toy, plumber's and oval turners. Brush turning is also a distinct branch. Of toy turning, I may promise, I gave an account in my Letter concerning the toy makers.

The work of the general turner consists principally in making articles required by joiners, chair makers, cabinetmakers, and upholsterers; such as door knobs, stair banisters and newels (the upright pillar supporting the scroll of the stair hand-rail), which are most for building purposes, and are usually turned out of deal. For cabinetmakers the general turner makes bed posts, table legs and pillars, drawer knobs, cornice ends, and different kinds of beadings, all kinds of wood being employed for these purposes, though mahogany is the principal. "Legs" are turned for the chairmakers, either for sofas, chairs, or stools. The upholsterers demands on the turner's skill are often identical with those of the cabinetmaker. The hard wood and ivory turner forms all the toys made of ivory, as well as chess-men, which they afterwards carve; they are also the artificers of billiard balls, pestles, twine boxes, skittle balls, and of similar articles made of the harder kinds of timber. The tassel and fringe turner is employed entirely for the upholsterers, who use the productions of their skill for the drapery with which our bed and window hanging are decorated. The last mentioned class of turners all use soft woods, principally alder, lime, and chestnut. The cotton bobbin, toy, and lace bobbin turners are occupied in the respective callings indicated by their appellations. The cotton bobbin and toy turners use soft woods, but the lace bobbins are made of hard woods, being polished, and sometimes highly ornamented. This is a trade, however, which is fast declining, as these bobbins are only used for lace made by hand, and they are hardly made at all in London now. At one time lace bobbin turning was a very prosperous occupation. The plumber's turner forms suckers and buckets for pumps, dressers (a kind of mallet with which the lead is "flatted"), wedges, mallets,and moulds for casting lead; beech, elm, ash, box, hornbeam, and alder being used for these purposes. British turners are employed in making the different kinds of broom heads, and on the stems of painter's brushes, all made of alder, or some equally soft wood, but principally of alder.

Steam turning is applied more or less to all the descriptions of labour I have specified. Steam machinery was first applied to turning in the metropolis about twenty-five years ago. It was in use in the manufacturing districts, however, some ten years before it was introduced into the London trade, its use is still far more prevalent in the great manufacturing towns of the provinces than here. "I remember," said a well-informed man to me, "that when I was a boy in the business, the notion of turning by steam was laughed at, and a man who thought it could be done was reckoned fit to *turn* into Bedlam. That's 35 years ago; but the trade has found it out since, and severely." Steam, is, however, only used now as the motive power, for a man must still be employed to "turn." Steam power, however, enables a man to do twice the ordinary quantity of work, and with less fatigue.

The trade of a turner is carried on by means of a crank, a wheel, and a collar-and-mandrel. The wheel is turned by the pressure of the foot (either the right or left, though the left is more generally used, as the body is thereby steadier). The big wheel turned by hand is now very rarely used, and only when the wheel usually employed and kept in motion by the turner himself is not of sufficient power; an assistant then turns the big wheel. The tool for cutting is held in both hands, but worked by the right hand. The wood to be turned is fixed to an spike chuck, with contrivances to affix it of any length. It is set revolving by the wheel and the apparatus attached to it. The wood is first "roughed" with the gouge as near as possible to the shape required before it is submitted to the chisel. The workman in turning applies his chisel (as a general rule) on a rest (which slides along the top of the bench), holding it in an oblique direction as it cuts the wood being turned. The same form of chisels and gouges as those now employed has been used within the memory of the oldest man in the trade. After this it is glass-papered, and so finished as regards the turner's craft. Polishing or painting is the business of the tradesman who requires the article. About fifty years ago the pole-lathe, which is worked without a wheel, was in general use. It is now confined to only one or two branches of the trade. With the pole-lathe the workman, by means of a treadle, can give the work a turn forward or backward. The pole, which is placed above his head, sinks or rises to the pressure of the treadle, so that the work is done by a series of cuts, with an interval of time between each, instead of one continued revolution. The pole-lathe is still used in the country, especially in Buckinghamshire, where "rapparee" (painted bedroom) chairs are principally turned out of the beech, which is plentiful there; it is used too in some parts of Yorkshire. The London flute-makers ·and the bobbin-turners still use the pole-lathe. The wheel-lathe has been in common use for forty years.

The general turner's part of the business is considered to demand the greatest exercise of skill. He has frequently to work from drawings, and to work to great nicety, especially in new patterns for bed-pillars and table-legs; and an experienced cabinet-maker or an upholsterer will soon detect any irregularity in the turner's work, or any deviation from the pattern. Toy turning is not considered so nice an art, and the turning of drawer knobs is about the easiest of all descriptions of turned work; on them, and on ball feet for plain tables, boys are generally instructed. Boys, however, are of little use at turning until they have had a year and a half or two years' practice. "I myself never knew a woman employed in turning," said a workman to me, "except one, and her husband used sometimes to make her turn the big wheel, as a punishment for drunkenness. There have been a few females who have 'turned' in London, however, and more in the country." They all belonged to the turner's family.

The ivory and hard woods, however, are "turned" by a different method, and different tools are used from those of the general turner. The commonest implements of the hard wood and ivory turners are the firmer (a kind of chisel), the round-mouthed tool, the point tool, and the screaver or parting tool. The firmer is used to accomplish the finishing work, and is equivalent to the chisel of the general turner. The round-mouth tool is used as a gouge, and the others are applied to effect the openings of elevations on the pattern. If the article turned in ivory be large, it is frequently made of separate portions, the slender part being screwed firmly to the more bulky, as in letter stamps, and by this screwing material is saved. All ivory is turned by "scraping," the tool being applied horizontally to the work, while wood is turned by "cutting." The trade distinction is, that the ivory is "under-handed" work, and wood turning "over-handed." Hard woods are turned like ivory. Metal turning is more under-handed than ivory or hard wood turnng, the turner applying his shoulder to the tool to keep it on the rest. In hard woods and metals, as in ivory, "scraping" is the process observed. It is impossible to lay hold of the metal, I am told, unless the tool be applied below the centre. As a rule, the application of the tool in general turning is above the centre — in metal turning below it — while in ivory and hardwood turning it is held even with it.

All the wares which the turner's craft is now called upon to form are paid for by the piece (they have, however, neither a price nor a log book), as far as the operative is concerned, in the regular establishments where men, and not merely boys, are at work. Some of the smaller articles, such as tassel moulds, are, however, paid for by the day, and the diurnal mode of payment is the rule also for very heavy work of the more skilled description, and for that the payment is 6d. an hour, but in the best shops only; 20 years ago it was 8d. The "East-end boys," or "the cut-and-run men" ((as I heard them indifferently styled), who are the slop turners, give, however, only about 1½d. for every 4d. paid by the honourable trade. The men thus underpaid are to be found in the Curtain-road, Spitalfields, Bethnal-green. The reduction in the prices paid by the honourable trade is very considerable in some articles, and the rate is unchanged in one only. The reduction is the greatest in drawer knobs; 36s. a gross was paid for turning them 30 years ago; now 7s. 6d. is paid for the same work, and even a lower amount. The decline was about 14 years ago, when the prices fell at once from 33s. to 7s. 6d., and since they have dropped to 2s. 9d. at the East-end of the town. Bedposts are reduced two-thirds; what were 7s. 6d. are now 2s. 6d., the fall having been gradual within these 12 years. A workman who brought me the accounts of his earnings for several years past showed me that in 1836 he was paid 2s. 6d. a dozen for deal columns with two pins, and now he gets only 1s. 6d. for the same articles. Chair and sofa legs alone maintain the old prices to the workman. An intelligent operative said to me:—

"I date the *very good* prices from 35 years ago, when a man could earn £3 or £4 a week. I've earned £1 a day myself occasionally, and it was a shocking day when I couldn't earn a crown; and I date the *fair* prices, when we could earn 35s. or 40s. a week regularly, from 8 to 12 years ago. Now, for the very same kind of work, and working the same hours, and the same every way, on the average I can't touch 20s. a week, tho' I may make 18s. and 19s."

I hereby subjoin a copy of his earnings for the last year:—

"1849.

	£	s.	d.		£	s.	d.
1st week	0	3	7	24	1	4	0
2 and 3	0	10	7	25	1	7	6
4	1	6	0	26	1	10	0
5	1	2	6	27 and 28	2	3	3½
6	1	8	6½	29	1	10	0
7	0	10	9	30	1	5	0
8	0	19	6	31	1	1	4
9	0	5	7½	32	1	10	0
10	0	8	6	33	1	4	6
11	0	4	8	34	1	4	5
12	0	9	6	35	1	6	0
13, 14 and 15	0	4	1	36	1	2	10
16	0	7	7½	37	0	19	0
17 and 18	1	0	0	38	1	0	0
19	1	5	0	39 and 40	1	5	0
20	1	12	9	41	1	2	6
21	1	2	6	42	1	0	0
22	1	10	4	43	1	0	0
23	1	1	5	44	0	3	9

45	1	10	0	49	1	3	0
46	1	5	0	50	1	10	0
47	1	3	8	51	1	10	0
48	0	17	0	52	0	17	0

Total £48 8 3

"Average of the above earnings per week, 18s 7½d. My books show
that's been my earnings for these last four years; and as I've kept an account
of my earnings I can prove the same as the 'very good' and the 'fair' prices.
Now, sir, there's door furniture, for 'turning' which six years ago I had 21s.
a dozen sets (a single set is two large knobs, with brasses, two roses, bolt
knob and rose, 2 escutcheons, and covers). These dozen sets the London
trade now get supplied from Birmingham for less than 15s., the material
included. Six years ago I was paid 21s. for my labour alone. The
Birmingham man for the same work gets about 4s. Our earnings were 400
per cent. better on most things, and the reduction has fallen principally on
the man, and not much on the master."

The fall, I am informed, was going on gradually, if not rapidly, from 1831
to 1841. During that period a change, before alluded to, took place in the
fashions of the cabinetmakers' trade. Many ornamental portions of
furniture, such as door and drawer knobs, the rings for cornices, and other
articles, were then made of wood in the place of brass, which went entirely
into disuse. Thus there was a greater amount of work than usual to be done,
and fewer hands to do it, and yet wages declined. Among the working
turners there is at present no society, nor has there been any since 1844. The
last was broken up in that year through a disagreement among the members,
as to whether or not little masters should be admitted "into society." There
are now no houses of call, or labour markets," so to speak, for the London
turners. One was opened by the last society, but there were only two calls
made from it. There are among turners, moreover, no superannuation,
sick, or benefit funds, and in case of permanent sickness, or in old age – for
only a few of the turners are saving men, one told me that not above a dozen
of them were so – there is nothing but the parish or the workhouse for them
to fly to for maintenance. This class has been very burdensome, I am told, to
the parish of St. Giles. I regret to add I am unable to show statistically to
what extent; for, strange to say, and much to our national disgrace, there
are as yet no returns as to the trades or occupations of those receiving parish
relief. In case of an accident to a turner, a collection is now made among his
brethren, a petition being carried round, and a praiseworthy liberality is not
unfrequently manifested by the operatives of this class towards their
suffering brethren. One man who had the misfortune to break his arm lately
received 55s. by this mode. The same process is observed for the burial of
any working turner. The operatives in this trade are nearly all married, the
very young being the only exceptions. Some of their wives work for the slop

tailors, under whose employ 7d. a day (less by the expense of thread, candle, &c.), is considered good earnings. The best class of workmen average about 18s. a week wages, nearly the whole being payments for piece work. (In the country the payment is almost always by the day.) The very inferior workmen, the East-enders, earn, it appears, from 3s. to 5s. a week less than the West-end men. Among the turners at the East-end there are few journeymen; they are nearly all little masters, and do their work in the hastiest and roughest manner, so as to gain payment for the largest possible quantity. They dispose of this work to the little masters in the cabinet trade and to the iron mongers. They or their wives hawk ball feet and small knobs, and feet of all kinds, to cabinet makers as well as to their own trade. They are subject to the usual distress of the underpaid classes, being kept waiting (the women more especially) before receiving any decisive answer until a Saturday night is almost spent, and the necessity of having *something* for a Sunday dinner allows a customer to purchase upon his own most niggardly terms.

Men out of work, or "on tramp" from one part of the country to another, can now only gain employment by calling at the turners shops. There is no arrangement for the assistance of a man "on tramp," but if he be known and in distress there is usually, in the different shops that he may call at, a gathering among the men at work for him. Some men give 4d. each – some smaller sums – when they think him a deserving object. Nothing was allowed to men on tramp when the society when the society was in existence.

The turners are instructed in their craft principally by means of apprenticeship. Some masters take a great many apprentices, and some of the little masters, whether they have the means of employing boys or not, make a traffic, I am assured, in apprentice premiums, being always on the look-out for boys apprenticed by parishes or public institutions. The object of such masters is to secure the fees; and instances have been known where a man has run off, leaving his apprentices behind him with their trade but half-taught to them, and the world before them. The apprentice system, indeed, appears to be one of the crying evils of all trades, and especially the underpaid ones. It is common for masters in the turning trade to have four or five apprentices at one time. The indoor apprentices, after payment of the premium, which was varied from £5 to £40, receive for their labour their board and lodging, but not their clothing or washing, nor the support during sickness. The plan of taking apprentices by the little masters has the injurious effect of throwing into the labour market a continued series of little-skilled workmen, brought up in the midst of poverty and hardship, and often with no aspirations to rise into a better condition. "Ill-treatment and half starvation, said a turner to me, "is more often these lads' lot than anything else. I've seen as much, both in town and country." I find, too, that gentlemen's servants not unfrequently become turners. I heard it attributed to some of them having acquired a taste for such work by having served masters who were amateur turners, of whom among the wealthier classes there are many. "Some of the first gentry, I assure you, sir," said a master, "are fond of a turn at the lathe, and some of them are very good hands, especially the late Lord Y——. He was excellent, and so is the present Lord ——, and Mr. G. T——, the rich banker in ——." In King's College there are about 25 lathes for the amusement and tuition of the pupils, many of whom are very efficient and tasteful workmen, especially some young Egyptians. Some of the gentlemen's servants pay a premium (one paid £20) to be instructed in turning, three years being devoted to that purpose; and they received a small sum per week at first, 5s. or thereabouts for the first year, and then the amount of their labour. It is supposed that there are now in London thirty turners who have been gentlemen's servants, some of whom are now masters.

There are not among the turners the brisk and slack seasons so prejudicial to the interests of the journeymen in other trades. The turner's work is one of tolerable regularity. There have been no strikes in London for forty years, and they are very unfrequent in the country. I heard no complaints from the men as to the prevalence of steam power being applied to their work. Their chief objection to machinery was, that but for steam, there would be employment for half as many more turners as are now in existence.

I met a few intelligent men among the turners, but intelligence is not the characteristic of the great mass of them. The poverty of the little masters tempts them, as I have stated, to take numbers of apprentices, who in their turn become little masters, and boys reared as I have described cannot be expected to attain tastes beyond such as can be gratified in the tap-room or the skittle-ground. Their ordinary amusements are skittles, cards, ("all fives" being their usual game), and dominoes, played in the tap-rooms for beer. Nor is there any distinction between the journeyman and the little master, except that he journeyman may be better off. Drunkenness is far less common among them than it used to be, but that I found to be mainly attributed to the scantiness of their means. "Most turners in small wares," said a fringe turner to me, "amuse themselves in the public-houses near where they work. I amuse myself with reading the papers or anything when I have a little spare time; but the Spitalonians (Spitalfields men) are rare fellows for skittles, cards, and dominoes, and, badly as they're off, numbers of them don't work on a Monday. I like a game at knock-em-downs (skittles) now and then myself. It's good exercise, and good for trade, as skittles is turners' work, but I hate cards without it be a hand at cribbage, and cribbage is a cut above the Spitalonians."

A highly intelligent man gave me an account of what he knew of the state of his calling:—

"I have known the trade upwards of forty years; and as soon as I was out of my apprenticeship, I could make £2 to £2 10s. a week on the average the year through. Some made more. I know one man who made £2 in one day, in turning 'pateras' for billiard tables, but that was an exception. Pateras were 6s. a gross then; they're now 3s. 6d. Wages have been falling gradually these last twenty years. They fell long before provisions did. Now there's hardly a job we do, but there's a reduction or an attempt at it. 'If you won't do it,' the masters say, 'there's plenty will.' 'Well, then,' I say, 'you'd better get them; I'll take no less; for I know, you see, that I'm a skilful hand, and that makes a man independent. I turn bed-posts, table and chair legs, and everything required in the furniture line, door knobs, and all those sort of things included. I average the year through 18s. a week, or hardly that; and them's the best earnings in the trade, excepting the turners employed by the best cabinet-makers, who have their own lathes and turners, and employ the men on their own premises. There may be seven cabinet-makers who do this, and their men may average 32s. to 36s. a week. The reduction in the wages paid to us since I have known the trade, amounts to between one-third and two-thirds of what we formerly received, and there are still attempts to lower our wages further. We feel the want of a society, but it's no use to raise one, as the men won't stick to it, and on the whole, the main body of us turners are not so intelligent as other mechanics. Our work is noisy, too, and no talk can be carried on, as in the tailor's shop, by which men can pick up a little politics or knowledge. We are now like the bundle of sticks after it was opened, and masters know that, and now we have nothing to fall back upon, and they treat us accordingly. I am married, but have no family, and have the good fortune to have a careful wife, and a comfortable bit of a home, but that can only be done by my being abstemious, for I often suffer from sickness, and that brings such a heavy expense that I can't save anything."

In connection with the general branch of the turning trade, there is engaged for the large work a "turn-wheel" (or man to drive the lathe by means of "the big wheel"). This man is usually paid by time, 3d. per hour being the ordinary rate of remuneration. Those hired for this service are frequently old soldiers, but blind men are generally preferred to all others. The reasons of this is, I am told, because men who are not deprived of their sight do not turn the wheel at one uniform speed. Their mind, to use the words of my informant, is wandering away from their labour, owing to their attention being taken of by surrounding objects. The blind man, however, like the blind horse in the mill, does his work without any alteration in his velocity. Formerly there used to be many blind men thus employed in the turning trade, and these were mostly soldiers who had lost their sight in Egypt. There were likewise many blind sailors gaining a livelihood in this manner. Now, owing to the use of steam power for the heavier work, there are no regular "turn-wheels" belonging to the business.

I am indebted for the following information concerning hard wood and ivory-turning, to a man to whom I was referred as a skilful and tasteful workman:—

"I have known the London *hard wood and ivory turning* trade," he said, "upwards of twenty-one years. I believe that there are now about 200 working men in my business. We have no society, nor superannuation fund, nor any provision of the kind. In sickness or distress each man must shift for himself. We all work by piece. There is no printed or acknowledged list of price. Masters and men understand, or agree, what should be paid for work, according to the character and scale of prices of the shop. I have worked at all branches of the business, and twelve years ago I could make, and did make, 12s. a day. Now-a-days an average workman can make 30s. a week in a good shop all the year through, for one season is about as good as another. The turning of chessmen in ivory is from £1 to £2 journeymen's wages, according to the size and quality. Wood chessmen, ebony and box, are, as a fair average price, 3s. 6d. the set, but they're not to compare, in form or work, with ivory. We turn — ivory and hardwood, ebony, rosewood, ebony, rosewood, satinwood, or any wood — pincushions, door handles, bellpulls, small boxes, and a good deal of work for carriages, such as the door handles. All flat work in ivory is done by hand, not by the lathe. (My informant then showed and explained to me the mode of working, which I have already described.) I have had advantages besides regular work. I have given gentlemen lessons in turning. Many gentlemen, and some peers, are very good ivory turners. I gave lessons to a gentleman who had the lathe and all the turning tools and apparatus that old George III used to work with. It cost £500 at a sale. I have seen some of the old King's turning, and it was very fair. With industry he might have made 40s. or 50s. a week as a hardwood and ivory turner. A first-rater at that time, when times and wages were good, would earn twice as much or somewhere on to it. The King's lathe and all connected with it was the best and the most beautiful I have seen. No women work at my trade. I ought to have told you before, that ivory turners, when they have skill enough, are employed to carve the chessmen — though that has nothing to do with the turning. Perhaps to make a handsome knight, or a good castle is the most difficult. Billiard balls are all made of ivory. We get 2s. the set for turning them in good shops, 1s. in inferior shops, and they're done for 6d. by the 'master-men,' as we call the low-priced men, or what you call the slop-workers. The billiard ball must of course be perfectly circular, and we form it mainly by the eye, so that ours is really a nice art. Any little unevenness is regulated afterwards by "papering," that is by rubbing it down with glass-paper; but I can do it without rubbing it down with glass-paper; but I can do it without papering. The ivory is first sawn, and by a very fine saw, to the size wanted. It is then roughed with the gouge, towards the shape required with the gouge, towards the shape required. Then, if it's for a good shop, it's laid by for nine months; for if it's worked wet – and ivory's like wood that way – it will cast (warp) or crack. I have known billiard balls made out of green stuff in ivory, go an eighth of an inch longer one way than another. But the 'master-men,' the cheap fellows, work it green, and so can do it, cheaper. They don't care whether their work stands true or not – not they. We don't call the 'master-men's' work 'slop,' we call it 'bad' work. These men's work is very inferior. It's hard to say to what degree they undersell a good master, for every shop has, perhaps, a different scale of prices. Say they work for one half the money, and with less than half the skill and pains. They hawk their goods to the toy and fancy shops, and to private houses. They take lots of apprentices, who grow as well into master-men. I know one man who has six, and another who has fourteen of these apprentices, and the fourteen man has got most of them from the workhouse. The Lord knows how they're treated. These master-men are very poor. They live chiefly in Clerkenwell and Bethnal-green. I don't suppose they earn more than 15s. a week, indeed not that the year through. These men expose the better masters to a very unfair competition. The foreign trade doesn't affect us much. One of our lathes costs from £4 to £5, and our tools may cost from £150 to £200; perhaps there is more than 200 of them of all kinds and substances, of firmers and the others. I'm speaking of the very best and handsomest sort of tools; such as gentlemen have; and it was this as made George III's lathe and kit so valuable. In our trade, however, the master finds tools (and they may generally cost half what I've mentioned), and the journeyman, if he's not a master-man as well, always works on the premises. The under-standing is, that when new tools are wanted the master finds the material, and the journeyman makes the tool. The wear and tear of them isn't 6d. a week. We turn bones as well as hard woods and ivory, but ivory's our main business. leg-of-beef and shin bones are turned into surgical instruments, such as syringes; calf shin-bones are turned into common chessmen, but they have a scrubby look with them. When an article's turned, it's polished off with putty-powder, or something of the kind. Some are dyed after they're turned. There's two men in London who do nothing but dye our work, and they must make £3 to £4 a week. They say they have secrets, but I dare say it's just chemistry. The demand for chessmen has increased in my time. There is half as many more required now as when I first knew the trade. The ivory we work is African, Siam, and East Indian, or Ceylon. The Ceylon is the finest grain, but the Siam is the largest.''

A man long familiar with the trade gave me an account of his experience as a *plumber's turner:*–

"I have known the trade 28 years in town and country, and have worked the last nineteen years in London. At first I was a general turner, and I am now a plumber's.'' (He described the nature of his work as I have given it previously). ''Ours is all piecework, except a few new models, and that's day-work; but it's very unfrequent. I could earn 8s. or 9s. a day 15 years ago, or rather more in winter, when I first was a plumber's turner in London; then it was my own fault if I stood still a single day, but I had to work very long hours for it, sometimes from 5 to 8 at night. Now, tho' there's no quicker hand in London, I must work harder to make 5s. than I did to make 9s. Wages have been so reduced, and the fall is on all the things mady by plumber's turners alike – they are all of one sort of work. I have earned 10s. a day in making plumber's dressers. I had 3s. 6d. a dozen for them, and now its 2s. 3d. There are now many things in my way, such as buckets and sockets, and plumber's tools in general, hawked about the streets for less than I have received for my labour on them. These cheap things are badly made; there's neither good workmanship nor good stuff in them, but they supplant better things.'' (I had from this man the same account of the want of a society as from the general turner). ''My wife does not go out to work, but then we have no family, or she must. I can still keep a pretty comfortable home, as I average 12s. a week the year through. My wife and I used to go the play now and and then six or eight years ago, and to Hampton Court sometimes, but, cheap, as those things are, it's out of the question with us at present. There's other things to think of – a decent sort of an appearance and tidyish room, and its only by being careful and steady that we can manage even that.''

A pale but keen-looking man gave me the following account of *tassel and fringe mould turning:*

''I have known the London trade from my childhood, and my ancestors have been engaged in it 100 years back, though not all that time in London. When I first knew the trade, twenty-three years ago, it was very prosperous. A good hand would then earn 36s. a week by piece-work at fringe moulds; and now, for the same amount of work, he wouldn't earn a third of that, not more than 10s., if as much. We were paid by the piece then as now, for 'fringes' so much the gross. Tassel-mould turning is the best part of the trade. These moulds are used for upholsterers' hangings, either for the drapery of beds or windows, for bell pulls, blinds, pulpit cushions, and similar things. There's numbers made for what's known as 'pulpit cushions,' but only a small part of them's used for parson's pulpit cushions; they're used for sofa cushions and such like. Trade was better when tassels were the fashion for the hammer-cloths of gentlemen's carriages, and indeed almost all our work is still for 'the nobs,' and yet it's most badly paid. We turn the wooden moulds in the usual way, treading and standing on one leg all day long, and the upholsterers' work-women cover these coulds with silk, velvet, worsted, or whatever's wanted. They're very badly paid. The fringe moulds are made for the same purposes as the tassel. The tassel is a plain mould and the fringe is rounded. We generally do tassels – and tassels only – by day-work, a good shop gives 25s. a week day-work (30s. to a very extraordinary hand), and inferior shops 20s. An average workman will do four gross a day of the easiest style of tassels, and short of a gross of the most difficult. It depends upon the pattern. The largest sizes are not the most difficult. It was all piece-work when first I knew the trade, but tassels hadn't come in then. I first worked on tassels ten years ago, and they'd come in a few years before that, perhaps. The wages haven't varied. We make about as many tassels as fringes; one tallies with the other. In turning fringes, we have, for 'short pipes' 9d. the gross; they are 9d. up to 3½ inches, and they rise at the rate of a halfpenny and a penny a gross through the different sizes, the highest being 4s. a gross for twelves inches, and 6s. for fourteen inches. Work night and day – and the men do so nearly – and they make from 15s. to 20s. a week. These prices are third of what they were twenty years ago, and they have kept falling gradually. I consider the fall is chiefly owing to so many small masters underselling each other, and eating one another up. When a lad's out of his apprenticeship, if he can only raise the expense of a lathe (and you can get a second-hand one for £1 – a good new lathe is worth £5), and can raise the tools required, which may be bought for another £1, these, with a bundle of wood, is all the stock in trade wanted for a start; and then the upholsterers and the cabinet-makers and the trade all know they have needy men to deal with, and make their bargains accordingly. The goods are hawked from shop to shop, and the customers put on the screw, and the little masters are left very little, hardly enough to pay just for their labour. I am a journeyman, but very few fringe turners employ journeymen, as their work is chiefly done by apprentices. I average 20s. a week. Among the apprentices a great many are parish boys, with whom a premium is given – I don't know what exactly. I know one who had several parish apprentices – it was for the sake of cheaper workpeople, not for the sake of the fees. The apprentices are bound for seven years generally, and must be kept all that time by the master. The little masters are drinking men frequently, and very poor. If anything happens to them there's nothing but the parish. Most of them have large families, and they live and work all in one room. The button-turners are amongst the worst off, but some button-turners are tassel-turners also, in which case they may take an apprentice. If they are only button-turners, I think an apprentice is almost beyond them. They live a good deal about Spitalfields. I can't say the turners I speak of are ever out of work, as they're little masters, and set themselves to work. But its only raking up an existence, it's not a living; not to be called one. As for myself, I'm not very partial to the turning business, only I'm among friends who are in it. I may cut it soon, as I have before now. Altogether I think I have worked eight years at other things, for I'm an independent sort of a man. Nobody whatever shall put upon me; a word, and I'm off. I've worked at repairing guns, and at shoemaking. I picked up the skill somehow by seeing others, and being quick. (Another turner told me that he was his own tailor.) I did tidy that way. But my main employ when away from my own trade – and I was never apprenticed to it, but was taught by my relations – was in having the care of steam-engines in factories. I've made 27s. and 30s. a week that way. I've had the care of a steam-engine at a great brewer's, so you perceive I can make a shift many ways.''

A man with a delicate look, and a stoop (not uncommon in his business, as the turners lean over their labour all day long), gave me the following statement concerning bobbin-turning:

"I am *a bobbin turner,* and may say I was born one, as I was born in Spitalfields, and have been in the trade all my life, and my father is 79, and has been in the trade since he was nine years of age. About 25 years ago my trade was good. I could live comfortably, and could have kept a wife and family comfortably. I wasn't married then, but I did marry 20 years ago, and at that time I had every prospect of keeping a wife and family well. It's a hard thing on working men like me, sir, that we marry when we find ourselves in a pretty good business, and of course we can't see why it should fall off, and then it does fall off, from no fault of ours, and so we are left to trouble and distress. It's a hard thing, sir; steam has taken away a great part of my labour, but how could I tell that? And yet I've often heard it said, that poor men shouldn't marry because trade was so bad. I have now a wife and seven children. I turn nothing but bobbins; that is a branch by itself. I turn cotton, lace, worsted, and silk bobbins. I work with the pole. The bobbins are made out of a sold piece of wood, always the trunk of the alder tree. The master supplies solid logs of wood, varying in length, which we cut into six or seven substances lengthways. We then cut these substances to the length required for the bobbins, and split them with a knife and mallet to the right thickness. The alder we use is grown chiefly in Kent and Berkshire. 'Reading staves' are the best in my trade. I am paid by the piece. 25 years ago I was paid 6s. a gross, journey-work, for silk bobbins, and could make five gross a week. I was paid 30s. a gross for large cotton bobbins, and could make a gross and a half a week, but for that work I had to find the material, which cost me from 12s. to 14s. Lace-bobbins were 8s. a gross, and I could make 4 gross a week. At that time, sir, I averaged 30s. a week. 20 years ago I could make about the same, but 17 years ago the fall began. Steam first began it. Silk bobbins first fell 6d. a gross, and the other in proportion. Our wages have kept falling and falling ever since, until last year we had 3s. For silks and for cottons and laces there's no demand; they're all country work, made mostly at Leicester, where wood's cheap, and steam power 10d. a day. They make cotton and lace bobbins, and find their own material, at one quarter the price we used to get. When I last worked on cotton bobbins, about 18 months ago, I had 8s. for the gross, and it's horse's work; they're too heavy for the foot, and with slaving like a horse or a slave, I could only make 12s. a week; but that was for the labour. The fall was gradual, from 30s. a week to 8s. I am now occupied only on silk bobbins, and last year they were 3s. a gross, and we then said one to another, 'They can't be lower anyhow,' but this year they are lower, only 2s. 9d., and as my master knows I'm a poor man with a large family (seven children), he's on the look out to reduce me to 2s. 6d., and I haven't full work at 2s. 9d. I can make five gross a week, but don't average more than four, that's 11s. Out of that I have to keep a wife and six children; one of my girls is in service. My wife works for a slop tailor, and makes 2s. 6d. a week by very hard work, and finds her own thread, too. One of my sons earns 3s. a week at glass blowing, he's grown up, but he's a cripple, and does it by night work; he can do nothing else. My other children are under nine years of age. My rent is 2s. 3d. a week for one room unfurnished. In that room I have to work, and in it my wife has to work, and we have to cook in it, but it's very little cooking does for us, though we have to keep a fire to heat the irons for pressing my wife's tailoring work. She works for a sweater, and is now making postmen's waistcoats at 6d. a piece. We have all to sleep in the same room, which is a goodish size. If I could afford it two rooms would be a great good to me. We live on bread and butter and tea, three times a day. That for breakfast at half-past seven, the same again between twelve and one, and the same again about seven at night. We may taste meat once in every four or five Sundays, mostly this time of the year" (this was said a few weeks ago), "for when the weather's so hot butchers are glad to get rid of meat at any price when they find it's a going, and really it's not fit to eat. As for clothing, the children have often enough to go without it, and so should I, if I hadn't an old thing given me by people my wife has nursed. I've never heard any particular reason for the reduction of our wages. Now the master weavers say that they can't afford the present wages, silk is so dear. The silk is wound ready for the weaver's use round the bobbins we turn. A great many in my trade have to live as I live. There's at least forty as badly off as I am in Spitalfields. I should have told you that I drink a great deal of water, and I really think that does me harm, for it's bad water, as one cock serves all the premises. I'm so weak in the evening I can hardly stand. My children play about in the court when it's fine, and when it's wet in the room. A girl of nine jobs and cleans about the house, or my wife could do no work at all. I have two children at a Ragged School. I can't afford to send them to any better place. They seem to like it very well. They are continually thinking of the loaf and bun they get at Christmas; last year they had a loaf and a twopenny pie; they often talk about that. All the families of the men situated as I am, live like mine. The little masters are a great cut-up to our business by underselling the better masters. I can't say that I know any drunkards among the journeymen in my trade. We're given over caring about politics since the time of the union, and then we didn't understand it. We are quiet men, and submit quietly to what we suffer. I can read and write, as I dare say most of us can. We have no fund, and no society, and never had. I see no prospect of better times, not at all; and if provisions were dearer, we might go to the parish, as we've done before, and in old age a man like me must come to the workhouse, and that's a sorrowful thought. A penny or a halfpenny a loaf makes a great difference to me; it does, indeed, sir – a very great difference, for bread's our great expense. It's dear eating, after all, is bread and butter for a family – there's no strength in it."

Another man in this trade told me that he was eighty or thereabouts, and had been married fifty-two years, and that he could still work at his trade, but could only make from 5s. to 6s. a week. He had never worked at anything but bobbins, and until within these nineteen or twenty years he could earn about 25s. a week. He could not work so well or so fast as he could a few years ago, he said, "but the fall in the prices is my great hindrance." "Yes," said his wife, "and if we ask a little help from the parish, they say, 'O, you can come into the house;' but then you see, sir, we should be parted, and that's a hard thing after being together above fifty years."

A *button mould trimmer,* living in a wretched room, told me that his trade was "sinking out." He made the button moulds which were covered with silk, and used for ladies dresses. He had, some years ago, he hardly knew how many, 4d. and 4½d. for what he had now 1½d. and 2d. a gross, and very little work he could get now even at those prices. He made 4s., 5s., or 6s. a week now, and 10s., 12s., or 14s. formerly.

I saw several of these humbler workmen, and found their rooms bare of furniture, but generally clean. The pride of the artisan to have "something to call a home," still exists.

Concerning the "little masters," I had the following information. There were very few little master turners in the general branch of the trade before 1823. The operative turners were, prior to that time, generally journeymen working for the respectable master turners, who were then four times as numerous as now. Each of these masters employed from three to half a dozen men on their premises, having very rarely more than one or two apprentices. The wages of the journeymen ranged from £5 to £2, the average earnings being between 50s. and 60s. per week. After the year 1823 the cabinet makers by whom the master turners were employed, finding that they could not get their work done owing to the drinking habits of the journeymen turners, determined on reducing the prices paid to the masters, on the plea that they gave too much money to their men; and no sooner were the masters' prices reduced than they lowered the wages of the men. The journeymen, however, knowing that it was the custom of the masters to charge one-third as profit upon the amount paid to the journeymen for their labour, determined not to submit to the reduction, and accordingly several started in business for themselves. These journeymen then solicited the custom of the cabinet makers who had employed their former masters, offering to do their work at a lower rate. The more respectable masters, finding themselves undersold by the journeymen who had left their employ, then went to work to reduce the prices of the men that still remained with them, and thus sought to get their work back again from the cabinet makers. This further reduction, however, caused more journeymen still to leave their masters' employ, and to start in business for themselves, seeking to obtain work at a lower rate still. And thus matters have been going on to the present time − journeymen trying to cut under the masters, and the masters, partly in self defence and partly in revenge, trying to cut down the wages of the men.

There are now, I am told, four principal reasons for turners becoming little masters. First, says my informant, the men are generally so fond of drink that a large master won't employ them. Then they commence business themselves, and work for little master cabinet makers. Another cause is, that it takes but a few pounds to commence operations on their own account. A third reason is, because they don't like to be under the control of an employer. And the fourth, because, when working for themselves, they can begin when they like, and leave off and have "a spree" when they please.

The little masters in the turning trade work the same long hours as the garret-masters in the cabinet trade. When a man begins for himself he gets a boy to tread the lathe, clean up the wood ready for turning. I heard of no boys working at a lathe who are less than twelve years of age. "You see, sir," I was told, "the work is so heavy that it requires a strong boy to do it."

The East-end turners generally, I was informed, labour at the lathe from six o'clock in the morning till eleven and twelve at night, being 18 hours' work per day, or 108 hours per week. They allow themselves two hours for their meals. It takes them, upon an average, two hours more every day fetching and carrying their work home. Some of the East-end men work on Sundays, and not a few either, said my informant. "Sometimes I have worked hard," said one man, "from six one morning till four the next, and scarcely had any time to take my meals in the bargain. I have been almost suffocated with the dust flying down my throat after working so many hours upon such heavy work too, and sweating so much. It makes a man drink where he would not. It is generally considered that about nine-tenths of the turners are little masters. In fact, nearly the whole of the general turners are little masters, and one-quarter of these hire the lathes they use, for which they pay from 2s. to 2s. 6d. per week. The little master turners seldom or never work upon their own materials. It costs about £3 to set up in the business in a little way. A lathe (second-hand) costs £2, and tools £1."

The little masters, I am informed, spend at least 4s. per week in beer; and almost all agree in ascribing the impoverishment of the trade to the drinking habits of the men. The Metropolitan Police returns, however, show the turners to be the least criminal in this respect, and, indeed, in all others, of the whole of the artisans that I have yet treated of. Striking the average of those taken into custody for drunkenness during the last ten years, the ratios have been as follows: sailors, 1 drunkard in every 13; labourers, 1 in every 31; carpenters and joiners, 1 in every 59; sawyers and tailors, 1 in every 63; weavers, 1 in every 75; carvers and gilders, 1 in every 89; shoemakers, 1 in 91; coachmakers, 1 in 106; and turners and cabinet-makers, 1 in every 580 of the entire body. The turners and cabinet-makers are also the least criminal; that is to say, there have been the least relative number of them taken into custody during the last ten years for manslaughter, rape, common assaults, and simple larceny.

LETTER LXVIII
Thursday, September 5, 1850

According to the last census the number of "Ship-builders, Carpenters, and Wrights" (terms between which it is not easy to distinguish, the builder, carpenter, and wright being, according to my informants, one and the same individual), were in 1841 20,424 throughout Great Britain. Of these 17,498 were residents in England and Wales, and 2,926 in Scotland. The number located in the Metropolis — with whom I have more particularly to deal — was then 2,309. Since that period the number appears to have increased nearly one-fifth, for, according to the best-informed persons in connection with the trade, the following may be taken as a correct estimate of the hands belonging to the different branches of the business at the present time:

	Society Men	Non-society Men	Total number of Society and Non-society Men
Shipwrights...............................	1,500	500	2,000
Shipwrights Joiners	110	230	340
Mast and Block makers................	110	140	250
Boat-builders............................	30	80	110
Barge-builders	—	150	150
	1,750	1,100	2,850

The building of a ship may be not inaptly compared to that of a house, as I have described it in my former Letters. The modeller executes the plans of the architect. The shipwright is the carpenter. The ship-joiner's department of the work is not very dissimilar in its character to that of his namesake ashore; while the labour of the mast and block makers, of the boat-builders, and the sail-makers, may roughly typify that of the cabinet-makers and upholsterers, and other furnishers and finishers of our dwellings.

It is not my intention fully to describe the whole process of the important art of ship-building, nor would the limits of a newspaper admit of such description. To show the divisions of the trade, however, and so to render the statements I give more clear and intelligible, I will very briefly explain the process as it was described to me by working men, to whom I was referred as being the most skilful and intelligent. Three classes of workmen are employed in the construction of a vessel, before it is "ready for rigging." These are the *shipwrights*, the *ship-joiners*, and the *caulkers*. The work (as regards the mechanical labour employed) commences with the shipwright; and he and the ship-joiner makes the whole "carcass" from "keel to gunal" (gunwale); the joiner's work being confined principally to the formation of the cabins. Drafts and plans are given out by the foreman for the guidance of all the operatives. The shipwright begins with the keel, which is always made of elm – sometimes American, but chiefly English, timber being used. They then "put in the floors;" which are the timbers that constitute the bottom of the vessel and float upon the water. These "floors" consist of first, second, and third "futtocks" (fuddocks), the form of which I described in my letter on ship-timber sawing, and they are made so as to give, when put together by the skill of the workman, the form, the bend, and sweep of the hull. The perfect construction of this portion of the vessel is the high art of the shipwright. "Top-timber" is then placed above the floors for the purpose of binding and strengthening them by an interior as well as an exterior connection; and when that is done – English oak being used as the material – the ship is said to be "in frame." She – for I found the feminine appellative applied, no matter in what stage the vessel might be – is then "ribanded;" that is, pieces of timber, five and six inches square, are affixed fore and aft, as a temporary hold or binding to the timbers, so that they may "set" properly, for which a month is sometimes allowed. After this the ship is in a state to be "skinned," or planked, the wrights commencing with "the wale," or continuation of the bottom; and thus they work on to the completion of the "top sides" which surmount the upper deck.

Thus far outside work alone has been spoken of. After this the inside portion is begun; but sometimes the outside and inside works are carried on simultaneously. The inside work is generally commenced at the lower deck clamp – the clamp being the part which holds and supports the beams. The lower deck beams are "crossed," or adjusted, in a way not unlike the adjustment of the girders and joists of a house; and the same labour is completed as regards the middle and upper decks (supposing the vessel to be 1,000 tons), but the planking is "left to the last to give the ship air." If a smaller vessel be built, the same method is practised. The next stage is to form "the poop," which comprises the outer portion, or carcass, of the captain's, officers', and passengers' apartments; and then that of the forecastles, or sleeping places of the crew. The beams, of English or African oak – English oak and sometimes teak having been used for all the previous portions – are then laid across, to form the quarter-deck, and the decks are afterwards "planked." The planks are of Dantzic fir, and are laid in a way very similar to that practised in flooring a room, but the shipwright must lay his planks with a nice adjustment to the curved and sweeping outline of the ship; while the outline to which the house joiner has to work in the floors is generally straight.

The ship-joiner, when the work is advanced as I have detailed, is required to ply *his* avocation. He makes and fits up the whole of the interior accommodation of the ship, such as the cabins for the officers and passengers, and the forecastles. Deal, which is afterwards painted, is the wood generally used for the cabins of merchant vessels; but when the fitting-up is in a superior style, handsome mahogany or maple gives a richness and elegance of appearance to the interior of the ship. I was told by an experienced person that the costly furniture and fitting-up of a cabin greatly reassured any timid passenger to whom sea voyaging was new, and who felt nervous and apprehensive before the hour of sailing. Such a passenger – a lady especially – I was assured, seemed to feel, and had not unfrequently expressed an opinion, that the owners of the ship were confident there was no danger of its being wrecked, or they would not have expended so large a sum in mere adornment. The saloon of a steamer, or the equivalent "cuddy" of a passenger sailing vessel of the first class, is often fitted up with mirrors, sofas, and expensive wainscotting, in a style that is known as the "gorgeous." The ship-joiner makes also the sideboards, the sofas, and every article of furniture which is fixed or stationary in the vessel, and so he must be able to work as a cabinet-maker as well as a joiner. On the very rare occasions on which the ship-joiner is required to work by the day his wages are 5s. 6d.; on piece-work, however, he earns somewhat more.

The caulkers are employed solely in "caulking" the vessel, the process required to ensure her proper floating. They drive a caulking-iron (not unlike a blunt square chisel) into the ship's seams, and then "horse it up;" that is, fill the interstice with oakum, driven in as close and tight as possible with a tool called "a horse." The surface is then pitched over, and the pitch is afterwards scraped and painted. But "caulkers," according to the divisions of artisans which I have here adopted, belong to a different class, and cannot be included among the workers in wood.

In the principal, and, indeed, in nearly all the ship-building yards, the men work by contract – a system which has been pursued for the last fifty years at the least. A shipwright contracts to do all the wright's work, or a portion of it, and employs men under him. In these cases no day-work is performed; all is done by the piece. In some yards, however, there is occasional day-work, and the payment for it is 6s. and 7s. a day. I am assured, moreover, that on piece work, in a good establishment, good workmen earn an equivalent amount at least, as the proprietors will not allow them to be ground down to swell the profits of the contractors. Nor, in the best yards of which I am now writing, are there any middlemen (beyond the contractor), or any subletting. The same system is pursued in the departments of the joiner and the caulker. Under the best management, however, and with all the checks adopted against abuse, the system of contract leads to the following grievance. Each contractor can employ his own men, or "mates" as they are termed, and of course he give the preference to his own friends and relatives, who may be young men, while wrights or joiners who have spent half a life time in working, "off and on," for the same firm, may stand by idle. In case of a discharge from one of her Majesty's dockyards, "the hands," as it was worded to me, "make for London, for river-work," and cause somewhat of a glut of ship-building operatives. Many of the men thus discharged may be friends and relatives of a contractor, and men who have superannuated pensions from Government are "put on" over the heads of workmen to whom long employment in an establishment has given what they not unreasonably consider a sort of prescriptive right of engagement. These cases are, I understand, exceptional, and in the ship-builders' yards, which may well be called of the "honourable trade," the contractor must not, and does not, use his power to employ underpaid workmen. Skilled labour is indispensable for employment. The only complaint of which I heard was that an undue preference was shown.

The shipwrights and all the mechanics employed in ship-building find their own tools. The wright's tools are not costly. The principal are the axe, adze, maul, mallet, saw, and chisel. A complete set is not worth more than 50s., and some work with tools of the value of 25s., carrying them all in a bag. The joiner's tools, which are similar to those of his brother operative on shore, are worth, in their fullest completeness, £20. I heard of one ship-joiner whose tools, along with the handsome mahogany chests in which they were contained, were worth £80, £10 may be the average value of the tool's that a ship-joiner possesses. A caulker's tools, however, cost only a few shillings.

The hours of labour are from six in the morning in summer, and from daylight in winter, until six at night, or until dusk. Out of this term of labour half an hour is allowed for breakfast, half an hour for luncheon, an hour for dinner, and half an hour for tea; so that the entire term of labour is at the utmost nine hours and half.

There is no special subdivision among any of the classes that I have spoken of, and they are employed alike in building steamers and every kind of sailing vessel. The contractor, or the foreman, who has the general over-looking and direction, will take care that a workman is employed on the work in which he is the most skilled, but no department of the labour must be strange to him. Some of the joiners, who may be less efficient than their fellows, are often "put to embossing" – that is to say, they work after the shipwrights, in planing the sides of the vessel, and in putting the ornaments to the head, side, and stern. When a joiner, even of the very best order, has completed the particular work given to him, he also – if no "job" that is more suitable to him be ready – is put to embossing, until other work can be given to him. The calling of the shipwright is exclusively his own. No house-carpenter can undertake – or rather would, in a good yard, be allowed to undertake – the execution of the shipwright's work. But the case is different with the joiner. A clever house-joiner readily becomes a clever ship-joiner, and is occasionally so employed by a befriending contractor. The ship-joiner in like manner can work as a house joiner, and did so before the house-joining sank into its present condition – a condition which I have fully predicted in my letters on the subject. Among the ship-joiners – I must still be understood to speak of the honourable trade – there are no "improvers," no "strapping," indeed none of the more serious grievances by which his less fortunate brother operative ashore is afflicted.

The work of the ship-builders is very hard, and demands not merely the customary skill and quickness of the handicraftsman, but great manual strength; they must either carry heavy beams or wood-work from the work-shops to the ship, or else they must convey ponderous timbers complete to the workshop for affixing in the ship, and with these they must ascend and descend the ladders. In the course of my inquiry the weather was very sultry, and the men suffered greatly by having to work in the broiling sun; for in many parts of the labour on the ship itself they could have no shelter. The work is always carried on in the "dry dock," where the vessel is being built, or in the workshops adjacent, where everything is made (such as doors, furniture, &c.) that is susceptible of admeasurement, and then taken to the ship to be "fitted." In the winter the men suffer much from exposure to the cold. In rainy weather they are employed as much as possible in the workshops, or under cover.

The caulkers' work is especially hard, so much so that they do not toil later than three in the afternoon. The greater fatigue of the caulkers is attributable to their having to caulk in all positions of the body – recumbent or half-recumbent. When the bottom of the ship, for instance, is caulked, the men have hardly room to stand. Accidents are not unfrequent among shipwrights, who work on "stages" (equivalent to the scaffolding of a house) lashed to the ships' sides. A short time before my visit to one of the yards, one of the chains of a stage holding four men broke, and they all were suddenly precipitated some twenty feet to the ground; all were hurt – one seriously – though no lives were lost. A fall of this kind is the more dangerous as the men work with sharp tools.

In point of intelligence, the ship-builders must be ranked high – quite as high as their fellow-labourers of the best class (I now allude to none other) ashore. One shipwright, however, thought that many of his fellows did not avail themselves so freely as they might of the munificent means for the education of children which an eminent shipbuilder has so generously provided – I allude to Mr. Green. I was assured, not withstanding, that every shipbuilder, not an "emigration" or "a lath and plaster man," or a "boiler-maker" – terms that I shall presently explain – could, at the very least, read and write.

The shipbuilders are, I found, great politicians. It is customary, during their half hour's luncheon at eleven o'clock, for one man to read the newspaper aloud in the public-house parlour; a discussion almost invariably follows, and is often enough resumed in the evening. The men for the most part go home to their dinners. The earnings of the shipwrights of the best class, are, while at work, from 40s. to 50s. a week; and those of the joiners and caulkers from 10 to 15 per cent. less; but it must be borne in mind that the average employment of the general body does not exceed nine months in the year. The majority of the shipbuilders are married men with families, residing chiefly in Poplar and the adjacent parts. Some whom I called upon had very comfortable homes, and in their apartments there was no lack of books – a very fair test, it may be said, of the intelligence and prudence of a working man. Not a few of the shipbuilders have brought up their sons to their own calling, or to some other branch of ship-building, or else to a sea-faring life. Within these twenty years the shipbuilders generally were hard drinkers – now, I am assured, there are 50 steady men to 1 tippler.

In some yards the workmen are paid once a fortnight, the money being disbursed to them out of the counting-house on a Friday evening, the payment being for all that was due up to the previous Tuesday night. In other yards they are paid at four p.m. on the Saturday. I was informed that it is common enough for a shipbuilder, with his wife and children, to enjoy his Saturday evening in some surburban excursion. Payment in public-houses, or anything approximating to the truck system, is unknown.

The average time now occupied before a ship of 1,000 tons can be built and launched is twelve months; but on an emergency an 800 ton ship has been commenced and launched in four months. Formerly, I was assured, ships were kept so long on the stocks for "seasoning" – especially the East India Company's large vessels – that the dry rot appeared in their timbers before planking. "Now," said my informant, "that's only the case in her Majesty's dockyards."

In the course of my inquiries, I heard the better class of shipbuilders speak of a description of work known in the trade by the very expressive title of "emigration work" – by which was meant the building of a vessel "just for a passage out." The men thus employed were either unskilful, or not respectable, but the demand for such vessels has now almost ceased – old vessels alone being fitted up for emigrants. "There's Mr. ——," I was told, "picks out old ships and prepares them, and sends them out. He supplies emigration companies." Another class of ships I heard described as "lath and plaster" ships. "They are thrown together," I was told – another informant said "blown together – in the north of England; made cheap, of Quebec oak and inferior stuff, and inferior work; the timber ain't squared, it's sided together with the sap in it, and so it'll shrink and warp." I was told, however, that some ships are built in a northern port, almost equal to those built in London.

The shipbuilders in London are – as regards the majority – natives of the metropolis. The others are principally Scotchmen, and west of England men, with a small proportion of north countrymen, and a very small proportion of Irishmen. In one large yard there was but one Irishman. All whom I saw, no matter from what part of the country, spoke of the London-built ships, in the goods yards, as being the best in the world.

There are two other classes of operatives connected with ship-building, to whom I need only allude, as my present inquiry is confined to the workers in wood – viz., the workers in iron. These are the ship's smiths (called blacksmiths in the trade), who make the bolts, knees, and other iron work of the ship, and who are a highly respectable class; as well as the iron shipwrights, or men employed in constructing the iron steam-boats. Between these last-mentioned workers in ship iron and the workers in ship wood, there is no cordiality. The iron workers are called "boiler-makers" by the regular shipwrights, who describe them as an inferior class to themselves, made up from all descriptions of workers in iron, and including many boys and unskilled labourers.

The first process usually observed in ship-building is the preparation of the model, showing the form and proportions of the vessel to be built. In large establishments a modeller is employed by the ship builders, and his services are confined to them alone. For the purposes of general trade this profession is very limited; only one name appears in the Post-office Directory as a *ship modeller*. This gentleman employs only the members of his own family in the business, and his calling seems so far hereditary that it has been pursued by his family from the time of his grandfather. A draft is first pencilled, and by that the modeller works. Until about twenty years ago one draft served from generation to generation for one particular kind of vessel. Now, a draft and model are prepared expressly for every ship. The art of modelling requires not only the exercise of the most patient and minute nicety, but a thorough knowledge of ship-building in all its ramifications. The artist, too, must give the precise form of the vessel, as well as every separate portion, called "sections," for the guidance of the builder. Moreover the model is sometimes "rigged," and the masts, blocks, &c., are shown according "to scale;" and further the tonnage of the ship to be built must be expressed by the admeasurement of it.

Ships are now registered according to the new plan of admeasurement (established about ten years ago). The great difference between the two systems is that the new is inside, and the old outside, measurement. To ascertain the tonnage by the new mode, the middle (or medium) length of the vessel inside, from stem to stern, is taken; also the depth amidships, one-sixth of the depth forward and one-sixth aft; the breadth, one-third from the deck amidships, and one-third from the bottom; the same forward and aft; and these respective admeasurements are then multiplied together, decimally, and when divided by 3,500 the result gives the "register tonnage." To show the tonnage by the old mode, the outside length "between the perpendiculars" (or from stem to stern) was ascertained; also the measurement of two-fifths of the main beam (which gives the length of the keel for tonnage); and these results being multiplied by the breadth, and by half the breadth of the vessel, and then divided by 94, gave the builder's measurement. I am informed that, notwithstanding every precaution, the tonnage measurement of a ship is hardly ever correct. Ships are "cramped," as it is called by the builder; that is, the proportions of the parts where the admeasurement takes place are so managed that the result shall, for purposes of registry, &c., be as favourable as possible to the shipowner.

The modeller works to any scale required. For a small yacht or schooner an inch to a foot has been worked; for a large ship, an inch to 20 feet. The woods he uses are the finest firs, holly, mahogany, box, and ebony. The pulleys and all the tackle for a full-rigged model are made if bone or any hard wood. Sometimes the model shows only what may be styled the exterior of the vessel, the holds and cabins being left to the discretion or the instructions of the builder. Sometimes every portion, down to the minutest part, is expressed. A model can, moreover, be taken to pieces, when made for that purpose, and all the component parts of the important process of shipbuilding are thus displayed individually. To show the labour and nicety required for such a model, I may mention that one of a West Indiaman, 350 tons burden, was made for a learned judge now on the bench, and when taken to pieces, the parts numbered 651. My informant attributed much of the greater care and attention now given to the production of ships' models to the improvements introduced by the Yacht Club, the members having frequently required models, both for experimental and practical purposes.

Another, and an important department of the ship-modeller's business, and one subjected to severe examination, is to prepare the models of vessels for the Admiralty and law courts, to illustrate collisions; and thus to show, as far as possible, by the nature and locality of the damage, if the vessels were on the right or wrong tacks, according to the regulations of the Admiralty and the Corporation of the Trinity House, and sometimes to demonstrate the extent of damage sustained.

A *ship-joiner*, whom I found in a very comfortable room with his wife and family, gave me the following account: —

"My father was in the business, and I was brought up to it by a friend of his. That's often reckoned a better way, as fathers are too severe or too indulgent. I was regularly apprenticed, and have never worked anywhere but in London, except once. I have always worked under the contractors, and have made my 33s., 36s., and 38s. a week when at work, according to the piece work — it's all piece work — that I get through. There is no fixed price — so much for the job, whatever it may be — and I've done all parts, I think. There's an understanding as to the pay. We know that we can make our living out of it. I may work rather more than nine months in the year altogether. In a good yard, after a ship is finished, there may be a slack of two or three months before we are wanted on a new ship. We are not kept going regularly at any one yard — only as long as a ship's in hand. We look out at all the yards. I'm a society man, and wish everybody was. I earn as much now as I did twelve or thirteen years back, when I first worked as a journeyman, and as provisions are cheaper I'm better off, or I could not give my children — there's three of them — good schooling as I do. I don't know that I can do better than bring up my boy — the others are girls — to my own trade, if he grows up sharp and strong; it's no use without. I know of no grievances that we have. I worked, not long since, in the joinering of an iron ship. There's more joinering in them than in wood ships, as there's a lining of wood to back the iron work. I don't mix with the "boiler-makers." I seldom stir out of a night, as I'm generally well tired after my day's work. I live near my work, and take every meal at home, except my luncheon, and that's a draught of beer, and sometimes a crust with it and a crumb of cheese, that I now and then put in my pocket."

The *carving of the figure-heads* of vessels is a distinct branch of the business of ship-building. In some yards this carving, as at present pursued, partakes more and more of the characteristics of a fine art, and in all it is less rude than it was. The monstrosities, the merely grim and grotesque, which delighted the seamen of the past age, are now almost entirely things of the past. In the figure-heads of the meanest vessels now built, some observance of truth and nature is displayed. The figure-head is ordered of the carver for the general trade (the greater builders usually comprising that department as well as others in their own establishments). Sometimes he works from a drawing — rarely from a model. A carver upon whom I called, had a spacious workshop in the corner of a large garden, immediately behind his dwelling-house, which was near the Thames. Ranged alongside the wall, at the top of the garden, were a row of colossal and semi-colossal figure-heads, exceedingly grim and dusty, and seeming singularly out of place, for they loomed down, with their unmistakeable seafaring look, upon the white and orange lilies, the many-tinted sweet peas and carnations, and the red and white roses. The figures were all of elm, and each had preliminary coat of paint of a dull brick colour, to prevent the wood from cracking, so that their uniformity of hue added to the curious effect that they presented. It was easy enough to recognise the features, or rather the approximation to the features, of the Queen, Prince Albert, and the Duke of Wellington; though there were several countenances which looked familiar enough, and yet puzzled the memory as to whose effigy was represented. Some figure-heads were robed, and starred, and coronetted, and some had the plain coats of the present day. With these were mingled female forms, some with braided hair, others with very rigid ringlets, carved out of the solid wood. I ascertained that it would have been idle indeed to speculate on the "likeness" of most of these figures, as they are ready for an emergency. Sometimes a "head" is demanded in a hurry – the name of the vessel not being determined upon until she is in an advanced stage of completion. Then the well-known effigies are ready; while the plain are available, with the least delay, for the "Williams" or "Georges" of the smaller merchant ships, and the decorated and coronetted for any given peer or potentate that may be popular for the time being; or else, with the addition of painting and gilding, and a little alteration at the hands of the carver, the general figures are ready to be converted into any given individual whose popularity attracts the shipowner's attention, or whose patronage ensures his regard. The female figures are in like manner convertible into any "Jane" or "Ann," or into the allegorical "Justice," "Peace," "Concord," or "Commerce," according as they are wanted at "the shortest notice."

Along the wall of the workshop were the same array of effigies, while in one corner, amidst heaped up timber, was a covered figure in a sitting position, which was much more elaborately worked than the others. A cornucopia rested on it's left arm, while the right hand grasped a snake, the head of which had been broken off, and lay close by. The carving of the thick curly hair was minute, and showed great painstaking. This, I found, was at one time a choice ornament of the Lord Mayor's state barge, and represented "Africa." An opposite figure, allegorical of another quarter of the world, I was told, became rotten and had to be removed from the barge, and "Africa" was removed at the same time, or she would have appeared isolated. When deposited in its present place the figure was gilt, but a great part of the gilding having been rubbed or fallen off, its new owner had it painted all over to resemble the others.

Figure-heads are generally made of elm; a few, however, are of fir, a material demanded by some builders from its cheapness. The largest English elms are used by the ship-carvers; the figure-heads are worked out of the solid trunk, except the arm, if it be extended in the act of pointing, as it often is. An arm, or a telescope, or any projecting portion, is then joined or "limbed" to the trunk. The ship-carvers make the cat-heads, for which elm is used; and until within these eight or ten years, they carved the ornaments required for the cabins, and the scrolls, or twisted snakes, or roses, thistles, or shamrocks that were sometimes demanded for the adornment of the ship's hull; but this department of their trade is now superseded, composition ornaments being almost universally in use.

The ship-carvers in the general trade are a small body of men, numbering only 5 masters, 15 journeymen, and 4 apprentices – all, I was told, London men. The work is by day, 6s. being the established day's wage. The employment of the men is tolerably regular. They have no society, and no benefit or sick funds among them. They all live near the river, and three-fourths of them on the Surrey side. Their character and habits in no respect differ from those of the shipwrights.

The price of an average-sized elm figure-head, exclusive of any cost in painting or gilding, is from £6 to £7 10s. – more sometimes, according to the work required. A figure-head of the more elaborate style is about a fortnight's work for one man. The men find their own tools, which are worth, in their completeness, £5 or £6. The tools are axes, saws, chisels, and gouges, but principally gouges. Among them are no slop-workers, and I heard of no grievances; but more than one workman expressed some apprehension of the proceedings of two men who were in the habit of frequenting the docks, and offering to get repairs to figure-heads executed below the established and fair prices. Of these men, mention is made in the following narrative, and the fact was confirmed by others.

A muscular, hearty, and hale-looking young man, whom I found at work in a shop, presenting many of the characteristics of one I have more particularly described, but not the same, gave me the following information:

"I was apprenticed to Mr. ——, and have never left London. My father was connected with ship-building, and so put me to this branch. I'm unmarried, and live with my friends. I have nothing to complain of in the way of business, as I have pretty good employment. We all drink beer – some of us, perhaps, too much, but nothing compared to other trades. Our's is hard work, but we don't drink much at work. Look you here, sir, this log of ellum, with just the sides taken off by the sawyers, to make it square, has to be made into a 'head' – into a foreign nobleman or prince – I don't remember his name, but it's a queer one. To do that is heavy lifting and hard work. None of these fellows here (pointing to the figures), is the proper size, hardly big enough, or I could easily gouge this one now into a lord. We first axe the log into a rough shape, a sort of outline, and then finish it with chisels and gouges. I sometimes work from a drawing, but mostly out of my own head, and direct myself by my eye. We have nothing to do with painting or gilding the heads. They're sent home in their own woods just with a coat of paint over them, to save them from cracking. Yes, you're right, sir, that head will do for the Queen; but if a Queen isn't wanted, and it's the proper size, I can soon make her into any other female. Or She might do for a 'Mary Anne,' without altering; certainly she might. The way the hair's carved is the Queen's style, and has been in fashion these eight or ten years. Ringlets ain't easy; particularly cork-screw ringlets, as they're called. The watch-chain and seals to a gentleman ain't easy, as you have to bring out that part and cut away from it. The same with buttons and stars. Perhaps we aren't as good at legs as at other carving. We generally carve only to the knee. The shipwrights place our work on the ship's knee caps. We have no slop-workers among us; but there are two men who keeps a look out at the docks for broken heads, or heads damaged any way, and offer to repair them cheap. They're not workers themselves, but they get hold of any drunken carpenter, or any ship carver that happens to be hard up and out of work, and put them to the job at low prices. But the thing don't satisfy, and they do very little; still, it's a break in upon us. I make from 24s. to 30s. a week the year through, oftener nearer 30s. than 24s. I make 36s. at full work."

The builders of ships' boats are a distinct body, as are the builders of wherries for racing or other aquatic amusements; and the general boat-builder constructs skiffs, lug-boats, lighters, and barges. These divisions, however, are not very precisely observed, for almost every master will undertake the building of any description of boat.

Six boats are the complement of a ship of 1,000 tons – the long boat, two cutters, gig, jolly boat, and life boat. The "long boat" is used for the lading and discharging of the cargo, and for the rescue of the crew when the vessel is in danger of being wrecked. The "cutters" are principally employed for communication with the shore when the ship is on a foreign station, or is moored out at sea. The "jolly boat" is made available for any temporary or unimportant service, and is more in use than any other boat – while the "gig" is the captain's boat. A merchant vessel of 350 tons carries four boats. Of these, the life boat must, by a recent Act, be one; the long boat is usually another; and the remaining two boats are provided according to the discretion of the captain, as he may judge that the nature of his service and the character of the ports or shores to which he is bound may require. Smaller ships have two or three boats.

The other boats are those used for carrying on the traffic of the river; for the conveyance of "fares," as persons who "take a boat" are styled by the watermen; or for the recreation of those who are fond of "boating," wherries being now almost entirely in the hands of amateurs. The "lug boat" is a large roomy boat adapted for the conveyance of luggage to and from a ship; the "lighter" is made to fulfil the same purposes as regards cargo; the barge is useful for general purposes, but principally for the conveyance of coal or any heavy material. The "skiff" is the boat with a round stem and a square stern, that the watermen now ply with. The "wherry" is the long, narrow boat, the character of which I have already indicated.

The first process in boat-building is the formation of the keel, which is of American elm or oak, and must be of good, long-grained, tough wood. The "timbers" (ribs) are next placed together, having been prepared to the proper sizes and shapes by the sawyers; they are "moulded," or fitted one to another, on the same principle as in shipbuilding. This done, the carcass of the boat is formed. Oak, elm, and (though rarely) fir are the materials of these carcasses – the majority being made of English elm. The carcass is then "skinned;" that is, the "streaks" (pronounced strakes), or exterior timbers, are placed to complete the work. For ships' boats the streaks are of mahogany or "wainscot" (as the Baltic oak is called in boat-building), or fir, which is the cheapest, and makes the lightest but the least durable vessel. The streaks of skiffs, wherries, lighters, and lug-boats are of English oak, as are those of the barges, with an occasional exception, where fir is so employed.

The London boat-builders are not now a numerous class – numbering only about 120, independently of the builders of wherries, who are not more than 35. Three-fourths of these operatives are London men; the majority of the others being from Deal and the north of England, especially from Whitby. They are a sober and far from ignorant class. "I really don't know one drunkard among us," said one of them to me, "and I think we can all read and write; but we are a downcast lot to what we were once." Another man, whose information I found corroborated, said, "I think the men in my trade are steady and domestic. Most of us have wives and families. I don't know a gambler among us, and there's only a few youngsters that care for a hand at cards. Generally of a Saturday night, if we've had a middling week in the yard, we pay 6d. a piece, and enjoy ourselves quietly over our beer or ale, or whatever we like, and our pipes, and our talk, and when the money's out we go away."

The boat-builders work by contract and by day; the contract or piece-work system greatly predominating. The payment by day, of ten hours' labour, is 5s. 6d. An operative contracts with a master to build a boat complete, which he does by his unassisted labour, or if it be a large-sized boat, or demanded in a hurry, two men undertake it. The employer finds all the material, and the work is carried on in his "yard," as the boat-building establishments are always called. The operatives engaged in this business have a list of prices agreed upon in concurrence with their masters in 1824, but now little regarded. The boat-builders have a society, but it is only for providing members' funerals, and for relief during sickness. They have no provisions for the regulation of wages, so that, according to the "honourable" or "screwing" character of the employer, there is a difference in the rate paid of 6d., 9d., and even 1s. a foot. The observance of the prices of 1824 is rendered (nominally) a dead letter by the following method: In the case of a gig of the first class 5s. a foot is the amount on the list of prices, and 5s. a foot is still paid; but in 1824, there were only nine streaks worked where there are now thirteen, and so, in a gig of the largest size, twenty feet being an average length, there is almost a week's extra work, and at the same rate of remuneration to the artificer. And thus through all the grades of boat-building. Nor is this all. Payment for "extras," such as a "shifting wash-streak," or board over the gunwale, was allowed to the workman, but that, with some others, has been gradually "knocked off." There are, however, still a few exceptions to this under-payment.

The boat-builders are not affected by the introduction of unskilled labour. Want of regular employment and uncertainty of remuneration are their principal grievances. The average work of those best employed is for about nine months in the year, realising 33s. a week during that time, or 22s. a week for the twelve. This uncertainty or irregularity of employment is a great evil to the working-men. "If we lives casual," said one man to me, "we grows careless."

The boat-builder finds his own tools, a complete set of which is worth from £3 to £4. Many manage to work, however, with tools worth not more than 25s. I am assured that their tools are now seldom pledged. A boat-builder will suffer a great deal before he resorts to the pawnbroker with his tools; some of them knowing, from woful experience, how difficult is the redemption of a pledge to a man whose employment is irregular. They seldom reside very near their place of work, but are scattered about wherever lodgings may be most economical. They are paid every Saturday night, nine o'clock being the very latest hour in the worst yards. They have no grievances as to payment in public-houses, or enthralment to a publican connected with a master or foreman.

The business is generally learned by apprenticeship to a master. Twenty-five or thirty years ago £50 was not an unfrequent premium for an outdoor apprentice; now premiums are never given, but a youth's labour is paid at a mere nominal rate, or not paid at all, for one year or eighteen months, and this is considered equivalent to a premium. Each master has his own scale of wages to his apprentice. In the last year of the apprenticeship, when the lad is often as good as a journeyman, and can be employed while the men are idle, the rate is usually 15s. The apprentices taken, however, are not so numerous as to be complained of by the journeymen.

I now give two statements from working boat-builders. The first is that of a highly intelligent man who has had great experience, and has observed many changes in his trade. For these changes he gave what he considered the causes, expressing himself with terseness and propriety. Many grievances also are specified; the depression of the trade is accounted for, according to the best of my informant's judgment, and a further account of the habits and social condition of the boat-builders is detailed or intimated:

"My trade," he said, "is greatly depressed to what it was. When I was out of my apprenticeship, thirty-three years ago, there was twice the employment for boat-builders that there is now. At that time I think boat-builders were doubly as numerous as at present, as well as having double the employment. I consider the change owing to the many railways and steamboats now in operation. When the Scotch steamers came up, between twenty and thirty years ago, the Scotch smacks plying to London and back were soon run off that coast, and the same with other coasts. These smacks were always knocking their boats to pieces, and wanting new ones, or wanting repairs. They had to get the boats out to get alongside the wharfs, but now the steamer goes right up alongside, and hardly ever wants boats, and can hang them up as in a parlour. The jetties and piers do away with the use of boats. At Ryde now, and in many a foreign part, the steamer goes right up to the pier, and the boats come home without a scratch. Before the piers came up, passengers, and luggage, and cargo, used to be landed in boats. Of course there's fewer wanted at present. I could and did earn 50s. a week the year through, thirty years back. At that time boat-builders were far better situated in having comfortable homes, and in being able to educate and provide for old age, or for families, than at present. There are more and cheaper schools now, certainly, but look at the difference of 50s. a week the year through, and 22s. or 23s., which I take to be the present average for those in the best work. I'm satisfied that boat-builders are an intelligent set now, but I think there was more intelligence among us in my young days. There's not much drinking among us at present, and there was less than. Indeed, the less a man earns, and the more he's out of work, the more he's tempted to drink. He's driven to drink by poverty and oppression. He's often afraid to face his home. We were far better treated, too, by our employers formerly. Now, we're bullied and sworn at by many a master, 'till a man's blood boils. We're exposed to degrading words, that lower a man. Not that all masters are such; for there's Mr. F——, I worked for him a few months back, and there's no under-working or under-paying there; it's a good yard, I wish to God there were plenty such; and there's your money early on a Saturday evening, and all proper treatment. With the cutting masters, however, a poor man has no check. If he says anything he gets abused. And now I'll tell you, sir, of a crying evil, and if it was necessary I'd get, in two hours from this time and place, twenty honest men's signatures to prove that I state nothing but the fact. It's a crying evil that captains and owners will go up and down the river and buy old rotten boats, and have them painted up to look viewy. Emigrants' ships are surveyed, to be sure, but the survey of the boats is often nominal. Why, how often do we read of an emigrant ship having been in distress in a storm, and how her long-boat was launched and was stove in no time, and how numbers of poor fellows' lives were lost? And why was the boat stove so soon? Just because she was 'nail-sick.' What do I mean by nail-sick, sir? Why, it's our word when the nails have rusted asunder in the old rotten wood, and so when there's a stress on the boat, and she gets a hard blow, why, she goes slap to pieces. She was all rottenness, paint, and putty, at start. There ought to be an officer to survey every boat, and atttend to nothing else, and who wouldn't be humbugged with paint. Owners and captains won't give anything like a fair price for necessary repairs. If a man asks £1, thought that may be only a reasonable price, they'll say, 'A pound, pooh! The ship's carpenter shall do it;' and then perhaps, and very frequently too, it's not done at all. When the act of Parliament, three or four years ago, required every ship to carry a life-boat, it caused good work for us, because ship-owners did provide life-boats at that time. Now, when they're wanted, owners and captains go up and down the river, and pick up any old rubbishing thing, and fit it for one. When it's trimmed up it looks very well. But, if any one were to go on board a ship that didn't belong to a good owner – some little shifty owner's ship – and if he would just try with a small knife under the bilge of the boat, why many's the time it'll go through it as if it was through a wafer. Or they'll find, perhaps, six or seven coats of paint, after a little scraping, for the paint holds the streaks together until there's stress and danger; so that when there is, down she goes with, may be, many a fine fellow in her."

Another boat-builder, employed at present in the building of ships' boats, gave me the following statement. He resided in a crowded neighbour-hood, not far from the river-side. His room was small and dark, but fully furnished, and a few numbers of a cheap periodical lay on the table. He was a grave good-looking man:

"I have been a boat-builder fourteen or fifteen years," he said, "and served an apprenticeship in London. My father was a waterman, and I wish he had brought me up to some better business; but they say no businesses are as good as they were once. He's been dead some years. There's no reduction in the wages paid me since I was out of my time, but I must do more work for less money. I lived with my mother until she died, four or five years back, and all I'd saved went to bury her. I don't think I could very well afford to keep a wife, though it's very lonesome having nobody to care about one. No doubt I could get a wife, but to keep her is another thing. I shouldn't like to to be in poverty instead of one, and I wouldn't like any decent girl I might marry to have to do work for the sweaters, to help us to make both ends meet when work's scarce. Some have to do it, though, to my knowing; and don't the girls find out the difference between that and being in good service, as some of them have been! I'm not employed – and very few of us are – three-quarters of my time; and, take the year through, I don't earn more than a guinea a week. I may be hard at work this month and have nothing to do for the next fortnight, but go from yard to yard and be told I'm not wanted. Now, suppose I've 21s. a week, and I'm a single man. I pay 2s. a week for this room, with a recess there for my bed. They're my own sticks. Then say 8d. a week for my washing, as I can't bear to be dirty. Well, then, I often work a good way off, and must live out. I can potter on cheaper at home. My breakfast, at the very lowest, is 3½d., and that's only 1½d. for half a pint of coffee, penny loaf, and penny butter. Properly, for a working man, it should be 7d. − pint of coffee, 3d., penny loaf, and penny butter, and 2d. for a rasher; but say 3½d. When one's hard at work one requires some refreshment before dinner time, and you can't have anything cheaper than half a pint of beer − a pint's not too much; the half pint's a penny. Then for dinner, half a pound of steak is 3½d.; if you get it cheaper it's tough and grisly, and no good. I get it cooked for nothing at a public-house if I take a pint of beer with it, and that's 2d., and a penny for potatoes, and a halfpenny for bread; altogether the lowest for a decent dinner, anything like satisfying, is 7d. Tea is a halfpenny more than breakfast; for it's tea instead of coffee, you see, sir. Then there's a pint of beer, and a penn'orth of cheese and a penn'orth of bread for supper, that's 4d. I know there's plenty of working men who go without supper; but I'm hearty myself, and feel I want it. That's 1s. 7½d. for a day's keep, and a boat-builder's is hard work, and we require good support. Seven times 1s. 7½d. − and indeed Sunday should be reckoned more, for if I have a good dinner off a joint with my landlord and his family, as I have every now and then, I pay him 1s. − but, say 7 times 1s. 7½d. that's how much? − 11s. 4½d. Well, then, there is my club money, and I pay 3d. a week for papers; and I go to chapel on a Sunday pretty regular, and there's often a collection, and I can't pass the plate without my 3d., and, indeed, I oughtn't; and I sometimes get a letter from a brother, a mason, I have in Australia, and I sometimes write to him: and besides there's 4d. a week for tobacco, at the very least, as a pipe's a sort of company to a lone man; and for such like things we can't say less than 2s. a week; indeed not less than 2s. 6d. Now, sir, what's that altogether? (I told him 16s. 6½d.) Then there's 4s. 6d. a week, he continued, left for clothes, and for any new tool I may want, and for everything else; and I couldn't keep a wife, let alone a family, on that." (He seemed to enter with great zest into these explanations.) "Besides, this is the most favourable way to put it; for when I have a good week's work, and make 33s. or 34s., or as much as 36s., I want more support, and my living costs me more, though I keep it as square as I can for a rainy day or a slack time. If I ask for work, and say I'm quick at clinch boats (ship's boats), a master will say, 'Now here's a long boat I want building, how much will you do it for? Don't tell me about prices, I can't get my price, and if you won't come down a peg, another will.' If I ask £4, he'll bid £3 3s., and will bargain, perhaps, for £3 10s., and it's from eight to ten days' work. I can't very well pass an offer, as I may not very soon have another. I have worked ten months and more in Mr. ——'s yard; but that was only once. I know men and families live on 12s. a week. It's not living, though; it's only tea and bread and butter, or no butter. There can be any strength in that."

The making of oars and sculls is a distinct branch from boat-building. The *oars* are used when two men row the boat; the *sculls* when one man is so employed. I need not further describe articles so well known. The oars are made of ash; the sculls of fir. The scull-makers, as they are generally called, make oars and sculls indiscriminately, unless a master chooses to employ them entirely on one branch, which is a rare occurrence. These operatives are about twice as numerous as the boat-builders. This seems an anomaly, but it was accounted for to me thus: Whilst a boat is in use many pairs of oars or sculls are lost or broken. When broken they can seldom be repaired, as no jointing, lashing, or dovetailing will sustain the pressure of the water. It is not unusual, too, for a ship to carry out at the least duplicate pairs of oars; sometimes more than that. The oars thus carried out, if the ship be bound to a warmer climate, must be of well-seasoned ash, or they will warp; and an oar that is not "true" is difficult of management, and the cause of excessive fatigue. The amateurs, who row their own wherries, are excellent supporters of the oar makers, as they are not unapt to lose or break their oars. Some of the river clubmen, however, I was told by a scull maker, were among the best of rowers, and would make capital watermen. This was not said scoffingly, but in the way of commendation. Then it must be remembered that to some wherries there are six pairs of oars, and to many boats two pairs. The scull-makers work by the piece, so much the pair. In their habits and social characteristics they do not differ from the boat-builders.

SUBJECT INDEX

Cabinet-makers – *contd.*

247